Theory as Method in R

While education researchers have drawn on the work of a wide diversity of theorists over the years, much contemporary theory building in these areas has revolved around the work of Pierre Bourdieu. *Theory as Method in Research* develops the capacity of students, researchers and teachers to successfully put Bourdieu's ideas to work in their own research and prepare them effectively for conducting master's and doctoral degrees. Structured around four core themes, this book provides a range of research case studies exploring educational identities, educational inequalities, school leadership and management and research in teacher education. Issues as diverse as Chinese language learning and identity, school leadership in Australia and the school experience of Afro-Trinidadian boys are covered, intertwined with a set of innovative approaches to theory application in education research.

This collection brings together, in one comprehensive volume, a set of education researchers who place Pierre Bourdieu's key concepts such as habitus, capital and field at the centre of their research methodologies. Full of insight and innovation, the book is an essential read for practitioners, student teachers, researchers and academics who want to harness the potential of Bourdieu's core concepts in their own work, thereby helping to bridge the gap between theory and method in education research.

Mark Murphy is Reader in Education and Public Policy at the University of Glasgow, UK.

Cristina Costa is Lecturer in Technology Enhanced Learning in the School of Education, University of Strathclyde, UK.

Theory as Method in Research

On Bourdieu, social theory and education

Edited by
Mark Murphy and
Cristina Costa

Routledge
Taylor & Francis Group

LONDON AND NEW YORK

First published 2016
by Routledge
2 Park Square, Milton Park, Abingdon, Oxon OX14 4RN

and by Routledge
711 Third Avenue, New York, NY 10017

Routledge is an imprint of the Taylor & Francis Group, an informa business

© 2016 Mark Murphy and Cristina Costa

British Library Cataloguing in Publication Data
A catalogue record for this book is available from the British Library

Library of Congress Cataloging in Publication Data
Theory as method in research: on Bourdieu, social theory and education/ edited by Mark Murphy and Cristina Costa.
pages cm
Includes bibliographical references.
1. Bourdieu, Pierre, 1930–2002. 2. Education – Philosophy. 3. Educational sociology – Case studies. 4. Educational leadership – Case studies. 5. Education – Research – Case studies. I. Murphy, Mark, 1969 June 17– II. Costa, Cristina.
LB880.B6542T54 2016
370.1 – dc23
2015013028

ISBN: 978-1-138-90033-2 (hbk)
ISBN: 978-1-138-90034-9 (pbk)
ISBN: 978-1-315-70730-3 (ebk)

Typeset in Galliard and Gill Sans
by Florence Production Ltd, Stoodleigh, Devon, UK

MIX
Paper from
responsible sources
FSC   FSC® C013056
www.fsc.org

Printed and bound in Great Britain by
TJ International Ltd, Padstow, Cornwall

Contents

About the contributors

Cristina Costa is Lecturer in Technology Enhanced Learning in the School of Education, University of Strathclyde, UK. Her research focuses on the intersection of education and the participatory web through a sociological lens, especially Bourdieu's key concepts. She is also interested in broader issues regarding the participatory web in the context of a changing society. Cristina has a research record that links social theory to emerging academic areas such as technology enhanced learning in an attempt to bridge the existing gap between theory and practice.

Scott Eacott is an educational administration theorist and Director of the Office of Educational Leadership in the School of Education at the University of New South Wales. He is widely published with research interests and contributions falling into three main areas: educational administration theory and methodology; leadership preparation and development; and strategy in education. His latest book, *Educational leadership relationally* (Sense, 2015) articulates and defends a relational approach to scholarship in educational leadership, management and administration.

Katie Fitzpatrick is Senior Lecturer of health education and physical education at the University of Auckland, New Zealand. Having taught in diverse multicultural schools for over seven years, she joined academia with an interest in issues of social justice. Bourdieu's ideas underscored her first, award winning book, which explores the place of health and physical education in the lives of urban youth: *Critical pedagogy, physical education and urban schooling* (Peter Lang, 2013). Her current research is focused on the perspectives of diverse youth on issues of health, physicality, ethnicity and gender/sexuality. She has published numerous articles and book chapters in these areas, as well as a recently co-edited new international collection on health education in schools *Health education: Critical perspectives* (Routledge, 2014).

Naomi Flynn is Associate Professor in Education at the University of Reading where she is a teacher educator. Naomi's research interests centre on the teaching of English in English primary schools, with a specific focus on how policy shapes teachers' practice. Her doctoral research centred on how teachers' practice was impacted by the changing pupil demographic in primary schools in the south of England following Eastern European migration to Britain after 2004. She would be happy to hear from others using Bourdieu in their analysis of education, or from colleagues with an interest in the teaching of children with English as an additional language.

Bruce Kloot is Lecturer in Academic Development in the Department of Mechanical Engineering at the University of Cape Town, and has a background in engineering and anthropology. His interests lie at the intersection of education, engineering and sociology and he is particularly interested in applying frameworks from the sociology of education to analyse higher education in post-apartheid South Africa.

Stephen May is Professor of Education in Te Puna Wananga (School of Māori Education) and Deputy Dean, Research, in the Faculty of Education, The University of Auckland, New Zealand. He is also an Honorary Research Fellow in the Centre for the Study of Ethnicity and Citizenship, University of Bristol, United Kingdom. Stephen has written widely on language rights, language policy, and language education and has had a longstanding interest in both Bourdieuian social theory and educational ethnography in relation to these areas. To date, he has published 14 books and over 90 academic articles and book chapters in these areas. His key books include *Language and minority rights* (2nd edn, Routledge, 2012), the first edition of which received an American Library Association Choice's Outstanding Academic Title award (2008). His latest book is a significant new edited collection, *The multilingual turn* (Routledge, 2014). He has previously edited, with Nancy Hornberger, *Language policy and political issues in education*, Volume 1 of the *Encyclopedia of language and education* (2nd edn, Springer, 2008); and with Christine Sleeter, *Critical multiculturalism: Theory and praxis* (Routledge, 2010). He is General Editor of the third edition of the 10-volume *Encyclopedia of language and education* (Springer, 2016), a Founding Editor of the interdisciplinary journal, *Ethnicities* (Sage), and Associate Editor of *Language Policy* (Springer). His homepage is www.education.auckland.ac.nz/uoa/stephen-may

Guanglun Michael Mu is a sociologist of education. He has worked as an academic in three countries – China, Australia and Canada. He currently holds the Vice-Chancellor's Research Fellowship at Queensland University of Technology, Australia. Dr Mu adopts methodological pluralism, with particular expertise in quantitative methods. He is engaged with research in diversity and inclusion, with a particular interest in Chineseness in diaspora. His work has been published in some prestigious journals, for example *Journal of Multilingual and Multicultural Development, Language and Education,*

International Journal of Bilingual Education and Bilingualism, and *Australian Educational Researcher*.

Many years ago, Dr Mu had an opportunity to have considerable contact with a group of young overseas Chinese – Australian Chinese, American Chinese, Canadian Chinese, British Chinese and Southeast Asian Chinese. He travelled with these young people around China. For these young people, this was not only a trip to learn the history, language, and society of their cultural motherland – China, but also a trip of anticipation, excitement, curiosity, and sometimes bewilderment. For Dr Mu, it was this very trip that prompted him to look at the subtle, multilayered identities and nuanced, interested language practices of overseas Chinese.

Mark Murphy is Reader in Education and Public Policy at the University of Glasgow, UK. Current research interests include accountability, public sector reform and the application of social theory in applied settings. His recent publications include *Habermas, critical theory and education* (paperback, with T. Fleming, Routledge, 2012), the four-volume *Social theory and education research* (Sage, 2013), *Social theory and education research: Understanding Foucault, Habermas, Bourdieu and Derrida* (Routledge, 2013), and *Research and education* (with W. Curtis and S. Shields, Routledge, 2014). He is Co-Director of the Robert Owen Centre for Educational Change at the University of Glasgow and is an active member of professional associations such as the British Education Research Association (BERA) and the Social Policy Association.

Kathleen Nolan is Associate Professor of Mathematics Education at the University of Regina (Saskatchewan, Canada), where she teaches undergraduate and graduate courses in mathematics curriculum, qualitative research and contemporary issues in education. Kathleen's current research focuses on mathematics teacher education, exploring issues of teacher identity, the regulatory practices of schooling, learning and knowing, and post-structural readings of scholarly texts. Kathleen is the author of *How should I know? Pre-service teachers' images of knowing (by heart) in mathematics and science* (Sense Publishers, 2007) and co-editor (with E. de Freitas) of *Opening the research text: Critical insights and in(ter)ventions into mathematics education* (Springer, 2008). In addition to publishing articles in the *Journal of Mathematics Teacher Education* and *Educational Studies in Mathematics*, Kathleen has also published chapters in books edited by M. Walshaw (2010) and T. Brown (2008).

Maria Papapolydorou is Senior Lecturer in Education and Childhood Studies at the University of Greenwich. Her research focuses on identities and inequalities (social class, ethnicity and gender) in the field of education. Maria is also interested in social capital theory, particularly from a Bourdienian point of view, and the way it can be used to explore teenagers' social networks. Her research outputs include articles published in the *British Journal of Sociology of Education* and *Youth and Policy*. Maria's PhD thesis examined the relationship between social capital and students' education. More recently, her research explores the way social class is understood as a concept and as an identity by higher education students.

Ravi Rampersad is Senior Manager in the Consulting Practice of the Deloitte & Touche (Trinidad office) where he leads the Education Consulting Practice. Prior to joining Deloitte & Touche, Ravi served as an academic with the state funded College of Science, Technology and Applied Arts of Trinidad and Tobago (COSTAATT) for over five years. His tenure focused on lecturing and engaging in curriculum and course development in the social sciences. Ravi remains a part time faculty member of COSTAATT. Ravi gained his PhD in Education from the Institute of Education, University of London, and is building an international profile of research, teaching and publications on issues of race, ethnicity, gender and identity. A common thread in his work relates to investigating and redressing issues of social justice and the marginalization of vulnerable groups in society.

Jo Warin is Senior Lecturer in the Department of Educational Research at Lancaster University and Co-director of the Centre for Social Justice and Wellbeing in Education. She teaches on the online Doctoral Programme in Education and Social Justice, and supervises many PhD students. Social justice in education is at the heart of Jo's research, which is focused on socio emotional aspects of children's lives in formal and informal educational contexts. She has published a book about her unique qualitative longitudinal research study (*Stories of Self. Tracking children's identity and wellbeing through the school years*) with several related journal papers. She also researches and publishes in the field of staff gender issues in early childhood education, drawing on theories of masculinities, bringing together research on the identities of male teachers and fathers.

Permissions

Sections of Chapter 3 have been published in a journal paper: Warin, J. (2013) 'Identity capital in school: an application from a longitudinal ethnographic study of self-construction during the years of school', *British Journal of Sociology of Education*. 1–18. doi: 10.1080/01425692.2013.849565. These are reprinted by kind permission of the publisher: Taylor & Francis Ltd, www.tandfonline.com.

Chapter 1

Introduction

Bourdieu and education research

Mark Murphy and Cristina Costa

Introduction

Over the years, education has developed a long and fruitful relationship with theory of all stripes, in particular the work of the French social theorist, Pierre Bourdieu. The impact of Bourdieu on the field of education research has been significant and sustained, his contribution to educational ideas arguably stronger than that of any other social theorist of the late twentieth century. This can be explained to some degree by his own research interests in the power of schooling and education, but it also reflects the strength of conceptual analysis that offers fertile ground for theoretically engaged researchers. Ideas developed and disseminated through his many and varied works – such as *habitus, cultural capital, field* and *symbolic violence* – have inspired countless education researchers over the years, a situation that shows no sign of abating. Within the sociology of education, for example, Bourdieu's work has been utilized to enhance our understandings of the ways in which the curriculum, both overt and hidden, along with pedagogies, and their implicit taken-for-granted cultural capitals, contribute to both the reproduction of inequality and its legitimation through the misrecognition of social experiences and cultural inheritance as individual capacities.

Given the breadth of his influence on education research it can be a challenge to understand how to explore the relevance and reach of his core concepts in specific settings – how does an education researcher successfully put Bourdieu's ideas to work in their own research? What are the mechanisms via which theory can translate into method? The objective of this book is to provide the reader with pathways to achieving such forms of 'application', while contextualizing his key concepts within the broader oeuvre of Bourdieu's theoretical approach. This contextualization will assist the reader in their efforts to build connections between the various theories.

Central to fulfilling the objective of this book is an exploration of the ways in which the work of Bourdieu has been applied in research contexts such as:

- educational identities
- inequality and schooling

- leadership and management
- teacher education.

How the concepts of Bourdieu have been applied in these contexts is illustrated via a set of case studies, each of which critically examines the challenges faced when 'bridging the gap' between theory and research method. The content of these case study chapters is designed so that the emphasis is on the practice of research; in doing so they exemplify the numerous inventive ways in which Bourdieu's core concepts, such as habitus, can be brought to life in research settings.

As a preface to these contributions, this chapter provides an overview of Bourdieu's work in the field of educational research, illustrating how educational issues weaved their way in to many aspects of his oeuvre and conceptual thinking. In particular, the chapter seeks to explore the ways in which Bourdieu himself attempted to overcome the theory/method dichotomy, and the ways in which he operationalized/developed his own concepts in research. The chapter also provides an overview of the chapters featured in this collection, illuminating in particular the fundamental question that this book aims to address: the application of Bourdieu as both theory and method in education research.

It should be noted that such theory/method challenges are not the exclusive domain of educational researchers grappling with Bourdieu's conceptual apparatus – most variants of social theory present challenges of application for scholars wishing to bring intellectual depth to their fieldwork. The case studies included in this collection could be seen as a sample of a much wider research agenda geared towards bringing theory and method closer together (see Murphy, 2013). Bourdieu's ideas have been put to work in numerous interdisciplinary contexts, with habitus, for example, helping scholars across a range of disciplines make sense of issues like inequality, crime, mobilities and migration (see Costa and Murphy, 2015). These wider applications have to some extent been explored via the website www.socialtheoryapplied.com, a site co-edited by this collection's co-editors. The developing interest in the website and its contributions is further testimony to the significance attached to the art of application by scholars keen on exploring the power of ideas, but uncertain as to how to realize their potential in the field of research. We see the production of books such as this edited collection and the website as overlapping parts of an ongoing project to make a focus on 'application', an essential component of research agendas such as those in education, while helping to raise its status in the binary world of theory/method distinctions.

Bourdieu and education research: a brief history

Bourdieu's considerable research output is a reflection of his desire to bridge theory and practice through method. Through a process of conceiving and apprehending the nature of the social world, Bourdieu aimed to depart from the classic dilemma of the object/subject divide. His contribution, in this sense, has resulted in an open framework of macro concepts that support the analysis of the interplay between structure and agency in specific contexts. This framework was not, however, conceived of in a vacuum nor established via a single study or research approach. Concepts such as field, habitus, capitals, doxa and symbolic violence were developed iteratively, reflecting his career-long endeavour in refining both his theoretical understanding of the social world and the methods through which he could arrive at such understandings. This is explicit in the evolution that marks his work, starting with his departure from classic ethnography (Bourdieu 1977, 2004a) – which he employed in his first sociological work in Algeria – through to more daring methodological approaches such as a variant of narrative inquiry, which he used in one of his later projects documented in *The weight of the world* (1999). Bourdieu was committed to methodological explorations that result in richer sociological explanations. Bourdieu's approaches to knowledge constructions theoretically and methodologically thus imply a knowledge of praxeology. They also involve an attempt to overcome the dichotomy between the objective and subjective dimensions of the social world by combining and distilling both through a practice of reflexivity. In other words, in order to overcome such antinomies, Bourdieu's research concerns were directed at devising mechanisms that would balance the distance as well as the proximity between the researcher and the researched.

More than anything else, Bourdieu's theorizing of the social intended to serve the purpose of critical inquiry. To achieve this goal Bourdieu was constantly engaged in the re-creation, re-examination and re-application of his own concepts with each new empirical work. His research translated into contributions across the social sciences, which have since been taken even further afield. Thematically speaking this translated into a vast and varied programme of research in which a social gaze was possible and necessary. Bourdieu himself explored a wide range of topics including social suffering, media, politics, the arts, taste and education.

Education was an area of study that cut across many of the topics to which Bourdieu devoted his research interest, thus occupying a special place in his research legacy. This is most likely because of his fascination in identifying the mechanisms of domination that prevailed in each and every social context he studied – a thread consistent across his work – and in which the education system plays a vital part.

Although Bourdieu centred most of his work and research on the French context, the theoretical critiques he put forward throughout his career have been applied to other contexts, giving his work a global dimension. This is particularly the case with regard to the study of educational issues, as educational researchers have demonstrated through the application of the Bourdieuian lens in the most varied contexts. This is so because Bourdieu's concepts are 'primarily social and metaphorical, not geographical' (Nowicka, 2015, p. 97). This is equally true because Bourdieu's key concepts are malleable (rather than vague), and therefore receptive to multiple and original applications. What Bourdieu offers us through his empirical work is the true essence of social theory, i.e. the construction of methodological and analytical frameworks through the application of one or more concepts to explore and understand social phenomena (Murphy, 2013, p. xxiii).

The appeal of Bourdieu's work to an international audience interested in educational research thus derives from the universality of his concepts in helping to unearth engrained educational issues, such as inequalities regarding access to education or educational trajectories of the social classes, and the ramifications of the different opportunities derived from such differentiations. The Bourdieuian community have a lot of examples from which to draw. In *The inheritors: French students and their relation to culture* (1964 [1979]), Bourdieu and Passeron disclose the paradox of formal education by focusing on the French system, which although attempting to provide a democratic pathway to education through open competition fails to acknowledge the impact of individuals' economic, social and cultural capitals on their scholastic success or lack of it. Individuals with higher levels of capitals possess a 'natural' competitive advantage in relation to individuals from disadvantaged backgrounds. This is because students from privileged social classes acquire 'knowledge and know how, tastes and a "good taste"' (p. 17); this is an inheritance of a refined habitus, the skills and attitudes that benefit them indirectly in the cultural system education aims to reproduce.

Bourdieu, in collaboration with Passeron, continued to study the French educational system. In *Reproduction in education, society and culture* (1979 [1990]) they again concluded that the transformative purpose of education is often overshadowed by its capacity to reinforce social inequalities – a topic that became prevalent in most of Bourdieu's work. For Bourdieu, cultural capital – especially in its embodied state – is of paramount importance with regard to school achievements. Cultural capital is, to a great extent, a family legacy that the school as a system fails largely to influence. As such, the values and attitudes individuals bring with them to school have a determining impact on how they approach and experience school(ing), with their expectations and achievements being more often than not linked to their unconscious interpretation of their position in the field in relation to their social class.

Bourdieu and Passeron also established relevant links between education, society, and culture not only through the notion of capitals – specifically cultural capital – but also through the concept of habitus, and the dispositions individuals acquire throughout their life trajectories, which orient their strategies towards social and professional practices. They describe the difference between primary and secondary habitus. According to them, the 'habitus acquired in the family [primary] forms the basis of the reception and assimilation of the classroom message, and the habitus acquired at school [secondary] conditions the level of reception and degree of assimilation of . . . any intellectual message'

(Bourdieu and Passeron, 1979 [1990], pp. 43–4). Hence, the Bourdieuian perspective understands education mainly as a system of reproduction of social practices and social privileges, with social classes being defined not only in relation to the position they occupy in the field, but also, and above all, through the cultural capital and habitus associated with that very same position. This is naturally converted into forms of symbolic power, such as distinction and the sense of identity individuals confer on their position in the field.

Later in his career Bourdieu studied distinction in taste, attitudes and social positions of social agents. In his book *Distinction: A social critique of the judgement of taste* (1984), he reflects on the economies of practices and cultural goods through 'the role played by the education system in mediating the relations between the status hierarchies associated with different tastes and cultural preferences on the one hand, and the organization and reproduction of the occupational class, on the other' (p. xx).

At the core of Bourdieu's argument is the idea that individuals' dispositions are (re)produced in relation and in response to the social, economic and cultural structures on which agents operate and with which they identify themselves or detach themselves from. As Bourdieu concludes, 'social identity is defined and asserted through difference' (ibid., p. 172), with education playing a role in reproducing such differences.

In *Homo academicus* (1988), Bourdieu once again makes education his field of study, only this time he sets out to investigate his own 'tribe'. Methodologically challenging, given his inevitable connection with the university that stages such a study, Bourdieu endeavours to observe the principles of reflexivity, 'the principal weapon of epistemological vigilance' (p. 15), in order to provide a sociological account of the French academy during and after the May revolution of 1968. He examines the field of academia, and its different faculties, as a space of struggle for forms of capital and power. But here he surprises us with his observation that the positions of dominant and dominated forces shift as the field undergoes transformations (p. 77) or faces moments of crisis (p. 189); this is an issue all too present not only in France, but also more globally in the period in which the study was conducted.

Indeed, as Bourdieu's work progresses, so does his work and thinking. Although his interpretation of field as a reproductive system persists throughout his career, with every new text Bourdieu also starts to account for change, even if in more implicit ways.

In *The state nobility: Elite schools in the field of power* (1996), Bourdieu looks at distinction through a perspective of deviant trajectories (p. 183). His argument is that the social mechanism of academic aggregation and segregation and the inevitable contention between the field and the habitus – the school and the students – is a determinant factor of change and transformation of both the field of power and the individual, and their distinctive identities through the opposite doxic approaches that each party represents and embodies.

In short, although the Bourdieuian interpretation of education has traditionally been associated with the institutionalization of a system of cultural reproduction, through which the dominant values and ideas become a form of domination and symbols of superiority of one social class over another, education, as a field, may also encourage change or transformation. Bourdieu himself was no stranger to such transformative experiences – see his self-portrait in *Sketch for a self-analysis* (2008).

What is probably most fascinating in Bourdieu's work, however, is that although he invites us to think relationally about theory and method to arrive at a robust understanding of (social) practice, he was more evasive about the processes through which theory can be applied to method. His most explicit explanation of this link can be found in *An invitation to reflexive sociology* (1992) where in conversation with Wacquant he outlines two different stages for examining the social world: the first deals with the surveying of the field and the spaces of positions it provides – the objective structures – by pushing aside any mundane construction (p. 11). The second consists of the re-introduction of agency, the lived experience that is (re)constructed intersubjectively. Additionally (and a constant in Bourdieu's work), there is a need to observe the principles of reflexivity, of being vigilant in attuning oneself to the relation between the researcher and the phenomenon at hand (see also Bourdieu, 2004b). Just like his research toolkit, his methodological approaches have been left open to experimentation, something that can be both daunting and liberating when trying to apply his key concepts to different contexts. Bourdieu himself did not follow one single line of inquiry, but experimented with many different ways of capturing and understanding the social world.

The organization of this book

A key objective of this collection is to illustrate the diversity of contexts within which Bourdieu's ideas have been put to work. For the purpose of organization, these contexts have been grouped under the following headings:

- Part 1: Researching educational identities
- Part 2: Researching equity in education
- Part 3: Researching educational leadership and management
- Part 4: Researching teacher education.

Each of the four parts comprises a number of chapters that explore Bourdieu's ideas and their applications from a range of theoretical and methodological angles, while also covering areas as distinct as digital scholarship, academic development, race and educational achievement, Chinese identity and English language teaching. The research included in the book has been carefully selected so that as wide an understanding of Bourdieu and his applications could be provided to the reader, although it should be noted that the list of topics included should be seen as a reflection of a much wider field of intellectual endeavour. We have also included a final chapter which summarizes and reflects on some of the key findings of the case studies across the sections.

Part 1: Researching educational identities

Part 1 on educational identities research includes three chapters, each one devoted to a specific Bourdieuian concept. Guanglun Michael Mu's chapter places habitus at the centre of a study on how Chineseness is negotiated through Chinese Heritage Language learning (CHL). Aiming to see such identities as neither fully predictable nor wholly malleable in the CHL learning process, Mu endeavours to straddle the schools of social psychology and post-structuralism. And in order to think through the social psychological and post-structural schools while employing diverse methods across quantitative and qualitative spectra, he draws on Bourdieu's sociological theory and methodological pluralism.

Mu considers habitus of Chineseness as a set of embodied dispositions structured in cultural history, coming to shape, and being shaped through, CHL learning. On the one hand, habitus of Chineseness is durable and transposable, hence quantifiable at least to a certain extent. The initial quantitative study rises to the challenge of quantifying the nebulous notion of habitus. It indicates that habitus of Chineseness serves as an underlying pattern that generates, and is generated through, Chinese Australians' choice of CHL learning. On the other hand, habitus of Chineseness is abstruse and elusive, hence mutable. The subsequent qualitative study diachronically discusses the 'unconscious consciousness' behind Chinese Australians' CHL learning shaped by the cultural history, the present social orders and the imagined future. In brief, the empirical evidence evolved from multiple data sources is in concert with Bourdieu's theorization of habitus, which is a system of 'structured and structuring structures', generating but not determining social practice.

Chapter 3 sees Jo Warin explore the concept of capital through a Bourdieu-informed methodological lens, specifically examining the production of identity capital through schooling. In what she refers to as an 'intermittent ethnography' – a longitudinal qualitative study conducted over a 14-year period with 9 children and young people from the time they were aged 3 to 17 – the findings showed that some children and young people had developed the capacity to produce a complex narrative of self while others had not. The narratives that developed around each child's school trajectory in relation to their identity building, revealed the existence of vicious and harmonious circles of social deprivation and social advantage. Seeking theory that would help her understand the differences between the nine targeted children with regard to the quality and frequency of the types of activity that are implicated in the development of identity, led to an engagement with Bourdieu's emphasis on forms of capital exchange and transubstantiation between schools and families, which for Warin have the explanatory power to reveal how forms of wealth become 'converted into an integral part of the person' (Bourdieu 1986, p.48). She suggests that there is a match between the longitudinal qualitative ethnographic approach she adopted and Bourdieu's incorporation of time, complexity and process in revealing how one form of capital may be transformed into another.

Her subsequent theorizing has relied on the concept of 'identity capital' to integrate individualized and therapeutic notions of self-construction into a political, economic and social context. The transubstantiation of interacting forms of capital explains cycles of social advantage and disadvantage within young people's trajectories through school and beyond.

Our own contribution to the collection is housed in Chapter 4 and explores the world of digital scholarship through a Bourdieuian lens. The chapter sets out to challenge assumptions about Bourdieu and determinism by engaging in a closer reading of Bourdieu's work, especially regarding the empirical under-standing of change. The chapter elaborates on the use of doxa and hysteresis in combination with reflexivity; these are research tools that have not yet gained the deserved prominence among Bourdieuian researchers, most likely because these constructs were less salient in Bourdieu's own writing. Yet, such concepts provide a lens through which the process of change can be explained. In this vein, this chapter examines how the combination of reflexive research practices with the concepts of doxa and hysteresis in the background allow the researchers to dig deeper into how change is perceived and enacted within the context of scholarly practices supported by the participatory web. The chapter also examines how this affects individuals' sense of identity.

Part 2: Researching equity in education

The first of the three chapters in this part (Chapter 5) sees Ravi Rampersad examine the underachievement of primary level Afro-Trinidadian boys via a combination of critical race theory (CRT) and Bourdieu's conceptual apparatus. Bourdieu's concepts provided a complementary partner to CRT in Rampersad's research, with habitus, field and capital positioned to capture the 'colours' of human agency. This theoretical synergy allowed for a greater appreciation of the contemporary manifestations of racialized structures in Trinidad, that of pigmentocracy. While CRT is strong on interrogating structures of oppression, the strength of Bourdieu lies with agency and issues of identity formation. It is argued that these two theories can be harmoniously applied in a complementary structure; this would see CRT used to centre race in analysis, while habitus, capital and field are employed to construct an intersectional schema of how race, social class and gender are embodied and enacted in both transformative and restrictive ways.

The theoretical thrust of his research underscores a specific methodological gaze, one which presupposed, to an extent, the valuing of certain types of data and collection methods. That being said, the use of both Bourdieu and CRT positioned data collection and analysis as an act of social justice, one which has the power to elevate the voice 'decibels' of the marginalized. In this sense, research is not seen as purely academic and extricated but as vested in championing social justice. Rampersad argues that concepts like habitus, capital and field allow an 'unpacking' and separation of social identity from dominant discourses of pigmentocracy and offer alternative views on differential educational outcomes.

Chapter 6 sees Maria Papapolydorou draw on a mixed methods research study that uses social capital as a concept, to map the ways in which social class and ethnic background cut across parents' involvement in their children's education. Bourdieuian frameworks lend themselves to an exploration of the relationship parental social capital has with their children's education, and the possible ways this is mediated by axes of inequality, such as social class and ethnic background.

Papapolydorou uses the chapter to explore what for her were two significant challenges in applying Bourdieuian theory in her research. First, Bourdieu mainly focuses on power differentials across social class groups but there is a relative lack of focus in his work on the topic of ethnic inequalities, especially in relation to social capital, which comprised an important focal point of her study. Second, although Bourdieu discusses cultural capital's relationship with education (Bourdieu, 1977), his concept of social capital is not considered with reference to the field of education. Instead, a generic definition is put forward but without elaboration as to how social capital might be operationalized for research purposes, let alone for research in the realm of education. In the chapter she discusses both the ways in which Bourdieu's frameworks informed the empirical undertaking of this research and the ways in which the theoretical and methodological challenges resulting from these frameworks were overcome. The chapter concludes by arguing that the findings of this study support some aspects of Bourdieu's social capital framework, while also suggesting ways in which his ideas can be applied further in future education research.

The final chapter in this part (Chapter 7) sees Katie Fitzpatrick and Stephen May flesh out in some detail what it means to do critical educational ethnography with Bourdieu. The key questions for them in this regard are: what does it mean to use Bourdieu's social theory to undertake ethnographic work in education settings? How do Bourdieu's ideas frame these methodological approaches in specific ways, and what are the implications of such framing? Given Bourdieu's own background in anthropological work, and his inherent interest in political and social issues, such a detailed exploration is welcome, especially in the educational field. They draw on critical ethnographic work in schools from their own work in language, health and physical education, and a range of other published studies. They use the chapter to focus specifically on how Bourdieu's notions of field, bodily hexis, and *méconnaissance* can be explored through critical ethnography in order to answer pressing contemporary political questions in education.

Part 3: Researching educational leadership and management

The two chapters in this part explore issues of educational leadership and management from different perspectives and also in quite different contexts. Based in Australia, Scott Eacott uses Chapter 8 to 'think anew' about his own field of endeavour, educational leadership research. According to him, mobilizing the work of Pierre Bourdieu in his scholarship has led to questions being asked of educational leadership research, posing serious methodological inquiry around the construction and ongoing maintenance of central research objects (e.g. leadership). For him, Bourdieu has helped erode the somewhat arbitrary division between theory and method and sustained a generative research programme concerned with the ongoing legitimation of the social world and its empirical manifestation in the administration of educational institutions. Eacott argues that engaging with, rather than necessarily overcoming, the methodological challenges in Bourdieu's work provides the basis for a rigorous and robust social 'science'.

Eacott's interest in the theoretical problem of the legitimation of the social world and its empirical manifestation in the administration of education draws heavily on his reading of Bourdieu, yet at the same time the challenges of mobilizing Bourdieu in a new space have led him to think it anew. Bringing Bourdieu into a different time and space, as he never explicitly wrote about educational administration per se, has required a rethinking of temporality and spatial politics. This chapter outlines the various ways in which Bourdieuian thinking has forced the author to think anew the construction of his research objects and how he can methodologically capture matters of temporality and space.

In Chapter 9, Bruce Kloot explores the use of narrative inquiry as a method for embedding Bourdieu's theoretical tools in educational research. It draws on empirical research conducted at two South African universities to demonstrate both the value and danger of using narrative inquiry in education research. According to Kloot, while narrative accounts typically illuminate the subjective reading of the social world, the ontological complicity between Bourdieu's notions of habitus and field means that multiple narratives can be used to reveal the contours of objective social structures. The result is a mapping of the field of South African higher education. Semi-structured interviews were performed with 21 individuals from various sectors of the field. These included interviews with seven mainstream professors from a range of the traditional engineering sub-disciplines, interviews with seven 'academic development managers' who were involved in administering or organizing foundation programmes, and seven more interviews, mainly with foundation programme staff.

Using Bourdieu as a starting point and the methodology of narrative inquiry, these interviews illuminated key aspects of the habitus of each individual, and these multiple habitus were then used to map the structure of the field. Given the close correspondence between habitus and field, the methodological issues at stake in this move are discussed by examining Bourdieu's own position on the theory–method relationship and some of the criticisms of his work that employs a similar methodology. The chapter concludes by drawing on one example from the study to demonstrate the possibilities as well as the potential problems of such an approach.

Part 4: Researching teacher education

Part 4 includes two fine examples of Bourdieu put to work in the context of teacher education and professional practices. Chapter 10 sees Naomi Flynn turn a Bourdieuian lens onto the teaching of English in primary schools. Specifically, she examines the use of Bourdieu's constructs of field, habitus, capital and doxa to deconstruct national policy and individual teachers' practice for the teaching of English in primary schools. Flynn takes as her starting point Bourdieu's work identifying language use and language ownership as the power brokers in relationships between teachers and pupils in order to uncover the range of influences operating unconsciously on teachers who, in England, face a developing demographic of children who do not speak English as their home language. Specifically, this chapter draws attention to the concepts of linguistic field, habitus and capital as potential interpretive instruments belonging to Bourdieuian theory. Furthermore it demonstrates how Bourdieuian thinking can be used in qualitative enquiry as the framework for coding in a constructivist grounded theory approach to data analysis.

She acknowledges in the chapter that using Bourdieu to explore classroom practice is not without its complexities, particularly in light of the view held by some that his theory presents researchers with a deterministic view of agency that suggests a fixed habitus in the face of change. However, for Flynn this of itself can be a helpful feature in uncovering how educational policy and practice play out together in either fostering or inhibiting developments in pedagogy. Her data illustrates how existing practices for the teaching of English influenced teachers' capacity to change their teaching approaches in order to accommodate second language learners. Using Bourdieu to expose the local and national fields operating as the architects of teachers' linguistic habitus provided a lens that questioned the received wisdom that has become common practice for English teaching.

The focus of Chapter 11 is on mathematics teacher education research, and sees Kathleen Nolan combine Bourdieu and the method of self-study in her research in this area. The qualitative research methodology of self-study has firmly established itself in recent years through its interrogation of pedagogy and practice in teacher education. Thus far, however, this methodology has been kept in relative isolation, deterred from engaging in rich conversations with a strong theoretical framing such as Bourdieu's social field theory. Nolan proposes that self-study and Bourdieu's social field theory (BSFT) create a productive pairing of methodology and theory, one that holds great potential for stimulating critical conversation in educational research.

Through the language and constructs of Bourdieu's social field theory, Nolan reconceptualizes a self-study methodology for mathematics teacher education research, highlighting the role of self and other(s) in/through pedagogic action and relationship. In doing so, she seeks to (re)define new relationships and conversations between methodology and theory – ones that resist privileging and separating the threads of methodology and theory in the research acts of data collection, analysis and representation. The purposeful weaving of methodology and theory in this chapter introduces a Bourdieu-informed discourse analysis (BIDA) framework, conceptualized as a tri-focal lens that serves to guide an interrogation of self-study data based in key Bourdieuian conceptual tools. Through this framework, Nolan identifies and consolidates the key threads of a dialectical methodology–theory construction and, ultimately, tackles the question of how the field of mathematics teacher education can study itself and unpack learning by inviting Bourdieu into the conversation.

The final chapter in this collection reflects on the different ways the preceding contributions have applied Bourdieu's ideas in educational research as both an object and means of investigation. We use this space to respond to some of the critical theory/method issues raised by the different contributions, in particular exploring the benefits and drawbacks of applying Bourdieu in real-life educational contexts that do not always lend themselves easily to intellectual investigation.

In order to facilitate this exploration, the chapter outlines some of the issues that arose when applying Bourdieu in the context of the four areas of education research included in the book: identities, equity, leadership and management, and teacher education. Such an approach, while summarizing and clarifying some of the issues raised in more detail, help us identify the ways in which research *context* matters in theory application – for example, are there different kinds of challenges when applying Bourdieu in leadership research as opposed to research in teacher education? The chapter reflects on the significance of context while also illustrating the ways in which such forms of applied research can be taken forward in future research investigations.

References

Bennett, T. (2010), 'Introduction', in P. Bourdieu, *Distinction: A social critique of the judgement of taste* (pp. xvii–xxiii). London: Routledge.

Bourdieu, P. (1977) *Outline of the theory of practice.* Cambridge: Cambridge University Press.

Bourdieu, P. (1984) *Distinction: A social critique of the judgement of taste.* Abingdon, Oxon: Routledge.

Bourdieu, P. (1986) 'The forms of capital', in J. Richardson (ed.), *Handbook of theory and research for the sociology of education* (Vol. 241, pp. 46–58). New York: Greenwood.

Bourdieu, P. (1988) *Homo academicus.* Stanford, CA: Stanford University Press.

Bourdieu, P. (1996) *The state nobility: Elite schools in the field of power*. Stanford, CA: Stanford University Press.

Bourdieu, P. (1999) *The weight of the world: Social suffering in contemporary society*. Cambridge: Polity Press.

Bourdieu, P. (2004a) 'The peasant and his body'. *Ethnography*, 5(4): 579–99.

Bourdieu, P. (2004b) *Science of science and reflexivity*. Cambridge: Polity Press.

Bourdieu, P. (2008) *Sketch for a self-analysis*. (R. Nice, trans.). Chicago, IL: University of Chicago Press.

Bourdieu, P. and Passeron, J.-C. (1964 [1979]) *The inheritors: French students and their relation to culture*. Chicago, IL: University of Chicago Press.

Bourdieu, P. and Passeron, J.-C. (1979 [1990]) *Reproduction in education, society and culture* (2nd edn). London: Sage.

Bourdieu, P. and Wacquant, L. (1992) *An invitation to reflexive sociology*. Cambridge: Polity Press.

Costa, C. and Murphy, M. (2015) *Bourdieu, habitus and social research: The art of application*. London: Palgrave.

Murphy, M. (ed.) (2013) *Social theory and education research* (4-volume set). Los Angeles, CA/London: Sage.

Nowicka, M. (2015) 'Habitus – its transformation and transfer through cultural encounters in migration', in C. Costa and M. Murphy (eds), *Bourdieu, habitus and social research: The art of application* (pp. 93–110). London: Palgrave.

Part I

Researching educational identities

Negotiating Chineseness through learning Chinese as a Heritage Language in Australia

The role of habitus

Guanglun Michael Mu

In every survey of human history, there is no shortage of discourses on the crucial role that language plays in identity construction. The increasing cultural and linguistic diversity has seen ethnic groups living together, negotiating an alloy of dynamic, different identities while striving to maintain their own group identity. The perplexity of identity construction for an ethnic group in a society has given rise to the salience of learning and developing the Heritage Language, a language other than the dominant language of that society that is associated with the cultural background of that ethnic group. There is a rich body of literature concerning the relationship between Heritage Language and ethnic identity, and the patterns and dynamics behind this relationship have been well debated (Mu, 2015a).

People of Chinese ancestry, due to their large scale, wide distribution, and demographic heterogeneity in diasporic contexts, have gained increasing scholarly attention. The mutually constitutive relationship between Chinese ethnic identity construction and Chinese Heritage Language (CHL) learning has been speculated on through classical social psychological and post-structural approaches. The current chapter differs, however, in its use of Bourdieu's sociology to dissect the CHL–ethnic identity link. In this chapter, I first present a panoramic overview of the social psychological and post-structural treatments of the relationship between CHL learning and Chinese ethnic identity construction. I then turn to a penetrating discussion of Bourdieu's key notion of 'habitus' to excavate the nature and nuances behind the aforementioned relationship through an empirical study that I did in Australia.

Chinese identity: ascribed, constructed or socialized?

The classical social psychological scholarship largely adopts a quantitative approach to examining Chinese Heritage Language learners (CHLLs)' self-identification and their CHL learning. In the United States, Chinese Americans' CHL proficiency was found to be positively related to their sense of belonging-ness to the Chinese ethnic group, their perceptions of the meanings attached to this membership, and their commitment to exploring Chinese heritage and culture (Kiang, 2008; Oh and Fuligni, 2010). Canadian studies tend to echo the US research. Canadian university students of Chinese ancestry considered CHL learning to be an integral aspect of their self-concept; the more they integrated CHL learning into their being, the more they were motivated to learn the language, and the more they considered their Chinese ethnicity central to their sense of self (Comanaru and Noels, 2009). Similar findings were reported in an early study in which Chinese Canadian university students related their CHL learning to a desire for participation in their ethnic community, the sense of connection to their ethnic homeland, and the motivation to be integrated into their ethnic culture (Feuerverger, 1991). These social psychological studies have an emphasis on how CHL learning helps to inform various dimensions of ethnic identity, such as nominal identification, group membership, shared patterns of communication, underlying beliefs, and philosophy of life within ethnic communities. In this vein, the social psychological scholarship tends to view the interrelation between CHL and Chinese identity through a predictable, linear and individualistic framework. Despite the meaningful findings from the social psychological research, this school oversimplifies CHLLs' life trajectories in relation to tensions and politics around CHL learning and identity construction.

In response to the oversimplicity of the social psychological school, post-structuralism challenges the understanding of ethnic identity as an individual trait of CHLLs. Chao (1997) reported that Chinese Americans' ethnic identity shifted along the process of their CHL learning, from their teenage desires to be integrated into American culture and English-speaking community to the gradual awareness of CHL learning as an undeniable part of their Chinese heritage during their young adulthood. This study indicated the entanglement of Chinese identity and CHL learning through an ongoing and changing process. He (2006) found that Chinese Americans studied their CHL to re-establish either similarities with ethnic Chinese members or differences from members of mainstream American culture, and that they were committed not merely to inheriting their CHL and maintaining their Chinese cultural identity but also to transforming and recreating their identity through CHL learning. This indicated that CHLLs' identity construction through CHL learning across time and space is a socialization process with multiple agencies, directions and goals. Ang (2001) discussed the predicaments of Chineseness in diaspora through an autobiographical approach. She failed to legitimize her Chinese-ness because 'not speaking Chinese' did not give her a recognized identity as a 'real' Chinese. To tackle the sense of alienation that took hold of her, she contended that 'not speaking Chinese' can cease being a problem for overseas Chinese in diasporic contexts. In other words, diasporic Chineseness cannot be envisioned in any unified or homogeneous way. Rather, it is a diverse, hetero-geneous and ultimately precarious hybridity. Different from the classical social psychological thesis, the post-structural school conceptualizes Chinese identity as contradictory, multiple, and fluid, contextually embedded and constantly constructed through CHL learning.

However, the post-structuralist concept of multiple identities without foundational basis has its limitations. The assumption that human identity is wholly malleable and that the body can be freely styled to assume an invented identity runs into problems when faced with the durability of human beings' internal schemata (Luke, 2009). These internal, bodily schemata enable human beings to remain in many ways the products of kinship and blood (Luke, 2009). In summary, both social psychological and post-structural schools offer thought-provoking insights into the identity–CHL link, while they inevitably receive critiques from other perspectives. To reconcile the tensions between the social psychological 'inside-out' approach and the post-structural 'outside-in' approach, it is useful to revisit Bourdieu's sociological notion of habitus, which underpins my investigation of the role played by habitus of Chineseness in CHL learning.

Habitus of Chineseness

Habitus denotes 'systems of durable, transposable dispositions, structured structures predisposed to function as structuring structures' (Bourdieu, 1977, p. 72). As a set of embodied dispositions, habitus is associated with continuity on the one hand and variability on the other hand. Its continuity has the tendency to perpetuate the durability and transposability of attributes across time and space, while its variability refers to the work of a 'generative principle of regulated improvisations' (Bourdieu, 1977, p. 78) through the internalization of the external (Bourdieu, 1984, 1988). In other words, habitus consists of enduring structures, or 'schemes of perception, conception, and action common to all members of the same group' (Bourdieu, 1977, p. 86); at the same time, habitus builds on basic dimensions of external conditions in social life that come to shape internal being, thinking and doing. The structural commonness within a group and the internalized external conditions can be considered a Bourdieuian approach to reconciling the social psychological and post-structural theses of ethnic identity.

Drawing insight from habitus, the ethnic identity of Chinese people, or Chineseness, can be conceptualized as a set of embodied dispositions associated with people of Chinese ancestry, embedded within their bodily attributes, rooted in their Chinese heritage and emergent from their family upbringing and social learning. These embodied dispositions, such as affiliated cultural, experiential, and historical memories, are 'structured structures' that may largely remain durable and transposable. That said, these dispositions are not immutable because they are 'structuring structures' constantly shaped and reshaped through socialization.

In order to identify some idiosyncratic representations of Chineseness, the notion of habitus warrants further scrutiny. Habitus works on 'the basis of the premises established in the previous state' (Bourdieu, 2000, p. 161). That is to say, habitus is acquired through culture (Bourdieu, 1984) and produced through history (Bourdieu, 1990b; Bourdieu and Wacquant, 1992). Confucianism can therefore be understood to constitute a cultural history or 'previous state' for Chineseness, because it is the bedrock, even the definitive core, of Chinese culture (Tan, 2008). A systematic review of Confucianism is provided by Mu (2015b), whose enumeration of Confucian dispositions includes, but is not limited to, valuing mathematics, handwriting and academic performance; maintaining strong family ties and social hierarchies; hoping to have sons to continue the family line; and feeling embarrassed to refuse requests.

Habitus endows individuals with durable cognitive structures and dispositional senses that direct them to appropriate responses to given situations (Bourdieu, 1998). As a system of dispositions to certain practice, habitus constructs an objective basis for predictable modes of behaviour because individuals equipped with a particular habitus will behave in a certain way in a given circumstance (Bourdieu, 1994). In this vein, habitus captures how individuals carry their culture, experience and history within themselves, and how they make choices to act in certain ways rather than in others. Accordingly, habitus of Chineseness is composed of a set of underlying tendencies and embodied predispositions to think and act in such a way as has been inculcated by Confucian heritage, and that represents a system of Confucian dispositions embodied in shared tastes, behaviours, values and ways of life. Specifically, Bourdieu (1991) theorizes that people make choices about languages according to the habitus they have. When Chineseness is conceptualized through habitus and CHL learning is considered a form of language practice, habitus of Chineseness, theoretically, becomes a generative mechanism that underpins CHL learning. This is the sociological tool that I use to delve into the relationship between Chineseness and CHL learning.

The mixed methods study

Different from the bulk of the extant studies conducted in North America, the current study sets its scene in Australia, an idiosyncratic cultural and social place for Chinese Australians, their ancestors and descendants. The 'gold-rush' age saw the agitation of European diggers towards Chinese diggers because of the lure of gold and the competition in gold mining. This agitation resulted in restrictive anti-Chinese legislation in the late 1850s and the early 1860s. Later, the so-called 'White Australia Policy' promulgated in 1901 constructed the legal basis for the racial superiority of 'whiteness' over 'Chineseness' and other 'colourness'. Nevertheless, the dismantlement of the White Australia Policy in the late 1970s saw the arrival of multiculturalism in Australia. Furthermore, the 2012 Australia in the Asian Century White Paper (Australian Government, 2012) increased the linguistic value of the Chinese language and favoured the cultural identity of Chineseness. In brief, Australia is a complex social place for

Chinese Australians who first suffered from the potholes and distractions brought by the historical discrimination against their Chineseness, and then enjoyed, consciously or unconsciously, the rejuvenation of this Chineseness brought by the multicultural social order. However, how the homogeneity, variability, and complexity embedded within this Chineseness as well as its associated social, cultural and historical ramifications come to inform and shape Chinese Australians' social practices, CHL learning in this case, is largely unknown.

To excavate the patterns, dynamics, and nuances behind this sociological phenomenon requires plural methodological approaches across quantitative and qualitative spectra. Such empirical research can not only 'grasp the particularity within the generality and the generality within the particularity' (Bourdieu and Wacquant, 1992, p. 75) but also uncover 'the universal buried deep within the most particular' (Bourdieu and Wacquant, 1992, p. 44). If habitus of Chineseness does build on the 'previous state' of the Confucian cultural history and does represent a set of structured structures that are manifest, to some extent, in a Confucian way of being, thinking and behaving, these historical patterns as well as the level of durability and transposability of these embodied Confucian dispositions should be discernible, and ultimately measurable, at least to a certain degree. That said, if these embodied Confucian dispositions are generated through the unconscious consciousness, the 'intentionality without intention' (Bourdieu, 1990a, p. 12), and the internalization of broad social structures, this habitus of Chineseness is associated with a set of nebulous dimensions that are difficult to measure in empirical research (Sullivan, 2002).

In brief, the theoretical nature of habitus prompts me to use a mixed methods research to dissect the relationship between Chinese Australians' Chineseness and their CHL learning. The initial quantitative sub-study considers habitus of Chineseness to be a set of 'structured structures' and relates the embodied Confucian dispositions to CHL learning, while the subsequent qualitative sub-study interrogates how the 'structuring structures' of Chineseness and CHL learning are mutually constructed.

The quantitative study

Much of the existing work attempting to use and apply Bourdieu is qualitative in approach. However, there is inevitably something missing by restricting the methodological focus to one mode of research when operating Bourdieu's theoretical package. In Bourdieu's original works, such as *Distinction* (Bourdieu, 1984) and *The state nobility* (Bourdieu, 1996), data were also quantitatively investigated by correspondence analysis to develop tendency, prediction and correlation. Although the argument against quantifying habitus has been prevalent in the literature for a long time (Sullivan, 2002), an increasing number of scholars (Cockerham, 2005; Cockerham and Hinote, 2009; Dumais, 2002; McClelland, 1990) have articulated less rigid views. The route of these colleagues inspired me to quantify the habitus of Chineseness.

To operationalize the habitus of Chineseness, a reliable and valid instrument of nine items was developed and validated to reflect various dimensions of Confucian dispositions (see Mu, 2014a, 2014b, 2015b). To gauge CHL proficiency, a reliable and valid instrument of four items asking participants to self-report Mandarin listening, speaking, reading and writing skills was developed and validated (see Mu, 2014b, 2015a, 2015b; Mu and Dooley, 2015). A 7-point unipolar Likert-type scale was used as a proxy interval level of measurement in line with common practice in educational research (Lehman, 1991; Tabachnick and Fidell, 2007). The scale ranged from 1 (not at all) to 7 (completely).

As widely used in heritage research (Gibbs and Hines, 1992; Hall, 1992; Kiang, 2008; Pao *et al.*, 1997; Root, 1992), snowball sampling was used to approach participants in my study. Eventually, 230 Chinese Australian participants, ranging in age between 18 and 35, responded to the online survey. To the best of my knowledge and belief, this is the largest national sample of Chinese Australians to date. Although snowball sampling does not guarantee the representativeness of the sample, it helped my study capture the demographic diversity of Chinese Australian population. The sample consisted of 47.8 per cent men and 52.2 per cent women. Of the participants, 111 were born outside Australia, with 95 born in China (the Chinese Mainland, Hong Kong, Macau and Taiwan) and 16 born in other countries (Indonesia, Malaysia, New Zealand, Singapore and Vietnam). Their age of immigration ranged between 9 months and 13 years – an age range consistent with the literature (Bhatti, 2002; Mu, 2015b; Zhang, 2009) for the first-generation immigrants to be considered as HL speakers. The Australian-born group consisted of 119 participants, including 73, 31, and 15 participants of second, third and fourth generation or further removed, respectively. Participants reportedly used a variety of languages at home, including English, Mandarin, Cantonese, other Chinese dialects, Indonesian, Vietnamese or a mixture of these languages. Their formal CHL learning varied from none at all to 15 years.

Regression analysis was used to predict the variance of CHL proficiency. To unveil the complexities of Chinese Australians' CHL learning, both Chineseness and selected demographic variables were treated as predictors for CHL proficiency. The demographic variables were language usage at home, place of birth, years of formal CHL learning and generation. Given the conceptual interest of my research, a hierarchical regression was performed by entering Chineseness first and the demographic variables subsequently. As indicated in Table 2.1, Chineseness was found to be a significant contributor to CHL proficiency. When Chineseness first entered the model, 44 per cent of the variance of CHL proficiency was explained. When demographic variables were added into the model, they made a further significant contribution by explaining another 20 per cent of the variance of CHL proficiency. In total, 64 per cent of the variance of CHL proficiency has been explained by the predictors.

Table 2.1 Variance explained by the predictors

Model	R	R2	Adjusted R2	R2 change	F change	df1	df2	p of F change	Durbin–Watson
1	.66[a]	.44	.44	.44	179.56	1	228	<.001	
2	.80[b]	.64	.64	.20	32.01	4	224	<.001	1.93

a Predictors: (constant), Chineseness
b Predictors: (constant), Chineseness, language usage at home, years of formal CHL learning, place of birth, generation
Source: reproduced from Mu, 2014b

Table 2.2 Significant predictors for CHL proficiency

Predictors	Unstandardized		Std. Beta	t	p	Collinearity statistics	
	Beta	SE. B				Tolerance	VIF
(Constant)	.10	.25		.41	.684		
Language usage at home	.54	.08	.40	7.02	<.001	.48	2.08
Years of formal CHL learning	.08	.02	.16	3.43	.001	.73	1.37
Chineseness	.45	.07	.34	6.82	<.001	.65	1.54

Source: reproduced from Mu, 2014b

Nevertheless, only three significant predictors were retained by the regression model. As indicated in Table 2.2, these significant predictors are: Chineseness, language usage at home and years of formal CHL learning. As evident in the data, Chineseness played an important role in CHL proficiency.

Of all the predictors for CHL proficiency, place of birth and generation were not significant. Interestingly, they were significantly correlated with CHL proficiency. Participants born in places where Mandarin has more legitimate value (Mu, 2015b) tended to have higher CHL proficiency than those born in places where Mandarin is less valued ($\tau = .40$, $p < .001$), while later generations tended to have lower CHL proficiency than early generations ($\tau = -.45$, $p < .001$). However, place of birth and generation became less powerful in the presence of other demographic variables. This result is informative. Chinese Australians were born into a particular place and a certain generation. These identities were given rather than chosen. Compared with place of birth and generation, particular language usage patterns at home and certain years of formal CHL learning can be choices either made by Chinese Australians themselves or imposed on them by their parents. In this respect, it is the agentive commitment not the static structure that comes to shape CHL practices.

Unlike these demographic variables, Chineseness is very unique. As a habitus, this Chineseness was both born and chosen. On the one hand, participants were born into a Chinese cultural history deeply rooted in Confucianism. Structured by the habitus, certain dispositions of Chineseness cannot be erased or made over and therefore stay durable and transposable. On the other hand, participants internalize basic dimensions of external conditions in their social lives, which, in turn, comes to shape their internal attitudes, values, perceptions and the dispositions that are structuring the habitus. This habitus, though durable and transposable, is not immutable. Instead, it is an open system of disposition 'constantly subjected to experiences, and therefore constantly affected by them in a way that either reinforces or modifies its structures' (Bourdieu and Wacquant, 1992, p. 133). Chinese Australians are 'open to the world, and therefore exposed to the world, and so capable of being conditioned by the world, shaped by the material and cultural conditions of existence' (Bourdieu, 2000, p. 134). Accordingly, dispositions, knowledge, and values associated with Chineseness are always potentially subject to modification, rather than being passively consumed or reinscribed. This is reflected in the data – participants reported different levels of attitudes towards Confucian dispositions ($M = 4.18$, $SD = 1.38$). In other words, different individual Chinese Australians capture or recapture dispositions of Chineseness at various levels in different contexts according to the social structures that they have internalized. Therefore, they will produce diverse forms of practices in relation to their CHL learning that ultimately lead to their different levels of CHL proficiency ($M = 4.21$, $SD = 1.84$).

Chinese Australians' Chineseness serves as an underpinning mechanism for CHL learning. However, this mechanism is generative but not decisive. The current regression model has explained 64 per cent of the variance of CHL proficiency with 44 per cent explained by Chineseness. Bourdieu's sociology may offer a theoretical framework to examine the remaining 36 per cent of the variance of CHL proficiency. According to Bourdieu (1984), routine behaviours and patterned sociocultural activities in which agents engage (practices) result from their dispositions (habitus) and their social resources (capital) within the current state of play of a particular social arena (field). In line with this Bourdieuian perspective, CHL learning, as a form of Chinese Australians' social practice, not only results from their habitus of Chineseness, but also may be attributed to the quantity and quality of resources they possess in proportion to which their opportunities for successful CHL learning vary. These resources are what Bourdieu means by capital. Therefore, the remaining 36 per cent of the variance of CHL proficiency may be (partly) attributed to various forms of capital invested by Chinese Australians (see Mu, 2015a).

The initial quantitative study unveils the underlying pattern that habitus of Chineseness underpins Chinese Australians' CHL learning. CHL learning is neither fully dependent on, nor completely free of, the habitus of Chineseness. The quantitative study, though informative, misses the nuances and minutiae behind the sociological mechanism of habitus. To uncover the niceties and details of how habitus of Chineseness informs CHL learning, I now turn to report the qualitative sub-study.

The qualitative study

At the end of the online survey, participants were invited to attend follow-up interviews. Five participants (Adam, Bob, Crystal, Dianna and En-ning) accepted the invitation. These participants offered 'maximum variation' (Patton, 1990) in their demographic features. The two male and three female participants ranged in age between 18 and 28. The three non-Australian-born participants moved to live in Australia at the age of 9 months, 12 years, and 13 years. The two Australian-born participants were both reportedly second-generation Chinese Australians. The home language/s of the five participants varied from English only, through a mixture of English and Chinese, to Chinese only. Their years of formal CHL learning ranged from 0 to 13. Interestingly, only one participant was proficient in CHL, while the others had relatively low CHL proficiency.

When I conducted interviews with these participants, I was very conscious of the definite asymmetry of power. As the researcher and the interviewer, I defined the situation, introduced the topics of the conversation and steered the course of the interview through further questions. This asymmetry was reinforced particularly when I occupied 'a higher place in the social hierarchy of different types of capital, cultural capital in particular' (Bourdieu, 1999, p. 609). To clarify, as an educated native Chinese speaker, I had conversations around topics associated with CHL learning experiences of the Chinese Australian participants. In this social field, the participants might assume that I had better Chinese language proficiency. This assumption entailed hierarchical field positions occupied by me and the participants based on different levels of Chinese language competence valued as cultural capital in this field. The lack of this capital might yield embarrassment or 'loss of face' and generate an uncomfortable environment for the participants during the interviews.

In order to control the effects of asymmetry of power, I practised naivety to characterize my special learner role. This learner role entailed a frame of mind to set aside any assumptions that the meaning of the participants has been known. The learner role was administered through verbal 'signs of feedback' or 'response tokens', such as 'yes', 'right', 'oh' and 'ok' (Bourdieu, 1999, p. 610), as well as putting forward explanations in a proposed rather than an imposed way, such as suggestions to offer multiple and open-ended continuations to the participants' hesitations or searches for appropriate expressions (Bourdieu, 1999, pp. 614–15), and non-verbal means, such as an open posture, approving nods, appropriate facial expressions and good eye contact. These verbal and bodily signs of attention, interest, approval, encouragement and recognition enabled my role as a listener and a seeker of knowledge during the whole interview process. It was the 'active and methodical listening' that led up to 'adopting the interviewees' language, views, feelings, and thoughts' (Bourdieu, 1999, p. 609) and signalled 'the interviewer's intellectual and emotional participation' (Bourdieu, 1999, p. 10).

Apart from 'active and methodical listening', 'proximity and familiarity' provided a condition of 'nonviolent communication' (Bourdieu, 1999, p. 610) during the interview. Common cultural and physical dispositions shared by me and my participants ensured this proximity and familiarity. I, a native Chinese, was culturally and physically close to my Chinese Australian participants, or 'linked to them by close familiarity' (Bourdieu, 1999, p. 611). When a young Chinese researcher interviewed these young Chinese Australians, the conversation could spring from the dispositions attuned to each other. The participants seemed to consider this situation as an exceptional opportunity to 'make themselves heard' and to 'carry their experience over from the private to the public sphere' (Bourdieu, 1999, p. 615). Their speech seemed to convey 'a joy of expression' (Bourdieu, 1999, p. 615). However, this relatively easy access and affinity with the participants did not necessarily lead to biased interpretation of the data to meet my own assumptions and expectations. As a scholar, I was more confined to university life and removed from the more complex lived worlds of Chinese Australians. Such social difference enabled me to step back as a listener from my participants' experiences. The aforementioned 'proximity' and 'social difference' helped me avoid the two problematic extremes: 'total divergence' between the interviewer and the interviewees where understanding and trust are not possible, and 'total overlap' where nothing can be said and questioned because everything goes without saying (Bourdieu, 1999, p. 612).

During the interviews, questions were asked around participants' CHL learning experiences. I now turn to a Bourdieuian interpretation to theorize participants' accounts of a CHL–identity link. As argued earlier, habitus is rooted in cultural history, or 'previous state' in Bourdieu's term (2000, p. 161). For some participants, the origins of their habitus of Chineseness reportedly carried deep meaning and relevance through their CHL learning. En-ning took the opportunity when she was learning Chinese in China to explore her family origin. She found and visited her grandparents' '老家' (hometown) in southern China. It should be noted that the Chinese word '老家' has a different meaning from the English word 'hometown'. '老家' is the 'root' of a clan, a native place where one's ancestors originated and were buried. It signifies not only the physical place itself but also the genealogical connections and the deep attachments to the land, customs and compatriots, forged through generations of shared ancestry, history, culture and language. The very visit to '老家' has 'totally changed' En-ning's life. As she said:

> I am so glad that I discovered this so early in my life. I do meet a lot of overseas Chinese who came to China much older, looking for something. But I am glad I came early . . . I think if we have the opportunity to explore

this other side of who we are or might be, that can be very empowering, which in turn can very much affect our life experiences.

En-ning seemed to attribute this trip to explore her cultural roots to her growing Chinese competence. As she explained, 'I wouldn't have managed if I didn't have at least some Mandarin. Even my parents have never been (there). It was incredible.' Clearly, En-ning made a link between her CHL and the historical foundation of her habitus of Chineseness. She also considered Chineseness an internal driving force behind learning CHL: 'For Chinese Australians learning Chinese, learning the language immediately raises issues of identity, belonging, culture and history.' Other participants provided similar accounts. Some examples follow.

When asked about the driving force behind CHL learning, Adam explicitly spoke of his Chinese ancestry and heritage.

> I am sort of trying to discover my heritage. . . . For me, Mandarin is a tool to enforce the Chinese identity . . . It's to satisfy my curiosity about my heritage and how history, culture, etc. have shaped who I am today as a part of my own 'who do you think you are' project.

It is worth nothing that Adam was referring to the TV genealogy programme *Who Do You Think You Are?* It is an Australian television documentary series, following the BBC series of the same name. Each episode profiles a celebrity tracing his/her family roots. Adam referred to this programme due to its promotion of genealogy, which resonated with his 'curiosity' about his 'Chineseness'.

When asked why he chose to learn Chinese in school, Bob said, 'Chinese is part of me.' When asked what the Chinese language meant to her, Dianna replied, 'It's also part of my identity, my Chinese identity. I was born into this culture, this colour, and this language, so it's part of my identity, my Chinese identity.' In this way, participants' CHL learning resonated with a constitutive dimension and sense of themselves. As such, CHL learning helped participants recapture or reinforce a habitus of Chineseness, which was embraced as 'part of' themselves or 'the other side of' themselves. These interview accounts evidently indicate that the family root, ancestral origin, and cultural heritage formulate the 'previous state' of habitus of Chineseness, an embodied identity that came to inform their CHL learning.

The 'previous state' of habitus integrates past experiences and functions at every moment as a matrix of dispositions, which generates infinitely diversified practices (Bourdieu, 1977). In this vein, habitus of Chineseness is not only a retrospective underlying pattern, but also a prospective sociological mechanism. All participants indicated that they intended to reproduce Chineseness in future through intergenerational Chinese learning. When asked, 'If you were to have children, would you like to encourage them to learn another language other than English?' all participants agreed that they would like their children to learn Chinese.

> I would love to see them learn Mandarin. Yes, I would love to see them learn Mandarin . . . It's definitely biased of course. (Adam)

> I wouldn't force them. They can decide what they want to know, like where their grandparents' heritage was from. But I won't force them. If they choose [Chinese] and they are interested, by all means I will support them and try to coach them . . . They can learn where their dad is from. (Bob)

> I would like my kids to learn Chinese . . . so that we don't lose it as time goes on. We are Chinese family and we should speak Chinese. (Crystal)

> I need to keep my home language going no matter where I am. So I will pass on to my children as well. (Dianna)

> I would encourage them to learn Chinese . . . I personally would like them to learn Chinese because of the personal connections they would have. (En-ning)

According to these accounts, the loyalty to CHL may persist over many generations of Chinese Australians who relearn CHL that symbolizes their ethnic identity, and in Bourdieu's sense, their habitus. This CHL learning is a strategy to reproduce the habitus of Chineseness in the next generation and even generations further removed. A habitus of Chineseness, to borrow a Bourdieuian metaphor, contains the genetic information which both allows and disposes successive generations to reproduce the world that they inherit from the previous generation (Bourdieu and Passeron, 1990). In this respect, this durable and transposable Chineseness is transmitted across generations and over historical time through CHL learning.

Interestingly, the choice of CHL learning as a form of social practice can be quite unconscious sometimes. When asked about the reasons for CHL learning, Adam said, 'I tried to learn Mandarin because I just wanted to learn it'. He added, 'I don't know how it happened but it just happened. It's a good weird thing that had happened.' When asked the same question, Crystal said, 'I like it because I want to.' She paused then added, 'I feel I just want to know it.' En-ning said, 'I don't know what came over me but I decided I wanted to learn it in school.' For Adam, Crystal, and En-ning, they did not have to know what drove them to learn CHL consciously. Their bodies knew. When Bob was asked why he chose to learn Chinese in school, he said it was 'because of my Chinese heritage'. By this account, it was his Chinese heritage rooted in his body that generated his intention for learning Chinese. As Bourdieu (1977) argues, agents' actions are the product of habitus of which the agents may have no conscious mastery because habitus always exceeds conscious intentions. As such, habitus of Chineseness produced these participants' CHL learning practices, without either explicit reason or signifying intent, to be none the less sensible and reasonable, and to be immediately intelligible and foreseeable, and hence taken for granted. This Chineseness was the immanent law laid down in these participants by their earliest upbringing and 'previous state', which were the preconditions for their CHL learning practices.

In brief, these participants' habitus of Chineseness operated at a level that was simultaneously conscious and unconscious. They did make language choices in strategic ways, and try to use the rules of different fields to their advantage, but at the same time they were influenced, or almost driven, by values and expectations that they derived from their habitus. Though they might be conscious of learning Chinese strategically, they might not be aware that their motives, goals, and aspirations were generated through their habitus of Chineseness.

Conclusion

Habitus as the system of dispositions is a past that survives in the present and tends to perpetuate itself into the future (Bourdieu, 1977). As habitus, Chineseness lays the groundwork for a set of embodied dispositions associated with the Confucian way of doing, being and thinking. These Confucian dispositions underpinned by habitus of Chineseness are durable with the passage of time and transposable with the changing of space, because the core Confucian values have an enduring impact on Chinese people today (Lee, 1996) and Confucianism is the dynamic force that determines the direction and form of Chinese life (Tan, 2008). Chinese Australians' Confucian deportment and manner are the products of their habitus of Chineseness, and therefore are dispositions belonging to and characteristic of themselves. As such, Chineseness is embodied and expressed through Confucian ways of 'standing, speaking, walking, and thereby of feeling and thinking' (Bourdieu, 1990b, p. 70). In this respect, 'history turned into nature' (Bourdieu, 1977, p. 78) and habitus is an 'embodied history, internalized as a second nature and so forgotten as history' (Bourdieu, 1990b, p. 56). Consequently, 'the active presence of the whole past' becomes 'the active presence' (Bourdieu, 1990b, p. 56) because what historic-ally needed to be durable and transposable through a process of continuous reproduction is now inscribed through social regulations, forms and norms. As 'inscribed in bodies by identical histories' (Bourdieu, 1990b, p. 59), habitus creates homogeneity in social groups. These Bourdieuian stances indicate that the habitus of Chineseness is historically informed by its cultural foundation, that is, Confucian dispositions. Consequently, Confucian perceptions, apprecia-tions and actions can be carried out and enacted not only by Chinese people living in China but also by overseas Chinese throughout the world, for example, Chinese Australians in this study. Therefore, Chineseness is the bodily inscription of Chinese Australians' past, present and future positions in the social structure that they carry with them, at all times and in all places.

The quantitative study suggests that when Chinese Australians have a stronger disposition of Chineseness, they tend to be more committed to learning their CHL, and therefore have a better CHL proficiency. As such, Chinese Australians' habitus of Chineseness captures how they make choices to act in certain ways rather than in others by virtue of their culture, experience and history within themselves. This strongly aligns with Bourdieu's (1991) contention that people make language choices according to the habitus they have. What evidently emerged from the qualitative data was that habitus of Chineseness was explicitly linked to past roots, present moments and future anticipations, willingly or unwillingly, consciously or unconsciously. This habitus of Chineseness, as a system of internalized cognitive and motivating structures (Bourdieu, 1977, 1990b), is produced by structures of past and present cultural and social environments and will be reproduced in future CHL learning through its generativity.

In summary, Chineseness is not a random or un-patterned structure but a systematically ordered one, comprising a set of embodied dispositions associated with Confucian values, which generate certain perceptions, appreciations and practices for Chinese Australians. Chineseness is durable in that it lasts over time and is transposable by being capable of becoming active within a wide variety of social worlds, and therefore functions as an enduring mechanism to generate Chinese Australians' CHL learning practices. However, this habitus of Chineseness is not immutable but changing constantly in response to new experiences. Therefore, Chinese Australians' habitus of Chineseness generates different CHL learning practices for different individuals in different contexts, resulting in variable levels of CHL proficiency.

References

Ang, I. (2001) *On not speaking Chinese: Living between Asia and the West.* London: Routledge.

Australian Government. (2012) *Australia in the Asian Century White Paper.* Canberra: Commonwealth of Australia.

Bhatti, G. (2002) *Asian children at home and at school: An ethnographic study.* London: Routledge.

Bourdieu, P. (1977) *Outline of a theory of practice.* Cambridge: Cambridge University Press.

Bourdieu, P. (1984) *Distinction: A social critique of the judgement of taste.* London: Routledge and Kegan Paul.

Bourdieu, P. (1988) *Homo academicus.* Stanford, CA: Stanford University Press.

Bourdieu, P. (1990a) *In other words: Essays towards a reflexive sociology.* Stanford, CA: Stanford University Press.

Bourdieu, P. (1990b) *The logic of practice.* Cambridge: Polity Press.

Bourdieu, P. (1991) *Language and symbolic power.* Cambridge: Polity Press.

Bourdieu, P. (1994) *In other words: Essays towards a reflexive sociology.* Cambridge: Polity Press.

Bourdieu, P. (1996) *The state nobility: Elite schools in the field of power.* Cambridge: Polity Press.

Bourdieu, P. (1998) *Practical reason: On the theory of action.* Cambridge: Polity Press.

Bourdieu, P. (1999) 'Understanding', in P. Bourdieu (ed.), *The weight of the world: Social suffering in contemporary society* (pp. 607–26). Cambridge: Polity Press.

Bourdieu, P. (2000) *Pascalian meditations.* Cambridge: Polity Press.

Bourdieu, P. and Passeron, J.-C. (1990) *Reproduction in education, society and culture* (2nd edn). London: Sage.

Bourdieu, P. and Wacquant, L. J. D. (1992) *An invitation to reflexive sociology.* Cambridge: Polity Press.

Chao, D.-L. (1997) 'Chinese for Chinese Americans: A case study', *Journal of the Chinese Language Teachers Association*, 32(2): 1–13.

Cockerham, W. C. (2005) 'Health lifestyle theory and the convergence of agency and structure', *Journal of Health and Social Behavior*, 46(1): 51–67.

Cockerham, W. C. and Hinote, B. P. (2009) 'Quantifying habitus: Future directions', in K. Robson and C. Sanders (eds), *Quantifying theory: Pierre Bourdieu* (pp. 201–10). Breinigsville, PA: Springer Science + Business Media.

Comanaru, R. and Noels, K. A. (2009) 'Self-determination, motivation, and the learning of Chinese as a Heritage Language', *The Canadian Modern Language Review*, 66(1): 131–58.

Dumais, S. A. (2002) 'Cultural capital, gender, and school success: The role of habitus', *Sociology of Education*, 75(1): 44–68.

Feuerverger, G. (1991) 'University students' perceptions of Heritage Language learning and ethnic identity maintenance', *The Canadian Modern Language Review*, 47(4): 660–77.

Gibbs, J. T. and Hines, A. M. (1992) 'Negotiating ethnic identity: Issues for Black-White biracial adolescents', in M. P. Root (ed.), *Racially mixed people in America* (pp. 223–38). Newbury Park, CA: Sage.

Hall, C. I. (1992) 'Please choose one', in M. P. Root (ed.), *Racially mixed people in America* (pp. 250–64). Newbury Park, CA: Sage.

He, A. W. (2006) 'Toward an identity theory of the development of Chinese as a Heritage Language', *Heritage Language Journal*, 4(1): 1–28.

Kiang, L. (2008) 'Ethnic self-labeling in young American adults from Chinese backgrounds', *Journal of Youth and Adolescence*, 37(1): 97–111.

Lee, W. O. (1996) 'The cultural context for Chinese learners: Conceptions of learning in the Confucian tradition', in D. A. Watkins and J. B. Biggs (eds), *The Chinese learner: Cultural, psychological and contextual influences* (pp. 45–67). Hong Kong: Comparative Education Research Centre.

Lehman, R. S. (1991) *Statistics and research design in the behavioral sciences.* Belmont, CA: Wadsworth.

Luke, A. (2009) 'Race and language as capital in school: A sociological template for language education reform', in R. Kubota and A. M. Y. Lin (eds), *Race, culture and identities in second language education: Exploring critically engaged practice* (pp. 286–308). London: Routledge.

McClelland, K. (1990) 'Cumulative disadvantage among the highly ambitious', *Sociology of Education*, 63(2): 102–21.

Mu, G. M. (2014a) 'Chinese Australians' Chineseness and their mathematics achievement: The role of habitus', *The Australian Educational Researcher*, *41*(5): 585–602. doi: 10.1007/s13384–014–0152–1.

Mu, G. M. (2014b) 'Heritage Language learning for Chinese Australians: The role of habitus'. *Journal of Multilingual and Multicultural Development*, *35*(5): 497–510. doi: 10.1080/01434632.2014.882340.

Mu, G. M. (2015a) 'A meta-analysis of the correlation between heritage language and ethnic identity', *Journal of Multilingual and Multicultural Development*, *36*(3): 239–54.

Mu, G. M. (2015b) *Learning Chinese as a Heritage Language: An Australian perspective*. Bristol/Buffalo, SD/Toronto, ON: Multilingual Matters.

Mu, G. M. and Dooley, K. (2015) 'Coming into an inheritance: Family support and Chinese Heritage Language learning', *International Journal of Bilingual Education and Bilingualism*, *18*(4): 501–15.

Oh, J. S. and Fuligni, A. J. (2010) 'The role of Heritage Language development in the ethnic identity and family relationships of adolescents from immigrant backgrounds', *Social Development*, *19*(1): 202–20.

Pao, D. L., Wong, S. D. and Teuben-Rowe, S. (1997) 'Identity formation for mixed-heritage adults and implications for educators', *TESOL Quarterly*, *31*(3): 622–31.

Patton, M. Q. (1990) *Qualitative evaluation and research methods*. Newbury Park, CA: Sage.

Root, M. P. (1992) 'Within, between, and beyond race', in M. P. Root (ed.), *Racially mixed people in America* (pp. 3–11). Newbury Park, CA: Sage.

Sullivan, A. (2002) 'Bourdieu and education: How useful is Bourdieu's theory for researchers?', *The Netherlands' Journal of Social Sciences*, *38*(2): 144–66.

Tabachnick, B. G. and Fidell, L. S. (2007) *Using multivariate statistics* (5th edn). Boston: Allyn & Bacon.

Tan, S. H. (2008) 'Modernizing Confucianism and "new Confucianism"', in K. Louie (ed.), *The Cambridge companion to modern Chinese culture* (pp. 135–54). Cambridge: Cambridge University Press.

Zhang, J. (2009) 'Mandarin maintenance among immigrant children from the People's Republic of China: An examination of individual networks of linguistic contact', *Language, Culture and Curriculum*, *22*(3): 195–213.

Chapter 3

The production of identity capital through school

Jo Warin

Introduction

This chapter applies a Bourdieuian theoretical lens to a research problem that at first glance appears to be rather more individual than sociological. The research study that forms the basis of this chapter aimed to examine how young children develop a sense of self during their introduction to formal schooling and how their practices of identity construction then continued throughout compulsory schooling. As Rawolle and Lingard (2008) point out, Bourdieu's theoretical emphasis on practice is distinctly social and differs from theories that treat practice as something best understood in terms of internal psychological states. They remind us that 'Bourdieu's entire theoretical and methodological approach is relational', and that his 'conceptual triad' of thinking tools: field, habitus and practice, refer to 'bundles of relations' (p. 731). My research adopted a relational approach, focused on the reflexivity practices of children and young people. I was interested in how they articulated their identities, and particularly how identities changed over time within the social context of school. I aimed to examine the construction of identity through the young person's participation in 'bundles of relations'. The emerging theoretical conclusion identified the value of self-awareness, emphasized as a relational concept produced through social situations, and defined as a capacity for developing and maintaining a narrative of self in relation to others. The relational lens revealed inequalities between the nine children and young people who participated in the study regarding their opportunities for engaging in advantageous self-building practices. This finding led to the identification of the concept of identity capital, which forms the focus of this chapter.

'Identity capital' is theorized to be the advantage gained through the reflexive capacity to articulate a narrative of self. The chapter will show how identity capital is developed through certain kinds of privileged discourses and through the opportunities provided within socially advantaged families and schools. It presents a further development of recent theoretical and empirically based research that has aimed to elaborate Bourdieuian theories of capital and ground them in real world applications. In particular, the chapter shows how identity capital operates in tandem with other forms of capital to entrench multiple social advantages during the course of childhood and adolescence. It also reveals the corollary of this social process: a compounding of multiple social disadvantages.

I begin by framing the chapter within Bourdieu's theories of capital and explain why I adopted this particular theoretical approach to illuminate my findings. This explanation necessitates an account of the study with a description of its aims, methodology, methods and findings. I then present some reflections on the relevance of Bourdieu's ideas to debates about matches and mismatches between the respective cultures and capitals of home and school. I focus especially on the ways that types of capital become transubstantiated across these fields and exert power in the reproduction of social advantages and disadvantages. I use two case studies from my data to illustrate the operation of multiple and compounding capitals through the school career. I then discuss some of the issues I confronted in bridging the theory–method relationship with a particular emphasis on the value of qualitative longitudinal research. Finally, I move on to identify the impact of my application of Bourdieu's theories to subsequent theorizing, and the planning of future relevant research with an emphasis on linguistic forms of capital and conclusions about the transformative potential of a Bourdieuian-focused approach for education policy.

Rationale for the selection of Bourdieu's theories of capital

The study that gave rise to the identification and theorization of identity capital was an ethnographic longitudinal study, undertaken by the author, and aimed at exploring children's capacity to construct a personal sense of self. It was designed in order to understand how children create an identity over time and how this process is influenced by key experiences such as the transition from one educational phase to the next. It involved working with children within the social context of family and school, incorporating pre-school, primary and secondary school (high school). The aim was to understand how children and young people build up a sense of identity, and to what extent their daily lives implicate the capacity to tell a story of self. The study belongs to the 'sociology of reflexivity' in that it constitutes an exploration of the capacity to 'self consciously and reflexively construct one's identity' (Kenway and McLeod, 2004). It was based on a critique of an essentialist and individualist discourse of self-concept so it was designed to capture processes of change across sociocultural contexts and across time for the duration of the school career.

A brief description of the study and main methods used

At the start of the study ten children and their parents were selected through initial contacts with pre-schools in a town in the north of England and they consented to participate. Sampling balanced a mix of criteria: types of social experience prior to compulsory schooling together with a mix of social class, gender and ethnicity backgrounds. Data collection methods varied over the course of the study influenced by the age of the children. These are described fully in a book (Warin, 2010) and a journal paper (Warin, 2011), which present a discussion of the methodological and ethical issues implicated in the longitudinal nature of the study and the changing relationship with the young people. The first phase of the research included observational study in pre-school and school settings as well as interviews with teachers and with parents in the child's home. Observational data were recorded in ethnographic field notes based on Emerson *et al.* (1995) and supported by video recording. Each child was observed for approximately 92 hours overall during this first 4-year phase of the study, with lengthier observations in the first 2 years. A parent and key school staff member was interviewed about each child during each of the first 3 years. A second phase of the study occurred 7 years later when the young people were in the second year of secondary school (aged 12/13) when I was able to re-engage nine of the original sample. During that year I visited them three times in their homes employing a range of interview strategies including the use of a time line, school photos and reports, and video material from the early phase of the study as triggers to prompt discussion about self-construction and change. A further round of interviews took place 2 years later, (age 15), again with an explicit focus on perceptions of identity and change. Finally, five of the sample consented to hold further conversations (age 17), in their family homes, focused on their understandings of self, a retrospective view of changes during their school years and their aspirations for the future.

The design, partly modelled on Pollard and Filer's longitudinal Identity and Learning Programme (Pollard, 2007) can most accurately be characterized by the term 'intermittent longitudinal ethnography'. It can be positioned within the emergent genre of qualitative longitudinal research (QLR) identified by Holland *et al.* (2006), which is sensitive to contextual issues, has the potential to focus on temporality and change (Thomson *et al.*, 2003, p. 185) and can illuminate important micro-social processes (Henwood and Lang, 2003; Finn, 2015). Analysis of the data was undertaken according to principles derived from grounded theory (Glaser and Strauss, 1967) but based on the elaborated 'constant comparison' version developed by Charmaz (2006) in which analysis is simultaneously data-driven and theory-driven. The detailed case studies of the children brought together socio-economic data concerning parental occupations, level of education, housing and family composition.

Inevitably, such a long lived study will see the researcher go through many changes as part of their intellectual research journey and will accommodate the absorption of new theoretical frameworks. When the study started its life I was unfamiliar with Bourdieu, coming from a social psychology background in relation to my research purposes, and drawing on theoretical approaches to identity that were derived from a synthesis between post-structural emphases on the fluidity and socially situated nature of self and temporal approaches to the building of a consistent self (described more fully in Warin and Muldoon, 2009; Warin, 2010). Originally, I adopted a socio-ecological approach to my understanding of the children's construction of identity based on Bronfen-brenner's model (1977), which emphasized the socially situated nature of child development within interacting communities and wider environments as a critical response to the traditional psychological essentialist theories that indi-vidualized child development. While this theoretical approach has the value of articulating the dynamism of change over time and change within 'bundles of relations' it fails to give sufficient emphasis to the influence and complexity of culture, social class and societal influence (Hill, 2009; Richardson, 2014).

My findings led to the articulation of a value for an ability to adapt and expand our narratives of self, producing a rich and differentiated identity. The study showed that some children and young people had developed the capacity to produce a complex narrative of self and that others had not. Consequently, I sought theory that would help me to understand the differences between the nine targeted children with regard to the quality and frequency of the types of practice that are implicated in the development of identity. The narratives that I developed about each child's school trajectory and their practices of identity building, revealed the existence of vicious and harmonious circles of social deprivation and social advantage. By the time the data collection was completed and I was analysing the complex sets of data collected throughout the course of the study, I had encountered Bourdieu's concepts and especially his work on capitals. I had become familiar with an expansion of his theories, for example in Lareau's work on the reproduction of cultural capital (1989, 2003), through the meeting of family and school worlds, and especially through Reay's development of emotional capital in understanding the perpetuation of social class disadvantages through schooling (2000, 2005).

As I engaged with these theoretical developments of Bourdieu, I was also aware of public media-led discussion in the UK about social capital, which was becoming a strong element of New Labour government discourse (Social Exclusion Task Force, 2007) and was based on the theories of Putnam (2000) and Coleman (1988). Discussing this turn in UK government policy, Halpern (2005, p. 284) suggested that social capital was seen as the 'magic ingredient that makes all the difference'. It governed the policy concerning the devel-opment of the Sure Start programme in England from 2000 as a method for helping socially deprived families to access advice, parenting skills and guidance through readily available forms of professional expertise. This view of social policy has also been represented as a form of 'linking' capital (Woolcock, 1998; 2001) as a way of discussing the advantages that accrue to groups and larger societies, and the advantages that accrue to small groups such as the family and individuals within families. I was also aware of an increasing trend to appropriate the concept of capital and use a myriad of descriptors of social advantages in this way, for example, the controversial use by Hakim of erotic capital (Hakim, 2011). I recognized a tendency to use the concept of capital merely as a synonym for wealth and that this was to ignore the complexity and especially the process aspects of Bourdieu's theories of cultural capital and its derivatives such as social capital. This exposure to the concept of social capital led to an engagement with Bourdieu's writings about capital. In particular, I was drawn to his theorizing about processes of capital exchange and transubstantiation between schools and families as they suggested a way of explaining differences in my sample of nine young people with regard to their social practices of identity construction. I recognized that Bourdieu's theories have the explanatory power to reveal how forms of wealth become 'converted into an integral part of the person' (Bourdieu, 1997, p. 48) perpetuating cycles of advantage and disadvantage.

Reflections on Bourdieuian theories about the reproduction of capital across the fields of home and school

Bourdieu has utilized the concept of cultural capital as a prism to reveal the inequalities that reside in home lives and that are exacerbated within education, drawing attention to the hidden and complex processes through which cultural capital is transmitted from one generation to the next: 'The reproduction of the structure of the distribution of cultural capital is achieved in the relation between familial strategies and the specific logic of the school institution' (Bourdieu, 1998, p. 19). He described families as corporate bodies who are animated by a tendency to reproduce their powers and privileges through a range of strategies such as matrimonial, inheritance, economic, and 'last but not least educational strategies'. The more cultural capital a family has the more they will invest in education. His description is focused on socially privileged families and the benefits they can accrue but this list of strategies can be generalized and applied to many kinds of families. This chapter applies Bourdieu's theory of the social reproduction of privilege to a range of young people and their families with markedly different class backgrounds.

Many current users of Bourdieu's concept of cultural capital are inclined to reduce it to a set of concrete and perceptible middle-class parenting practices such as museum trips, theatre and concert visits, and family engagement with highbrow cultural practices and knowledge, a simplification that loses sight of the buried and complex ways in which it operates. However, the concept has much more explanatory power and potential for providing us with under-standing of the apparent intransigence of social inequalities, as revealed in some of the richer and more detailed Bourdieuian analyses (for example, Cheadle, 2008; Devine, 2004; Lareau, 1989, 2003). These more detailed analyses show the operation of cultural capital through the relationship between families and education, through parental uptake of informal educational opportunities and through an understanding of, and engagement with formal schooling. For example, an increasing body of work shows how parents can take up a range of extracurricular educational activities (Covay and Carbonaro, 2010), including private tutoring (Erickson *et al.*, 2009; Lee and Shouse, 2011; Vincent, 2000; Yamomoto and Brinton, 2010), and summer programmes (Burkam *et al.*, 2004; Chin and Phillips, 2004). Researchers, who have examined parent–school relations in the light of Bourdieu's theories, reveal that various forms of capital come to be *transformed* into educational capital through parental involvement in their schooling (Domina, 2005; Reay, 1998; Vincent, 2000) and show that parental cultural capital impacts positively on school success.

Three aspects of parental investment in schooling can be identified that reveal the interactions of capital and shed light on the transformation of capital into academic advantage: parental choice of school by skilled choosers (Vincent, 2000; Vincent and Ball, 2006); communication between home and school based on shared 'currency' of values (Gewirtz *et al.*, 1995; Pollard and Filer, 2007; Power *et al.*, 2003; Reay, 1998; Vincent, 2000) and parental influences on children's discursive practices that enable optimal relations with teachers (Domina, 2005). Lareau (2003) following Bernstein, reveals how middle-class children are trained to negotiate with parents and other adults through a process of 'concerted cultivation' thereby developing a sense of entitlement rather than an acquiescent response to those in authority, and enabling good relationships with teachers.

While critics of Bourdieuian analyses of cultural capital have pointed to the limited articulation of capital in Bourdieu's original workings, suggesting they are incomplete (Sayer, 2005) and vague (Jaeger, 2011), the body of work referred to above has begun to apply and elaborate Bourdieu's approach. We are now beginning to have a much more highly developed and nuanced account of forms of human capital, their relationships with each other, and their operation, especially in relation to educational processes to do with the reproduction of social advantage.

Understanding differences in identity construction practices through a Bourdieuian lens

Looking across the case studies there was an inconsistency in the extent to which children were able to articulate 'self' and the degree to which they seemed to be concerned with the production of self. The analysis showed that the capacity to self-reflect interacted with socio-economic and cultural influences, and particularly exposure to opportunities to participate in a discourse of self-reflection. This finding led me to pay much closer analytical attention to social class differences between the young people, which in turn led to a need for a complex theory that could explain the dynamic reproduction of social advantages and disadvantages across time and field. I needed a theory that could reveal how bundles of capitals interact within bundles of relations throughout the young person's progression through school. Adopting a Bourdieuian focus enabled this. I was able to view the longitudinal case studies through a linking of identity development and human capital with an emerging focus on the concept of identity capital.

The term 'identity capital' is derived from Côté (1996), who used it to capture a specific form of advantage that resides in the psycho-social attributes of an individual's life pathway and that is particularly relevant in order for a person to steer a path through increasing consumer led choices. Drawing on the theories of Bourdieu, Coté described identity capital as the extent to which a person 'invests in who they are' (p. 425). He acknowledged that a higher social class background bestows advantages in acquiring identity capital.

Case study comparison based on different forms of capital and their interactions

The methods employed in this study allow for a detailed understanding of the *interactive* effect of capitals working together to entrench cycles of social advantage and disadvantage. I illustrate how identity capital is intertwined with other forms of capital within two case studies: Martin and Liam, separating out the different forms of capital (economic, cultural and social) that have been elaborated by Bourdieu, following definitions in Bourdieu (1997). I also harness the concept of emotional capital now well established by Reay and others. My aim here is to demonstrate the interdependency of these forms and reveal how they compound each other.

Martin

Martin's parents were both employed throughout the study, his father as a bank manager and his mother in various middle management banking positions. When the study began, they owned their own house then upgraded to a large detached house with garden. The family owned two cars and several computers. Their economic resources supported Martin together with his younger sister and two older siblings, a half-brother and half-sister. Turning from a focus on Martin's economic capital to his social capital, he benefited from the family's strong links with one of the local Anglican churches where his choir member-ship put him in touch with the middle-class congregation, including peers and adults. The church association then provided access to a local secondary school (high school) that had a very good reputation for school academic success and offered a rigid system of pupil selection on the basis of church membership. This 11–18 school had a sixth form (for pupils aged 16–18) creating an expectation that pupils would carry on with their studies post 16, gain A-level qualifications and then university entrance. The majority of Martin's peer group were from a similar background and held a common assumption about educational goals. Martin accessed a further dimension of social capital through his mainly positive relationships with his secondary school staff. At age 13 he mentioned he was able to talk easily with some of them, and again at age 17 he told me that some of the teachers were his 'friends'. This expression of familiarity with staff illustrates the findings of Lareau (1989, 2003), who showed how middle-class children are trained to negotiate with parents and other adults, developing a sense of entitlement rather than an acquiescent response to those in authority. Stearns *et al.* (2007) also see positive bonds with teachers as a crucial element of social capital and a mitigating influence on student dropout. The family's cultural capital took a number of forms including holidays abroad, family trips and family meals, which provided opportunities for communication with parents. Reay's analysis of emotional capital (1998, 2000, 2005) emphasizes maternal attention to the child's educational opportunities through being 'school savvy', the exercising of choice within the UK's education market, together with a reinforcing of school values through such activities as assistance with homework, and investment in aspirations for HE opportunities. These forms of emotional capital were very much to the fore in Martin's family. Both parents had the previous education, positive attitude to Martin's schooling, and excellent rapport with his school staff that were likely to enhance his chances of school success.

Liam

The economic resources of Liam's family were the lowest in the sample. At the start of the study Liam lived with his teenage mother Donna and her parents. Liam's biological father was known to him but never visited the family and did not provide any financial support. Throughout the study Donna received a disability benefit due to her mental health problems and remained unemployed. When Liam was 11 years old, she found a new partner, Jason, who provided, briefly, some financial support to the family. However, he and Donna separated after 2 years. When I first visited the family during the second phase of the study, when Liam was 12, they were living in a very small 1950s council house in a very poor state of decorative repair. The family's next home was a trailer in a park housing many families who were on income support, at a considerable distance from Liam's school. It was very cold and comfortless and it was during this phase of temporary accommodation that Liam told me he was worried about leaving his mother alone in this home. Donna did not possess a car and Liam was taxied to school at this time. The family were then moved into a larger trailer and then, finally, to the council house where they remained until the end of the study. Liam's social capital, among his own peers, family and his mother's friends, illustrates the 'dark side' of social capital, the accrual of negative influences (Portes, 1998). This was particularly apparent during Liam's mid-teenage years when the family moved to the Banks housing estate and he was drawn into gang membership. His neighbourhood peer group also influenced his school absence as there was a culture of 'skiving' school. The social capital of his immediate family provided further examples of negative influence as demonstrated in Liam's account of his grandfather's collusion in his school absence: 'I used to go to my Granddad's and my Granddad would have a laugh and say "skiving again" but he couldn't do anything because I didn't like school'. Liam had informal mentors among his mother's circle of friends who taught him to fish but who also inducted him into the illegal pursuit of poaching. As a school absentee, Liam was not able to form relationships with school staff so was not able to benefit by accessing their social capital. Reflecting back on his school experiences at age 17 he told me he saw the teachers as his 'enemies'. During the years of adolescence Liam spent little time in his home, choosing the company of his peers on the street or in the local playground so there was a decrease in his access to cultural capital through the adult members of his family. He was thrown back on the peer culture of his young, working-class, white male peer group. This implicated participation in risky and often illegal behaviour such as substance abuse, stealing cars and a shared resistance to school. With regard to emotional capital, while Liam benefited from close and positive family relationships with his mother, sister and grandfather he did not have access to the kind of emotional capital that Reay identifies and that is geared towards school success. Donna told me she could not exercise any control over Liam's school absence although she clearly wished she could.

Identity in 'intersecting multiple capitals' in the cases of Martin and Liam

The above presentation of different types of capital in each of these two cases makes it clear that these influential strands of each child's life are interwoven and become firmly embedded in creating a spiral of social advantage or disadvantage. This becomes apparent if we attempt to pull out one strand of the weave. For example, if we tease out the social capital strand of Martin's life that concerns his family's church membership we see how this is entangled with their economic capital through the geographical location of their house, neighbourhood and proximity to their church, together with their other social networks of middle-class friends and family, and access to a very successful and well regarded school and gateway to higher education. Looking rather more closely at this web of interacting capitals it is possible to discern the strand of identity capital on which I will now focus. My account of the intersecting forms of capital in these two examples supports the idea that some young people have considerable advantages when it comes to the opportunities and resources for articulating an identity.

Martin demonstrated a high degree of emotional literacy (Weare, 2004), especially as he matured, and harnessed a rich emotional vocabulary – for example, frequent use of the word 'sensitive' to describe himself. He also appeared to relish discussion of his personal relationships and opportunities for self-reflection. His facility for emotional literacy and his familiarity with a discourse of moral and therapeutic values for the production of an authentic self were tied up with his family's social class and their cultural capital. He spoke about conversations with trusted close friends among his school peers as well as with trusted teachers. These were opportunities for accommodating new self-understandings and remaking his story of self. Children like Martin have privileged access to particular discourses and vocabularies that enable a richer and more elaborated story of self.

Liam's responses to the research strategies that were intended to prompt self descriptions frequently met with a failure to articulate a story of self. For example, when asked at age 13 to 'bombard me with words that describe you' Liam found this challenging: 'Don't know really . . . don't know really it's hard to think . . . I don't know I can't think'. He resorted to the more concrete strategies used by younger children, describing his preferences and abilities, for example emphasizing his sporting abilities: running, doing stunts on his bike and roller blades. At 13, Liam also struggled to respond to the request to put himself in the shoes of significant others in his world and imagine how he might appear to them, suggesting an 'impoverished self'. This rather problematic term is used by Harter (1999) in her developmental account of children's capacity to construct identity and implies a belief that some children are deficient in having the necessary vocabulary or evaluative concepts to describe the self. Her account suggests this deficiency is located within the individual child rather than in their social context and the forms of capital they can access. Liam's responses indicate that he had experienced few opportunities for such exchanges. However although these direct strategies designed to elicit self statements were unsuccessful with the 13-year-old Liam, at 15 he was able to communicate some self aware insights, making statements that showed he was capable of both imagining and expressing ideas about how he came across to others, for example 'disruptive' to describe his imagined perceptions of his Pupil Referral Unit teachers. In comparison with some of the other young people, Liam seemed less concerned with constructing self within our conversations. Liam's poor school attendance, plus the fact that he spent much of his time in the company of peers rather than adults, limited his access to the discourse needed for building identity capital, and the kind of abstract talk that produces a stock of rehearsed insights into self, an interpretation that is well supported by Bernsteinian sociologists of social class and language.

The construction and maintenance of a sense of self emerges from this analysis as a form of capital which influences, and is influenced by, other forms of capital within a nexus of interacting multiple capitals. This view chimes with those sociologists who have suggested that the regular introspection implicated in the production of identity is the privilege of those who have the time and space to engage with it (Côté, 1996; Henderson et al., 2007; Rose, 1997; Skeggs, 2004). For example, Skeggs suggests that the activities implicated in self-reflection and self-construction, presuppose access to cultural resources, techniques and practices necessary for producing and knowing a self, and these are not available for all. Similarly, Henderson et al. point out that 'individuals are not simply free to choose who and what they want to be' (p. 14), while Kenway and McLeod

(2004, p. 529) suggest a strong association between the capacity to self-reflect and the opportunities presented in intellectually privileged arenas. The implication is that the capacity to construct identity can be portrayed as another form of capital, a significant resource for coping with and controlling one's life.

Challenges in bridging the theory–method relationship in applications of Bourdieu

As explained above, this study did not commence with the intention of testing out Bourdieu's theories. Instead Bourdieu was accessed in order to theorize findings concerning differences between the young people's identity construction practices and their opportunities for developing the socially advantageous capacity to tell a story of self. This data-led foray into Bourdieu was necessarily selective within the large canon of his work. My focus was specifically concerned with his identification of and discussion of the interaction of forms of capital to perpetuate social inequality especially through educational practices and processes. An interesting question emerges about using Bourdieuian theory as a *starting* point for designing a study with the same aim: to examine practices of identity construction through the years of compulsory schooling. What would I do differently if I were to design the study from this theoretical starting point? How would I advise others with similar research aims?

I would want to preserve a qualitative longitudinal research approach (QLR). I would defend this methodological decision on the basis of Bourdieu's criticism of the instantaneous nature of much sociology. He suggests we need to recognize that the 'structures sociology deals with are the product of transformations which, unfolding in time, cannot be considered as reversible' (Bourdieu and Passeron, 1977, p. 88). There is a good match between the type of methodology I adopted, a longitudinal qualitative ethnography, and Bourdieu's incorporation of time, complexity and process in revealing how one form of capital may be transformed into another. The power of interacting multiple capitals to produce social inequality lies within the fluid processes of capital transubstantiation and these are buried. Ethnographic work has a particular strength to offer this body of knowledge as it has the potential to unearth connections between different forms of capital, and can draw out the detail of their interactions. Longitudinal ethnography allows for an examination of the process of the reproduction of compounding social advantages (or disadvantages) as it gathers momentum over time. The application of Bourdieu presented in this chapter indicates a commitment to this type of research.

Subsequent theorizing and the planning of future relevant research

I conclude this chapter by offering some reflections on the possibilities for theoretical development with an emphasis on linguistic forms of capital. I also offer brief conclusions about the transformative potential of a Bourdieuian-focused approach for education policy. Since developing the concept of 'identity capital' my subsequent theorizing has relied on this concept to integrate individualized and therapeutic notions of self-construction into a political, economic and social context. The idea of interacting forms of capital is essential to a sufficiently deep understanding of influences on children's life chances and a fuller understanding of the impact of social experiences and practices across the twin fields of home and school on young people's trajectories through school and beyond. In particular my findings have thrown up the importance of access to the kinds of discursive opportunities that bring about the production of identity capital. This requires further research into Bourdieu's theories about linguistic advantages as part of cultural capital, and implications for schooling.

Bourdieu and Passeron (1977) argue that mismatches between the language of home and school are an important cause of educational failure, drawing on a legacy from Bernstein and Labov. Collins (1993) emphasizes Bourdieu's approach to linguistic forms of capital and advantage, and reminds us of his discussion of class codes, where Bourdieu distinguished between the 'bourgeois' (a literary orientation, Latinate vocabulary and constructions, and a striving for rare and novel expression) and the 'common' (a situational orientation, non-learned vocabulary, and the reliance upon shared figures of speech). Collins points out how the former kind of language is the language closer to that which is expected in educational settings and so creates a linguistic capital in the educational field and in the educational marketplace. We need research that can support Bourdieu's claim that: 'The educational mortality rate can only increase as one moves towards the classes most distant from scholarly language' (Bourdieu and Passeron, 1977, p. 73).

Collins' discussion takes us into the old territory of debate about 'linguistic deficit'. Conclusions from my study suggest that we need to understand linguistic capacity not as a disembodied individual ability, or deficit, but more as a set of opportunities (or lack of opportunities) that reside within human relationships. A particular focus on language as it is embedded in the social and emotional relationships between parents, teachers and pupils will further our understanding of the interaction of capitals to reproduce social advantage and disadvantage. Here we could follow the lead of researchers who have noticed how some children and young people acquire capital through managing a form of familiar and easy-going communication with their teachers (Black, 2004; Domina, 2005; Stearns et al., 2007). In the comparison of studies presented in this chapter there was a stark contrast between Martin's descriptions of teachers as his 'friends' and Liam's as his 'enemies'. Another related and potentially fruitful way forward would be to look at the concept of emotional literacy (Weare, 2004) within the light of Bourdieuian theory. This would also require a relational approach, rather than an emphasis on individual ability, an emphasis that is apparent in some discussions of this concept.

The transformative potential of adopting a Bourdieu-focused approach

The presentation of the case studies in this chapter, and illustration of the complex and compounding nature of different kinds of capital working together, suggest the impossibility of interventions to halt the social reproduction of advantaged and disadvantaged lives. Indeed, Bourdieu has been criticized for the pessimistic determinism of his theories (Mills, 2008). We need to see empirical applications of Bourdieu that can inform us about the possibility of strategies for halting, transforming, and perhaps even reversing the cycles of reproduction that have been described here. Mills puts forward a strong case for the transformative potential of Bourdieuian constructs and argues that school teachers can become agents in the transformation of cultural capital rather than its reproduction, improving the outcomes of marginalized school students. In a similar vein Richardson (2014) presents a discussion of the transformative role of outreach workers who engage with parents in the location of Sure Start children's centres in the north of England. She describes the relationships that these professionals create with parents of young children as a form of 'bridging capital', a term used by Woolcock and Narayan (2000) to portray relationships that help people to 'get ahead'. She shows how this form of intervention creates access to advantages such as health advice and financial services that are not accessible within immediate families and communities. Richardson depicts the imaginative and time-intensive efforts of the outreach professionals who engage with 'hard-to-reach' individuals living in challenging circumstances. These skilful and usually undervalued efforts represent a form of intervention, which has the potential to transform cycles of social disadvantage. However, transformation can only begin to take place when professionals are trained to recognize rather than neglect the cultural inequalities that exist within children's lives, including buried inequalities in forms such as disparities in identity capital.

A warning is sounded however by Gorski (2014) in his review of 30 years of research on the greatest barriers confronting students in poverty in the United States. He criticizes interventions that ignore the gross structural social inequalities that are the roots of educational outcome inequalities and explains that these include not only unequal access to educational opportunity, but also 'unequal access to healthcare, safe and affordable housing, and living wage jobs . . . in a nation that can afford to provide them to everybody' (p. 16). The discussion of Bourdieu's theories of capitals that has been presented in this chapter also emphasizes the need for social, educational and health services to be 'joined up'. In reflecting on the case of Liam, who was eventually unable to access school-focused strategies, it is possible to imagine how inter-professional collaboration from professionals outside of school might have helped to change his poor educational outcomes. A theory that identifies the complexity of interacting forms of capital implies interventions that weave together a web of services.

References

Black, L. (2004) 'Differential participation in whole-class discussions and the construction of marginalised identities', *The Journal of Educational Enquiry*, 5(1): 34–54.

Bourdieu, P. (1997) 'The forms of capital', in A. Halsey, H. Lauder, P. Brown, and A.S. Wells (eds), *Education, culture, economy, society* (pp. 46–58). Oxford: Oxford University Press.

Bourdieu, P. (1998) *Practical reason*. Cambridge: Polity Press.

Bourdieu, P. and Passeron, J.-C. (1977) *Reproduction in education, society, culture*. Beverly Hills, CA: Sage.

Bronfenbrenner, U. (1977) 'Towards an experimental ecology of human development', *American Psychologist*, 32: 515–31.

Burkam, D. T., Ready, D. D., Lee, V. E. and LoGerfo, L. F. (2004) 'Social-class differences in summer learning between kindergarten and first grade: Model specification and estimation', *Sociology of Education*, 77(1): 1–31.

Charmaz, K. (2006) *Constructing grounded theory: A practical guide through qualitative analysis*. Thousand Oaks, CA: Sage.

Cheadle, J. E. (2008) 'Educational investment, family context, and children's math and reading growth from kindergarten through the third grade', *Sociology of Education*, 81: 1–31.

Chin, T. and Phillips, M. (2004) 'Social reproduction and child-rearing practices: Social class, children's agency, and the summer activity gap', *Sociology of Education*, 77(3): 185–210.

Coleman, J. S. (1988) 'Social capital in the creation of human capital', *American Journal of Sociology*, Supplement: Organizations and Institutions: Sociological and Economic Approaches to the Analysis of Social Structure, 94: S95–S120.

Collins, J. (1993) 'Determination and contradiction: An appreciation and critique of the work of Pierre Bourdieu on language and education', in C. Calhoun, E. LiPuma and M. Postone (eds), *Bourdieu: Critical perspectives* (pp. 116–38). Cambridge: Polity Press

Côté, J. E. (1996) 'Sociological perspectives on identity formation: The culture-identity link and identity capital', *Journal of Adolescence*, 19: 417–28.

Covay, E. and Carbonaro, W. (2010) 'After the bell: Participation in extracurricular activities, classroom behavior and academic achievement', *Sociology of Education*, 83(1): 20–45.

Devine, F. (2004) *Class practices: How parents help their children get good jobs*. Cambridge: Cambridge University Press.

Domina, T. (2005) 'Leveling the home advantage: Assessing the effectiveness of parental involvement in elementary school', *Sociology of Education*, 78(3): 233–49.

Emerson, R., Fretz, R. and Shaw, L. (1995) *Writing ethnographic fieldnotes*. Chicago, IL: University of Chicago Press.

Erickson, L. D., McDonald, S. and Elder, G. E. (2009) 'Informal mentors and education: Complementary or compensatory resources?', *Sociology of Education*, 82(4): 344 –67.

Finn, K. (2015) *Personal life, young women and higher education: A relational approach to student and graduate experiences*. London: Palgrave Macmillan.

Gewirtz, S., Ball, S. and Bowe, R. (1995) *Markets, choice and equity in education*. Buckingham, UK: Open University Press.

Glaser, B. G. and Strauss, A. L. (1967) *The discovery of grounded theory: Strategies for qualitative research.* Chicago, IL: Aldine.

Gorski, P. C. (2014) 'Poverty, class, and the cultivation of economically just educational policy: The role of ideology', *Research Intelligence, 125*: 15–16.

Hakim, C. (2011) *Honey money: The power of erotic capital.* Allen Lane.

Halpern, D. (2005) *Social capital.* Cambridge: Polity Press.

Harter, S. (1999) *The construction of the self: A developmental perspective.* London: The Guilford Press.

Henderson, S., Holland, J., Thomson, R., McGrellis, S. and Sharpe, S. (2007) *Inventing adulthoods: A biographical approach to youth transitions.* London: Sage.

Henwood, K. and Lang, I. (2003) *Qualitative research resources: A consultation exercise with UK social scientists.* A report to the ESRC.

Hill, M. (2009) 'Ways of seeing: Using ethnography and Foucault's "toolkit" to view assessment practices differently', *Qualitative Research, 9*(3): 309–30.

Holland, J., Thomson, R. and Henderson, S. (2006) *Qualitative longitudinal research: A discussion paper.* Families and Social Capital, ESRC Research Group Working Paper No. 21. Swindon, UK: ESRC.

Jaeger M. M. (2011) 'Does cultural capital really affect academic achievement? New evidence from combined sibling and panel data', *Sociology of Education, 84*(4): 281–98.

Kenway, J. and McLeod, J. (2004) 'Bourdieu's reflexive sociology and "spaces of points of view": Whose reflexivity, which perspective?' *British Journal of Sociology of Education, 25*(4): 524–44.

Lareau, A. (1989) *Home advantage: Social class and parental intervention in elementary education.* Lewes, UK: Falmer Press.

Lareau, A. (2003) *Unequal childhoods: Class, race, and family life.* Los Angeles, CA: University of California Press.

Lee, S. and Shouse, R. S. (2011) 'The impact of prestige orientation on shadow education in South Korea', *Sociology of Education, 84*(3): 212–24.

Mills, C. (2008) 'Reproduction and transformation of inequalities in schooling: The transformative potential of the theoretical constructs of Bourdieu', *British Journal of Sociology of Education, 29*(1): 79–89.

Pollard, A. (2007) 'The identity and learning programme: "Principled pragmatism" in a 12-year longitudinal ethnography', *Ethnography and Education, 2*(1): 1–19.

Pollard, A. and Filer, A. (2007) 'Learning, differentiation and strategic action in secondary education', *British Journal of Sociology of Education, 28*(4): 441–58.

Portes, A. (1998) 'Social capital: Its origins and applications in modern sociology', *Annual Review of Sociology, 24*: 1–24.

Power, S., Edwards, T., Whitty, G. and Wigfall, V. (2003) *Education and the middle class.* Buckingham, UK: Open University Press.

Putnam, R. (2000) *Bowling alone: The collapse and revival of American community.* New York: Simon and Schuster.

Rawolle, S. and Lingard, B. (2008) 'The sociology of Pierre Bourdieu and researching education policy', *Journal of Education Policy, 23*(6): 729–41.

Reay, D. (1998) *Class work: Mothers' involvement in their children's primary schooling.* London: UCL Press.

Reay, D. (2000) 'A useful extension of Bourdieu's conceptual framework? Emotional capital as a way of understanding mothers' involvement in their children's education?', *The Sociological Review*, *48*(4): 568–85.

Reay, D. (2005) 'Gendering Bourdieu's concept of capitals? Emotional capital, women and social class', *The Sociological Review*, *52*(2): 57–74.

Richardson, A. (2014) The impact of Sure Start children's centres on social capital and exclusion, PhD thesis. Leeds Beckett University, Leeds, UK.

Rose, N. (1997) 'Assembling the modern self' in R. Porter (ed.), *Rewriting the self: Histories from the Renaissance to the present*. New York: Routledge.

Sayer, A. (2005) *The moral significance of class*. Cambridge: Cambridge University Press.

Skeggs, B. (2004) *Class, self, culture*. New York: Routledge.

Social Exclusion Task Force (SETU) 2007. *Reaching out: Think family*. www.cabinet office.gov.uk/~/media/assets/www.cabinetoffice.gov.uk/social_exclusion_task_ force/think_families/think_families%20pdf.ashx (accessed 19 August 2008).

Stearns, E., Moller, S., Blau, J.R. and Potochnik, S. (2007) 'Staying back and dropping out: The relationship between grade retention and school dropout', *Sociology of Education*, *80*(3): 210–40.

Thomson, R., Plumridge, L. and Holland, J. (2003) 'Longitudinal qualitative research: A developing methodology', *International Journal of Social Research Methodology: Theory and Practice*, *6*(3): 185–7.

Vincent, C. (2000). *Including parents? Education, citizenship and parental agency*. Buckingham, UK: Open University Press.

Vincent, C. and Ball, S. (2006) *Children, choice and class practices: Middle class parents and their children*. New York: Routledge.

Warin, J. (2010) *Stories of self: Tracking children's identity and wellbeing through the school years*. Stoke-on-Trent, England: Trentham Books.

Warin, J. (2011) 'Ethical mindfulness and reflexivity: Managing a research relationship with children and young people in a fourteen year qualitative longitudinal research (QLR) study', *Qualitative Inquiry*, *17*(9): 805–14.

Warin, J. and Muldoon, J. (2009) 'Wanting to be "known": Re-defining self-awareness through an understanding of self-narration processes in educational transitions', *British Educational Research Journal*, *35*(2): 289–303.

Weare, K. (2004). *Developing the emotionally literate school*. London: Sage.

Woolcock, M. (1998), 'Social capital and economic development: Toward a theoretical synthesis and policy framework', *Theory and Society*, *27*(2): 151–208.

Woolcock, M. (2001) 'The place of social capital in understanding social and economic outcomes', *ISUMA Canadian Journal of Policy Research*, *2*(1): 11–17.

Woolcock, M. and Narayan, D. (2000) 'Social capital: Implications for development theory, research, and policy', *World Bank Research Observer*, *15*(2): 225–49.

Yamomoto, Y. and Brinton, M. (2010) 'Cultural capital in East Asian educational systems: The case of Japan', *Sociology of Education*, *83*(1): 67–83.

Chapter 4

Doxa, digital scholarship and the academy

Cristina Costa and Mark Murphy

Introduction

Pierre Bourdieu's work on the conceptualization of social practices is commonly associated with habitus and its relationship with field and forms of capital. Yet – and although popular – these are not the only concepts in his toolkit that allow us to understand and apprehend practices both theoretically and method-ologically as social phenomena conveying a sense of identity. Taking the criticisms of Bourdieu's work seriously – especially the claim that Bourdieu's work takes a rather deterministic view of the social order – this chapter aims to challenge such assumptions by engaging in a closer reading of Bourdieu's work, especially regarding the empirical understanding of change. The chapter elaborates on the use of doxa and hysteresis in combination with reflexivity; these are research tools that have not yet gained the deserved prominence among Bourdieuian researchers, most likely because these constructs were less salient in Bourdieu's own writing. Yet, such concepts provide a lens through which the process of change can be explained. In this vein, this chapter will look at how the combination of reflexive research practices with the concepts of doxa and hysteresis in the background allow the researchers to dig deeper into how change is perceived and enacted, while using the context of scholarly practices supported by the participatory web as an example.

This chapter is divided into four sections. First, we provide an overview of the social context of the phenomenon explored in this chapter: the field of academia and the emergence of new technologies with participatory features. Second, we reflect on the concepts of doxa and hysteresis in conceptualizing practice. After that we will elaborate on the application of such concepts to devise a research methodology for 'capturing' and analysing instances of change. We conclude the chapter with a discussion on the methodological and theoretical implications of our research.

The web: a changing field

Web technologies are reportedly creating new forms of communication and distribution of social and intellectual capital (Gauntlett, 2013). And although there is a tendency to make generalized assumptions about the possibilities of the web as revolutionary and transformative (Selwyn, 2014) – to the point that such rhetoric loses its persuasive capacity – the scholarly practices developed on the web are starting to challenge the norms and conventions of established workplaces even if not much effective change has resulted from it yet. Such is the case of digital scholarly practices and academia as their ultimate place of legitimacy.

The spaces of congregation the web offers as well as the possibilities for the co-production of cultural and intellectual artefacts are encouraging the development of a new epistemology of practice (Costa, 2014a). In the context of academia this means that the emergence of the web as a space of agency is challenging the canons of academic work with activities that lie outside of what is considered the norm. For example, the rise of a participatory culture online, epitomized by the instant communication and publication of information in different formats and across platforms, is questioning the notions of traditional knowledge gatekeeping (Jenkins, 2009) and, by default, authority. And while the open access movement aims to widen the accessibility of knowledge and resources to different communities, independently of their economic power, the Creative Commons initiative is fomenting new forms of (re)distribution and (re)usability of cultural content that take the notion of authorship to a new level (Lessig, 2004, 2009). It is undeniable that the 'do it yourself' features of the web have added a new dimension to the relationship between authors and audiences. This is characterized by the fluidity of roles and distribution of leadership regarding the production and publication of content, and the repurpose of it. Yet these innovative online practices seem to have limited currency beyond the field in which they are conceived and realized: the web. Even though these new technologies are starting to redefine the purpose and source of intellectual work, the dissonance between the practices developed on the web and in academia – as fields of cultural production – is still pronounced. As such, this inferred field rivalry implies competition rather than complementarity of the two social places.

Notwithstanding the symbolic power of the academy in maintaining its structure, the openness of cultural production to the masses via the web raises important issues for academia as the main provider of intellectual knowledge. When seen from this perspective, the practices the web supports not only challenge the conventions that characterize scholarly practices historically and traditionally, but also the perceptions of academics with regards to the meaning they ascribe to their profession as knowledge workers. The norms associated with academics' research activity is a good example of it given that it places a special emphasis on the publication of research findings in prestigious journals that cater for a specific readership, a practice that has become engrained in academic culture for centuries (Talib, 2002; Miller et al., 2011). Such assumed norms have an impact on academics' sense of professional identity and how they perceive their academic role.

The digital dimension of scholarship however confers a new sense of (professional) self, especially in individuals who exploit the affordances of the web to develop unconventional forms of knowledge working (Costa, 2014b). These are especially associated with the concepts of open and networked scholarship practices, which aim to rejuvenate the meaning of the university within the context of a society that is embracing digital technologies to live, learn and work. In defining this new approach Weller (2011) coined the term 'digital scholars' to describe academics whose approaches to scholarly work involve using the web to push the boundaries of what is currently expected and accepted as academic contribution. Engaging in digital scholarship practices and 'being' a digital scholar thus denote a form of differentiation that is embodied in practice. This digital distinction in turn implies a certain rupture with the structure of the academic field not exclusively because of its digital characteristics but mainly, and above all, because of the approaches to practice implicit by the digitization of the academic habitus that becomes inscribed in one's sense of identity (Costa, 2015).

As noted in previous publications on the changing impact of the web on academia (see Costa 2014b, 2014c), the web as both a tool and environment serving to transform scholarly practices is dividing the scholarly community into, at least, two distinctive groups of academics: those who adhere to the academic conventions associated with the institution and those who move away from traditional forms of scholarly work in an attempt to put their web inspired principles into practice. However, this division cannot be explained in such linear or simplistic fashion because at stake is not only the distinction of two competing practices but also the imposition of a field's habitus on another field as a way of legitimating academics' (new) sense of identity and agency. The intention of changing a field's habitus with the proposal of a habitus from another field is more often than not met with suspicion, not least because it implicitly calls into question the taken-for-granted practices that define that field, i.e. the field's doxa.

Doxa and hysteresis: tools for understanding fields in change

Even though Bourdieu did not live to see the development and effect of the web on social fields and its agents, his theoretical and methodological legacy provides us with tools that help us explain the changes in meaning and in practice that are slowly occurring in academia with the support of the web. Bourdieu looked at strategies of differentiation as a form of distinction (Bourdieu, 1996) that can be more easily recognized in relation to what it diverges from. Distinction denotes difference, and can be seen as a break with the norms of a field and the habitus that characterizes it. Hence, it is when this ontological complicity between the field and the habitus – that the field sup- ports – reaches a point of disagreement that change is likely to occur. Bourdieu

(1977) explains the misalignment of the field and the habitus through the concept of hysteresis. The hysteresis of habitus, Bourdieu asserts, 'is one of the foundations of the structural lag between opportunities and the dispositions to grasp them' (p. 83). In the context of the digital scholarship phenomenon, this mismatch between digital scholars' habitus and the field of academia is achieved through a crisis of meaning between what academia acknowledges as academic contribution and the possibilities the web offers for creative and intellectual input. The distance between the two social fields is reflected through their distinctive logics of practice. At stake there are two competing views concerning what scholarship practices should be, how they should be conducted and whom they should serve. The contrasting approaches demarcate the intellectual space of struggle where two distinctive habitus meet. The web as a social field facilitates the deviation of scholarly practices from their place of legitimacy, i.e. academia. This departure from orthodoxy consists of a break with the doxic approaches the field uses to impose itself as habitus.

In his work Bourdieu noted that social practices are often typified by doxic experiences that denote acceptance of norms through the body. In other words, doxa is the embodiment of beliefs belonging to a field of practice, which are assimilated by the habitus, and conveyed through the dispositions individuals display and materialized through their practices. As such, the struggle between fields is made apparent through their competing doxa; what is accepted and what characterizes each field. This is visible in the battle for openness (Weller, 2014) in which individuals who incorporate the dominant practices on the web – a social field – as their newly acquired scholarly dispositions, expose the doxa of the academic field with yet another doxa; one that symbolizes their reformed habitus. This difference between individuals' developing habitus and the established social space in which they envisage their new practices to be realized results in a hysteresis of the habitus (Bourdieu, 1977, 1990, 1992), a sense of displacement with the field that substantiates academics' professional practice and, through association, their professional identity. The hysteresis effect is more likely to occur in times of transition in which agents struggle to impose new practices in the field while remaining relevant within the field's structure.

The emergence of digital technologies is without doubt creating a hysteresis effect in that it is changing how communication and culture are produced, distributed and used. And although the current generations have lived to witness this incredible shift – a moment that as McLuhan (1964) anticipated is likely to disappear as the novelty of new media wears off to become the new orthodoxy – nothing has prepared these generations for the unpredictability of digital technologies in creating alternative conduits of communication from which new roles and forms of agency have derived. These changes become challenges as they transform the meaning of social practices. Moreover, these changes are not only marked by new possibilities of production of knowledge or accessibility to it; they are also, and above all, typified by the emergence of a whole new ecology of participation, creation and communication of information that tests the stability of traditional monopolies of knowledge production with new practices. Digital technologies have thus encouraged new forms of agency that shake the recognized order of things.

Doxic approaches are specific to each single field. Therefore, they do not represent a system of beliefs characteristic of an entire society, but of a given social space. Taking this understanding of doxa into account, our aim is to examine how the concept of hysteresis (effect) can be operationalized in the context of digital scholarship practices. In doing so, we have to ask ourselves if Bourdieu's theory is capable of capturing change and the effects of it on individuals' practices. In trying to find answers to this question, we look at Bourdieu's empirical endeavours and reflect on our own experiences with regard to the development of methodological instruments that allow us to achieve such purpose. This reflective work is done in the light of previous studies on digital scholarship (see Costa 2013, 2015) and work on professional identities in higher education (Murphy, 2011) as we prepare to design a new study combining professional cultures and digital scholarship practices. The purpose is to take forward the lessons learned from such research experiences. The next section aims to do just that by elaborating on the methodological challenges of bridging theory with methodology when trying to understand changing scholarship practices.

Preparing for fieldwork with Bourdieu: the role of reflexivity

Bourdieu placed special attention on the methods he applied to access social reality as a construction rooted in a specific context. In conversation with Wacquant (1992), Bourdieu describes the ways through which his empirical research is developed to 'recapture the intrinsically double reality of the social world' (ibid., p. 11). Bourdieu's theory-method is developed in two complementary moments. The first moment consists of mapping out the space of social relations and actions. This involves identifying the nature and features the field displays and which determine agents' actions and positions from within. Once the properties of the field have been critically examined; i.e. the social context, the researcher should then turn his/her attention to the qualities of agency. The emphasis placed on agents' lived experiences allows us to access agents' categories of perception and appreciation. Such subjective observations should not, however, take primacy over the understanding of the structure of the field; rather, they should be analysed in tandem with the objective understandings developed in the first instance, which allows us to render explanations of individuals' dispositions as well as their relationships with the fields of power in which they operate. Bourdieu's advocacy for the relational nature of theory-method is further enhanced by his fixation with reflexivity, which also highlights the position and role of the researchers and the social and intellectual understandings they unconsciously transfer to the operationalization and analysis of the research. This is of particular importance in the contextual case of the phenomenon addressed in this chapter, as the study of the academic profession by fellow academics – which we are ourselves – requires a trained awareness of our own position in the field of study. Reflexivity goes, however, beyond the concepts of self-reference and self-awareness that serve the purpose of distance from the role to which we are professionally aligned. It deals most, and above all, with the systematic exploration of the 'unthought categories of thought which delimit the thinkable and predetermine the thought' (Bourdieu and Wacquant, 1992, p. 40); i.e. our own doxa. Reflexivity calls for the development of robust methodological tools that allow reflexivity to be embedded in the way social reality is accessed and 'acquired' for study and how the analysis that proceeds excavates beyond our own bias as social agents embodying specific social, intellectual and technological backgrounds. Reflexivity thus equates to thinking sociologically about both the researcher and the researched through methodological instruments developed for that very purpose. With this in mind, we need to devise a set of questions that will lead to the development of methods of inquiry conducive to the exploration of the phenomenon of digital scholarship beyond our own doxic approaches as well as the taken-for-granted assumptions that may be offered to us. In the next section we will elaborate on how we can take the work of Bourdieu forward to devise research tools that allow us to understand instances of change and the effects they have on individuals' professional lives.

The application of theory as method: the mapping of fields to understand their agents

The study on digital scholarship practices was first inspired by the extensive literature on the influence of digital technology on the scholarship of teaching and learning, and the gap it unveiled in proving any useful knowledge about its impact on the scholarship of research or engagement (Costa, 2013). However, the literature available offers contrasting accounts of how technology benefits education. If, on the one hand, studies report about the possibilities of emancipation and learner-centred approaches new technologies provide (see for example Beetham and Sharpe, 2013), on the other hand, research asserts more pessimistic approaches of how technology becomes a tool of distraction or is more often than not used for procrastination (Booth, 2013). Parallel to this there are a large number of studies on resistance to innovation and obstacles to change (Bryant et al., 2014), which offer very little beyond the descriptive analysis of the impasse that is created between institutional norms and individuals' new outlooks on practice. The voice of those who embrace technology to challenge engrained practices, how that came to be so and the impact it has on their professional lives and identity are aspects that are missing in published research. As such, this illustrates the doxa of research in theorizing this field of inquiry, opening a gap regarding more critical understandings of how agents work with and for the change of dispositions brought about by the web within the field of academia. It also does not explain why they deviate from the field that validates their academic practice and identity. And so we are left wondering about what happens when academics bring their online experiences into their professional practice? How do social spaces mediated by digital technologies change academics, their practice and the way they perceive their role and contribution as intellectuals? Are their newly acquired ways of approaching practice incorporated into the activities traditionally associated with academia? What role do digital scholars, as change agents, play in academia?

If the gaps in the literature provide us with the opportunity to formulate new research questions, the research questions themselves set the ground for the development of the necessary methodological and analytical tools given that they set both the context and purpose of the research. In wanting to look beyond the instrumental aspect of technology as tools enabling or disrupting practice, we need, first and foremost, to consider its role in mediating spaces of congregation of social capital, i.e. alternative social fields, and how such additional social spaces are structured. This precedes the analysis of agents' dispositions in incorporating unconventional practices in their academic portfolio, so as to understand 'where they are coming from'. In looking at agents operating between fields we then need to shift our attention to their relation with and between the two social fields; what links and sets fields and agents apart? In returning to the analysis of the objective structures, it is imperative we look at the web and academia and the distinctive roles both fields play in competing with and/or complementing one another. In this sense, Bourdieu's double lens not only allows us to surpass the binary divide between structure and agency by looking at the interplay between the two social spaces, but also by comparing and contrasting two fields with two different logics of practice. We know from previous studies (see Costa 2014c) that it is through the lack of coordination of the two fields in supporting the same dispositions that the hysteresis of the habitus becomes more pronounced as both fields' doxic approaches are brought into question. In this sense, what the analysis of doxa and hysteresis offers us is an understanding of how change occurs and is negotiated across fields precisely because of the dynamics established between fields and between fields and agents.

It is perhaps not surprising that there is a tendency in the social sciences in general, and education in particular, to look at the obstacles of change rather than how change occurs and affects those implied in it. Research on the reproduction of practice has a long tradition and Bourdieu's research is a good example of it. With much of his work devoted to the analysis of the reproduction of social practices – especially the examination of the dominant order and the place and role of the dominated – the understanding of change offered in his work is arrived at by chance, as an explanation of divergence from the norm, rather than intentionally. Yet, Bourdieu's work does provide scope to understand change even if it was not his primary intention, because of the malleability of his sociological tools.

Bourdieu proposes that change has its roots in individuals' crisis of meaning, which is subsequently understood as a form of reflexivity with regard to participants' own practices and the significance they assign to it. Bourdieu, in conversation with Wacquant, goes on to claim that change is a form of heterodoxy that exists in the 'universe of discourse (or argument) while doxa resides in the universe of the undiscussed' (1992, p. 168). Although vague, this understanding of how change can be represented is useful in devising mechanisms through which accounts of change – and the effects they may have on agents – can be elicited. Core to the expression of heterodoxy through discourse is the idea of emancipation through reflection. Bourdieu does not discard the idea of deliberation as a form of liberation that can in turn lead the individual to fight for change in both practical and symbolic ways. Yet, Bourdieu is cautious to note that such practices are dependent on socio-economic and also historic circumstances (1990). Hence, critical to this research are digital scholars' own perceptions of agency within the structures of practice offered by each field and both. In studying digital scholars' dispositions (Costa, 2014a) in relation to the fields of academia and the web, we are able to perceive how their habitus is incorporated or rejected by which field, thus disclosing the hysteresis of habitus and the doxic approaches at play. To access such modes of deliberation and production we need to look at methodological instruments that allow us to elicit such reflections. In doing so we need to depart from quantitative and holistic methods and look at techniques that encourage the narrative of experiences in the first person so that we can have access to agents' own views and perceptions. Nonetheless, there is a need to be mindful of the bias such narratives carry as they portray individuals' vested interests, which are likely to be inconsistent with the practices promoted in and by the field and which are decreed by the field's policies.

Bourdieu too was faced with similar methodological questions. His empirical work neither denied the use of quantitative research nor did it discard the value of qualitative data, so much so that Bourdieu has often employed both to create a richer narrative of the phenomenon under study. What is more, he also used less conventional methods, especially for his time, such as photography – in literally trying to capture the stories and the different angles his research could unveil (see Bourdieu, 2012). In *The weight of the world* Bourdieu (1999) used participants' narrations as a method that allowed him and his team to elicit autobiographical reflections as research texts, which were then objectified through short, sociological essays. Although criticized for what was assumed to be a less scientific approach (Nowicka, 2015), Bourdieu's effort to give voice to his research participants was equally powerful in creating instances of reflection and reflexivity for both the researcher and the researched. This marks the last evolution in Bourdieu's own work, which hints at his ambition to explore new ways of capturing the voice of agency through individuals' own words. This is not surprising given that the search for a method that would place research practice closer to the social phenomenon being studied was a constant in Bourdieu's approach. In this vein, we too feel compelled to look for less traditional methodological approaches when capturing the voice of agency, and a way of looking beyond doxified forms of research practice and exploring new techniques of data collection that might be more conducive to the social context being studied. The web itself is a space of personal storytelling where individuals, consciously or unconsciously, create a footprint of their online trajectories through participation in different environments.

In wanting to understand what happens to scholars engaged in digital activities, we will borrow from narrative inquiry a technique to both survey the fields in question and understand the place of (digital) practices in it. As a way of 'constructing and representing the rich and messy domain of human interaction' (Bruner, 1991, p. 4) through a first person voice, narrative inquiry does not aim to merely look at what happened, but rather what meaning is given to it (Clandinin and Connelly, 2000). Thus, narratives as interpretations of practice become social meanings of 'longitudinal and lateral aspects of experience' (Dewey, 1934, p. 44) through which individuals can 'claim identities and construct lives' (Reissman, 2007, p. 2).

Core to narrative inquiry as a research method is the wish to understand the contexts (Webster and Mertova, 2007, p. 32) – social, cultural, economical, political, professional, institutional, technological, etc. – in which the phenomenon takes place, a goal familiar to Bourdieuian scholars. The use of narrative inquiry to help bring out doxified positions of both individuals and the fields in which their experiences are realized is further justified by the fact that it gives narrators a central position (Larson, 1997) as main actors and first interpreters of their own experiences. For this project, in particular, the access to personal narratives provides an opportunity to get closer to perceptions of agency and the meaning that is attributed to them in the contexts in which participants' activities are enacted.

As Clandinin and Connelly (2000) understand it, narrative inquiry can be simultaneously a method and an object of study that offers an opportunity to explore, construct and reconstruct research participants' narratives of experience through reflexive accounts of their professional lives. Narrative inquiry helps unveil experiences that have remained untold by situating individuals' stories in a given context and raising awareness of the circumstances research participants narrate (Brooke, 2002; Stahl, 2011). This results in the questioning of the realities it tackles (Howcroft and Trauth, 2004). The job of the researchers then is to exercise reflexivity in that they seek new ways of thinking to address the issues the narratives bring out (Steinberg and Kincheloe, 2010). At the same time the access to personal trajectories can be helpful in tracing individuals' habitus; such narrations are, by the same token, likely to unveil participants' encounters with the field's doxa as well as their own doxified approaches, even if in an unconscious way. This is so because narrations of the 'self' carry in themselves points of view that have become naturalized practices, thus lacking awareness of their own partiality. In the context of digital scholarship practices, for example, it is anticipated that academia's cultural and intellectual traditions may be questioned with the proposal of deviant practices – digital scholarship practices – that expose the hysteresis of the habitus through the contestation of the doxa. By doing so, however, participants are also declaring their own doxified approach in relation to digital practices. Using doxa as a filter of analysis allows us to highlight the hidden assumptions that can only be made visible when we seek different ways of problematizing the reality presented to us, rather than taking such accounts at face value. In this sense, what narrative inquiry offers us is a multidimensional way of understanding the social reality being narrated as researchers can look at the data from different angles and categories.

Narrative inquiry does, however, present us with some issues. Although narrative constructions, as a method to capture change, are able to fulfil the purpose of organizing, sharing and collecting lived experiences as they have happened and been apprehended, and as they are told and understood, they 'can only achieve verisimilitude' (Bruner, 1991, p. 4). This is so because practices are codified through the interpretation individuals attribute to the realities they narrate (Kramp, 2003, p. 4). Narrative inquiry thus raises questions of validation because it relies on individual perceptions. Mishler (1990) talks about the validation of narrative research through a process of 'trustworthiness'. This return us to the argument that knowledge is socially constructed (ibid., p. 417) and that inquiry-guided research needs to oversee a process of practice that is reliable. The trustworthiness of this form of inquiry does not end with the research methods employed. In the case of theory-method application *à la* Bourdieu it covers the commitment towards reflexivity, and the submission of the reality presented to the critical and unfamiliar eye of research. Hence, the need to look beyond the understanding of habitus as embodied practice attached to a field. Doxa and hysteresis offer additional research filters that allow us to go even deeper into the meanings conveyed through the narratives told. In taking this approach forward, there is a need to prepare a robust plan of analysis that encompasses different iterations of working with the data. The first phase consists of looking at the data to capture its literal meaning. This gives us an overview of the field as well as a surface understanding of the phenomenon exposed to us through its social actors' discourses. It also provides us with an understanding of the intention of the narrators, which carries, in itself, conscious and unconscious elements. The second phase of analysis calls for depth. There is a need to examine what is beneath the first layer of analysis by searching for aspects unknown to research (and the researcher). This requires us to enter the universe of the undiscussed experiences through those that are discussed in order to bring to the forefront any 'pre-reflexive grasp of the social world' (Deer, 2008, p. 202). In doing so, we face two challenges. The first is represented by the difficulties researchers face in abstracting themselves from their own assumptions. The second consists of recognizing the assumptions that reveal and identify the doxa, and in some cases, the hysteresis effect that derives from it.

Operationalizing doxa has always been one of Bourdieu's conceptual black boxes; it is one that although presented in Bourdieu's work has remained relatively undiscussed. Even though doxa and hysteresis are part of Bourdieu's theoretical and methodological weaponry, these concepts are more often than not presented to illustrate the relational dynamics (or lack of them) between field and habitus. And although it is in the gap between field and habitus (hysteresis) that change is more likely to occur, it is often unclear how change does happen or what triggers it. Thus, it could be argued that these concepts occupy a more concealed, hidden position in Bourdieu's sociology. This is curious if we think that the main function of such conceptual tools is to support exactly the opposite, i.e. to give visibility to the hidden structures and perceptions that lie underneath any apparent or first explanation of the social world. The change of social practices in Bourdieu's work is thus regarded tacitly whereas their reproduction is made explicit more often. As such, this symbolized a doxified preference for the study of dominant practices to the detriment of deviant ones.

Final reflections

The paper has aimed to flesh out a programme of application of the concepts of doxa and hysteresis by reflecting how the sociology of Pierre Bourdieu can be useful in operationalizing and explaining change. Throughout his career Bourdieu endeavoured to develop a rigorous understanding of social practices by devising ways of apprehending and (re)presenting social realities both theoretically and methodologically. Bourdieu was as concerned about explaining the social world without falling into fallacious assumptions concerning the subjective reality he studied, as he was in constructing sociological instruments that allowed him to excavate the tacit knowledge implicit in social structures and their agents. Bourdieu clarifies this objective well in *Outline of a theory of practice* (1977) where he states that his goal is 'to bring to light the theory of theory and the theory of practice inscribed (in its practical state) in this mode of knowledge' (p. 3). The result is a series of theoretical constructs derived from his empirical work across different areas. These constructs support the reflexive purpose of the social sciences in explaining social phenomena as well as the role of the researcher in constructing such understandings.

Bourdieu's theory has acquired an almost universal currency given its application possibilities across multiple contexts. Despite the integration of his sociology across the social sciences and beyond, the criticism of his work with regards to the vagueness that his concepts depict is still felt strongly. However, what Bourdieu's work offers by giving us scope of manoeuvre within his concepts is a considerable degree of autonomy to look at the social world through different lenses and perspectives that might have otherwise been taken for granted. It is this aspect of disclosing familiarity and of acknowledging the role of the researchers in stepping outside their own assumptions that this chapter deals with. In doing so, we look beyond the popularized Bourdieuian concepts of habitus and fields whose inevitable dialectical relationship has often been criticized as offering a limit explanation of social action.

This chapter has proposed precisely the reverse. Bourdieu's sociology is capable of accounting for change and transformation. Yet, to reach such understandings we must address the meaning of habitus beyond its function of reproduction of practices and consider how the hysteresis of habitus – that is generated by the crisis of meaning – can lead to the renovation of dispositions that may or may not agree with the different social spaces in which agents are inserted. To exemplify this point we made use of the growing phenomenon of digital scholarship practices that is being stimulated by the pervasiveness of web technologies in both the workplace and individuals' social and cultural lives.

References

Beetham, H. and Sharpe, R. (2013) *Rethinking pedagogy for a digital age: Designing for 21st century learning*. Abingdon, Oxon: Routledge.

Booth, F. (2013) *The distraction trap: How to focus in a digital world*. Harlow: Pearson UK.

Bourdieu, P. (1977) *Outline of a theory of practice*. Cambridge: Cambridge University Press.

Bourdieu, P. (1990) *The logic of practice*. Stanford, CA: Stanford University Press.

Bourdieu, P. (1992) *Language and symbolic power*. (G. Raymond and M. Adamson, trans., J. Thompson, eds). Cambridge, MA: Harvard University Press.

Bourdieu, P. (1996) *The state nobility: Elite schools in the field of power*. Stanford, CA: Stanford University Press.

Bourdieu, P. (1999) *The weight of the world: Social suffering in contemporary society*. Stanford, CA: Stanford University Press.

Bourdieu, P. (2012) *Picturing Algeria*. (C. Calhoun, trans.). New York: Columbia University Press.

Bourdieu, P. and Wacquant, L. J. D. (1992) *An invitation to reflexive sociology*. Chicago, IL: University of Chicago Press.

Brooke, C. (2002) 'What does it mean to be "critical" in IS research?', *Journal of Information Technology*, *17*(2): 49–57.

Bruner, J. (1991) 'The narrative construction of reality', *Critical Inquiry*, *18*: 1–21.

Bryant, P., Coombs, A. and Pazio, M. (2014) 'Are we having fun yet? Institutional resistance and the introduction of play and experimentation into learning innovation through social media', *Journal of Interactive Media in Education*, 2.

Clandinin, D. J. and Connelly, F. M. (2000). *Narrative inquiry: Experience and story in qualitative research*. San Francisco, CA: Jossey-Bass.

Costa, C. (2013). *The participatory web in the context of academic research: Landscapes of change and conflicts*. PhD thesis. University of Salford, Manchester, UK. Retrieved from http://usir.salford.ac.uk/28369/

Costa, C. (2014a) 'The habitus of digital scholars', *Research in Learning Technology*, *21*: 1–17.

Costa, C. (2014b) 'Outcasts on the inside: academics reinventing themselves online', *International Journal of Lifelong Education*, *34*(2): 194–210. doi: 10.1080/ 02601370.2014.985752.

Costa, C. (2014c) 'Double gamers: academics between fields', *British Journal of Sociology of Education*, *12*: 1–21. doi: 10.1080/01425692.2014.982861.

Costa, C. (2015) 'Academics online: Fighting for a new habitus' in C. Costa and M. Murphy (eds), *Bourdieu, habitus and social research: The art of application* (pp. 151–67). London: Palgrave Macmillan.

Deer, C. (2008) 'Reflexivity' in M. Grenfell (ed.), *Pierre Bourdieu: Key concepts* (pp. 199–212). Abingdon, Oxon: Acumen Publishing.

Dewey, J. (1934). *Experience and education*. New York: Free Press.

Gauntlett, D. (2011). *Making is connecting*. Cambridge: Polity.

Howcroft, D. and Trauth, E. M. (2004) 'The choice of critical information systems research', in B. Kaplan, D. P. Truex, D. Wastell, A. T. Wood-Harper and J. I. DeGross (eds), *Information systems research* (pp. 195–211). Boston, MA: Kluwer Academic.

Jenkins, H. (2009) 'Confronting the challenges of participatory culture: Media education for the 21st century', *Program*, *21*(1): 72.

Kramp, M. (2003) 'Exploring life and experience through narrative inquiry', in K. B. deMarrais and S. D. Lapan (eds), *Foundations for research: Methods of inquiry in education and the social sciences* (illustrated edn) (pp. 103–21). Mahwah, NJ: Routledge.

Larson, C. L. (1997) 'Re-presenting the subject: Problems in personal narrative inquiry', *International Journal of Qualitative Studies in Education*, *10*(4): 455–70. doi: 10.1080/095183997237034.

Lessig, L. (2004). *Free culture: How big media uses technology and the law to lock down culture and control creativity*. New York: Penguin Press.

Lessig, L. (2009). *Remix: Making art and commerce thrive in the hybrid economy*. New York: Penguin Books.

McLuhan, M. (1964) *Understanding media: The extensions of man*. London: Routledge.

Miller, A. N., Taylor, S. G., and Bedeian, A. G. (2011). 'Publish or perish: Academic life as management faculty live it', *Career Development International*, *16*(5): 422–45.

Mishler, E. (1990) 'Validation in inquiry-guided research: The role of exemplars in narrative studies', *Harvard Educational Review*, *60*(4): 415–43.

Murphy, M. (2011) 'Troubled by the past: History, identity and the university', *Journal of Higher Education Policy and Management*, *33*(5): 509–17.

Nowicka, M. (2015) 'Habitus – its transformation and transfer through cultural encounters in migration' in C. Costa and M. Murphy (eds), *Bourdieu, habitus and social research: The art of application* (pp. 93–107). Basingstoke: Palgrave Macmillan.

Riessman, C. (2007) *Narrative methods for the human sciences* (1st edn). Thousand Oaks, CA: Sage.

Selwyn, N. (2014) *Digital technology and the contemporary university: Degrees of digitization*. New York: Routledge.

Stahl, B. (2011) 'Critical social information systems research' in R. D. Galliers and W. Currie (eds), *The Oxford handbook of management information systems: Critical perspectives and new directions* (pp. 199–228). Oxford: Oxford University Press.

Steinberg, S. R. and Kincheloe, J. L. (2010) 'Power, emancipation, and complexity: Employing critical theory', *Power and Education*, 2(2): 140.

Talib, A. A. (2002) 'The Research Assessment Exercise and motivation: A note on the difference in the impact on the active researchers and the non-active', *Higher Education Review*, 34(2): 51–9.

Webster, L. and Mertova, P. (2007) *Using narrative inquiry as a research method: An introduction to using critical event narrative analysis in research on learning and teaching.* Abingdon, Oxon: Routledge.

Weller, M. (2011) *The digital scholar: How technology is changing academic practice* (1st edn). London: Bloomsbury.

Weller, M. (2014) *The battle for open: How openness won and why it doesn't feel like victory.* London: Ubiquity Press.

Part 2

Researching equity in education

Operationalizing Bourdieu, interrogating intersectionality and the underachievement of primary level Afro-Trinidadian boys

Ravi Rampersad

Introduction

The theoretical and methodological 'relationship' with Bourdieu is the platform used to analyse the highly emotive, yet little understood issue of the achievement of Afro-Trinidadian boys at the primary level. 'Little black boy go to school', the title of a highly acclaimed calypso sung by Winston 'Gypsy' Peters symbolizes the debate on Afro-Trinidadian boys and achievement. The song labels young Afro-Trinidadian males as antisocial and anti-achievement for not focusing on education in their pursuit of other things. This 1997 song is perhaps the first public articulation of a perceived crisis of black masculinity in Trinidad and mirrors the sentiment of noted Caribbean scholar Errol Miller (see Miller, 1986, 1991).

In this calypso, social delinquency is evident in criminal activity, drug abuse, unemployment and destitution, which are pathologically linked to the academic failings and perceptions of social deviance in the culture of Afro-Trinidadian males. The general crux of this song represents a deficit model of thinking (Valencia, 1997), one which reflects the nature of arguments in public discourse. This deficit model situates the genesis of societal ills in the believed apathy of Afro-Trinidadian boys towards education and normative cultural values in general, as compared to other groups.

My research seeks to debunk this deficit model through a more nuanced appreciation for the factors affecting the education of Afro-Trinidadian boys. This is underscored in an understanding that Afro-Trinidadian boys cannot be classified as a monolith, but rather are reflective of a differentiated experience born of different socio-historic trajectories and social positioning in society. In attempting to fully comprehend this picture the research sought to analyse not just race, but importantly, the intersections of race, social class and gender. This required a theoretical and methodological model capable of capturing both this intersectionality and the micro-details of human agency as this complex racialized system is embodied and enacted in day to day life.

The research: a tale of two schools

The research centred on two Trinidadian public boys' primary schools, St George's and Pinehill (names disguised). St George's was associated with the middle and upper class and regarded as a centre of excellence, with students routinely placing within the top one hundred of national examinations. This school is highly sought-after and tends to have a lengthy waiting list for acceptance. Pinehill boys school is a community-based school located within the heart of the Pinehill working-class community. This school is often chided as a seat of male delinquency and a failing school, and students are primarily community residents and rarely from outside the area. The research participants included 8–10-year-old Afro-Trinidadian boys, their teachers, head teachers and parents. Data were collected over the course of one school term through a triangulation of methods including participant observation, focus group sessions (based on photo elicitation) and individual interviews.

Establishing context: demography and race in the Trinidad context

For one to further understand and appreciate the journey towards Bourdieu it is important to first grasp the context of this sojourn. Deconstructing the context lays the foundation for this chapter as it aims to create a narrative that will walk the reader through methodological and theoretical considerations in interrogating intersectional issues of race, class, gender in a postcolonial society and, ultimately, the connection with the sociology of Pierre Bourdieu.

Trinidad is the larger island in the twin island republic of Trinidad and Tobago; the islands are located in the southern Caribbean, off the coast of Venezuela. The current population (2014 estimates) stands at approximately 1.2 million with what can be considered a co-majority of racial groups of Indo-Trinidadians at 35.4 per cent and Afro-Trinidadians at 34.2 per cent; the next statistically significant group is the 'mixed category' at 23 per cent, and there are smaller groups of whites, Chinese and Syrians accounting for under 2 per cent of the total population (source: www.cia.gov/library/publications/the-world-factbook/geos/td.html).

Much of the modern history of Trinidad is connected to the racialized competition for resources, influence and political control, largely between the co-majority races (Meighoo, 2003). This is not to suggest that the other racial groups are not involved in this struggle for dominance and control, far from it. It is argued that the 2 per cent of the population that is white, Chinese or Syrian are disproportionately represented in the upper socio-economic spheres of Trinidadian society, while the working class is comprised predominantly of the co-majority groups (Coppin and Olsen, 1998). This racially etched status quo is the product and legacy of colonialism, which forged a society that married race and class into a system where whiteness and light skin colour are equated with normative capital and greater social opportunities; this is known as a pigmentocracy (Bonilla-Silva and Dietrich, 2008). In a sense, with pigmentocracy social class becomes interchangeable with skin colour as a classifier, so the higher up in society you go the lighter the skin colour (Bonilla-Silva and Dietrich, 2008; Braithwaite, 1953; Johnson, 2004; Mohammed, 2000). These patterns are also reflected in education with the creation under colonialism of a dual system of prestige schools versus government schools. The prestige schools are those which are associated with educational excellence and the white and lighter skinned middle and upper classes, while the government schools are typically stereotyped as self-fulfilling sites of delinquency and failure, with enrolment concentrated in the darker-skinned working class.

The terms used to denote racial categories provide a useful insight into the context of race in Trinidad. The prefix terms Afro and Indo are used to denote persons of African and Indian (subcontinent) Trinidadian heritage respectively. While this term may appear anachronistic, arguably it is reflective more of an enduring product of a racialized system than a cultural lag. The points of reference are North America and the UK where racial category identification terms may be periodically updated in line with changing societal discourses and debates (Lynch, 2006). Trinidad's experience with this is embedded within a racialized system born and reborn of colonial and postcolonial constructs, which obfuscates open dialogue and discourse on race and racial discrimination.

As such, race in Trinidad, as in much of Latin America, is seen as a taboo subject, a 'no go' area (Bonilla-Silva and Dietrich, 2008); it is an 'absent presence' (Tomlinson, 2008). It is suggested that countries in the Americas, such as Trinidad follow an 'ostrich approach' to racial matters, 'that is, they all stick their heads deep into the social ground and say, we don't have races here. We don't have racism here' (Bonilla-Silva and Dietrich, 2008, p. 152), we are all Trinidadians. Lowenthal (1967, p. 580), in his seminal piece on race and colour in the West Indies, written close to fifty years ago, similarly asserts that

> central to this image is the notion that West Indians enjoy harmony and practice tolerance among manifold races, colours and creeds. In the outside world, Caribbean race relations are often termed exemplary. Local governments industriously promote this impression to attract foreign investments, to emphasize social progress, and to vaunt their achievements. Guyana, once the 'Land of Six Peoples', now proclaims it is 'One People, One Nation'; Trinidad's coat of arms reads 'Together We Aspire, Together We Achieve', and the ruling party's slogan is, 'All o' we is one'; Jamaica proclaims 'Out of Many, One People'.

This view on race arguably contributes to the dearth in literature and statistics emanating from Trinidad and the Caribbean, which centre on race and skin colour (Bonilla-Silva and Dietrich, 2008; Coppin, 1997). England (2009) emphasizes this point with a newspaper quote from an Afro-Trinidadian calypsonian turned politician, Winston 'Gypsy' Peters on his accusation of being a race traitor by joining an Indo-Trinidadian-dominated political party. Peters challenges,

> What race you talking about in Trinidad? Trinidad have any race? Half of my family mix up with Indians. And my great grandfather is a White man from Scotland, George Steele. You understand what I am saying? My aunt and uncle dem is Indian too. Who the hell in Trinidad and Tobago could talk about race? When you want to talk about race you have to go to a place where one race can't even walk where another race lives. All of us does go and eat by one another, so when they point fingers at me it has nothing to do with race. It's more to do with jealousy than anything else. I am convinced of that. If Trinidad has to do with race, what am I going to do with my little Dougla[1] nieces and nephews?
>
> (*Sunday Mirror*, 1 October 2000
> as cited in England, 2009)

Accordingly, the reality of race today in Trinidadian society is not a black–white binary, one against the other, but rather the often intangible 'shades of grey' in between; that reality is pigmentocracy (Fanon, 1967; Hunter, 2002).

Accordingly, the nature of race and its position as a non-discourse makes it difficult at best to interrogate how it is embodied and enacted on a daily basis. On a practical level, as a social researcher, the daunting question arose early on, 'how can I analyse race and achievement when no one will talk about race, much less talk openly about it?' What was needed was a platform that could both appreciate and engage with the macro level of racialized systems and structures and how these are manifested on a daily basis in human agency. The non-dialogic climate of race in Trinidad dictates that race has to be carefully unpacked and deconstructed in order to fully grasp the nuances and essence of racialized structures and its significance for different socially situated groups. This is where Bourdieu's work is important as a flexible theoretical and methodological platform able to engage with and appreciate these nuances of a pigmentocratic society. Through adaptation and deployment of concepts of habitus, field and capital I was able to observe and digest the daily human agency of race, performed and expressed often indirectly through words and bodily disposition.

Why Bourdieu?

Before moving on to the appropriateness of Bourdieu for my research it is important to elucidate my particular epistemological foundation as a scholar; this is something which indeed shapes the nature of my research, in regard to conceptualization, design and treatment of data. In engaging with my research I am predisposed towards a particular worldview. This orientation is premised on an understanding of the centrality of three interdependent machinations: the salience of historical process in shaping the contemporary postcolonial world; the intersectionality of race with social class and gender as an organizing principle of postcolonial societies in the continued subjugation of minoritized groups; and the positioning of research as an act of social justice. With this in mind, one may 'label' me as a postcolonial critical race scholar.

Arriving at Bourdieu

One can argue for an approach that is itself similar in nature to the context of race in Trinidad, that is, flexible and multidimensional. In grappling with these demands, my theoretical journey initially took me into the fold of CRT. The early part of my research process focused centrally on the issue of race and led me to CRT as a discourse, one which has a similar gaze. CRT is an American-based theoretical discourse (for a more detailed view of CRT see Delgado and Stefancic, 2001), which centres an understanding of race and racism as pervasive constructs in the analysis of social phenomena (Delgado and Stefancic, 2001). There is equally a focus on intersectionality where race is constructed as a mediated structure interwoven with other layers of oppression such as gender and social class (Parker and Lynn, 2002). CRT developed as a transformative model in not only understanding marginalization, but also aiming to positively change the world (Delgado and Stefancic, 2001; Ladson-Billings, 1999; Taylor, 1998, 2000). Central to CRT is a firm belief that racism is not an anathema in society, but is part and parcel of the historical process of subordination of peoples of colour (Taylor, 2009). Delgado and Stefancic (2001, p. 7) suggest that racism is ordinary, not aberrational – 'normal science', the usual way society does business, the common, everyday experience of most people of colour in this country.

This discourse proved strong in appreciating the structural and socio-historical nature of racialized systems. This made it a 'natural' choice for engaging with the issue of Afro-Trinidadian boys and achievement. CRT was used to assemble an overall structural view of society as racially configured in nature, where race cannot be reduced to a simple construct of ideas and attitudes, but should be seen as being at the heart of a society's structuring. Bonilla-Silva (2005) argues that racialization of social groups constitutes a partial imposition (along with gender and class) of social relations vis-à-vis other groups in terms of access to and control over social, economic and political resources. Therefore, CRT facilitates an analysis of the education of Afro-Trinidadian boys that centres race and racism at the heart of their experience, by focusing on the structurations of the education system and of their communities.

While it became apparent that CRT was primed to engage with social phenomena on a more structural level, there was also the need to ascertain how race itself was embodied and enacted on a daily basis in the identity formation of Afro-Trinidadian boys. I was faced with the methodological dilemma of the structure–agency divide. Crafting an accurate picture of the educational experience of Afro-Trinidadian boys required grasping both the structures of society and how they are manifested on the individual level, the interplay between the macro and micro. This is where, for me, the sociology of Bourdieu emerged as an equal partner for CRT in the creation of a theoretical hybrid. Arguably, Bourdieu works to bridge that gap between objectivism and subjectivism, structure and agency (Jenkins, 2002).

Addressing issues in using Bourdieu

Is Bourdieu overly deterministic?

Bourdieu's use in my research was not a completely linear process without any concerns; before full commitment in applying Bourdieu, critiques had to be addressed. One of the main critiques levelled against Bourdieu posits a deterministic logic underpinning his concepts. The perspective that counters this criticism and allows for Bourdieu's use in my research hinges on an interpretation of Bourdieu. This interpretation sees Bourdieu's perspective as a view of human behaviour – directed but not determined. Bourdieu's concept of habitus provides a useful point of reference. Habitus, according to Connolly (2004, p. 83, emphasis added) can be defined as a 'combination of habits as they are internalized within the individual child as a coherent set of schemes that are *reflective* of the broader social structures within which they are located, that forms the basis of the notion of the habitus'. Reay (2004, p. 439) concurs, affirming a view of habitus as 'a means of viewing structure as occurring within small-scale interactions and activity within large-scale settings'. Habitus then is the conceptual tool that Bourdieu uses within this methodological framework of structuralist constructivism in an attempt to reconcile these dualisms' (Reay, 2004, p. 432). Key to the habitus is understanding that it is embodied; Bourdieu attempts to demonstrate both how the body is in the social world and how the social world is in the body (Reay, 2004). The generative schemes of the habitus are not merely reflected in the human psyche but are also subconsciously embedded and expressed through durable ways of acting: walking, talking, standing and eating (Reay, 2004).

However, Bourdieu is sure to emphasize that the habitus should not be construed as a schema that generates automatic responses and behaviour; that is to say, location within a particular field cannot in a linear manner predict practice (Bourdieu and Nice, 1993). Bourdieu's understanding of practice relates to human behaviour as inseparably both contextual and temporal in time and space, and not consciously, or not wholly consciously, organized and orchestrated (Jenkins, 2002, pp. 69–70). Equally, conceptualizing the significance of habitus requires an understanding of its relational dynamic within the field and the resources or capital at stake within that field. As such, Bourdieu, in conversation with Wacquant defines a field as a network, or a configuration, of objective relations between positions objectively defined, in their existence and in the determinations they impose upon their occupants, agents or institutions, by their present and potential situation (situs) in the structure of the distribution of species of power (or capital) whose possession commands access to the specific profits that are at stake in the field, as well as by their objective relation to other positions (domination, subordination, homology, etc.). Each field presupposes, and generates by its very functioning, the belief in the value of the stakes it offers.

(Wacquant, 1989, p. 39)

These contested resources or goods are classified into different categories of capital, such as cultural, social, economic and symbolic. As Bourdieu states, it is the nature and conditions of the different fields which imbue meaning and legitimacy in different forms of capital for different groups, groups which are socio-historically located in specific social spaces (Wacquant, 1989). Capital is primarily a relational construct where one type of capital is transferable or translatable into other forms (Bourdieu, 1986). For instance, social capital, defined as the benefits derived from membership in a social grouping such as a family, can be translated into economic capital (wealth and economic resources) through the use of familial connections and support in the labour market or in commerce. Therefore, when constituted together the relations of capital explain social advantage or disadvantage, and hence the status quo (Reay, 2005b).

Bourdieu (1990, p. 116) counters criticisms of determinism in three points; first, that the habitus becomes active only in relation to a field and that it can produce very different behaviour depending on the stability of that setting. Second, habitus is a product of social conditioning; interaction with the field either reinforces its generative schemes or transforms them. Thirdly, Bourdieu (1990, p. 116) argues that not only can the habitus be transformed, 'it can also be controlled through awakening of consciousness and socioanalysis'. I am inclined to disagree with Jenkins (2002, p. 83), when he states that Bourdieu's response cannot answer this critique as it situates the source of change as external to the social actors concerned. Jenkins' perspective, in this case, appears to be premised on the construct of the social world as external from social actors and their actions; that is, the habitus is not in the social world. I believe the crucial factor is the range, limited as it may be, of probable practices in the interplay of possibilities and constraints within a social context or field. In bridging the divide between structure and agency, the formation of habitus invokes the idea of embodiment where the social world impacts on behaviour, but also where behaviour structures structure (Crossley, 2001). This suggests that inherent in the limited choices that an actor has within certain circumstances, sits a vehicle for change. Accordingly, Bourdieu and Nice (1993, p. 87) stress that the habitus, 'is something powerfully generative'.

On a practical level, the indeterminacy of habitus is expressed in my own simple analogy. I ask you to imagine a situation where an eight-year-old British white working-class girl is given a sheet of paper and a pen and placed in a room for an hour and told she can do whatever she wants with the time. Realistically speaking, the girl can only behave within the realms of 'possibilities of practice'; that is to say she can do literally hundreds of different things, but she cannot do what does not fall into her habitus, for example write a story in Latin or Sanskrit, unless she has been exposed to these languages. If this is indeed determinist, it is latent on a very broad scale, similar to ascertaining that the amount of sand on a beach is finite, thus begging indeterminacy.

This counter-critique of Bourdieu is vitally important for any model that incorporates a CRT focus. CRT aims to counter any discourse that marginalizes or oppresses the voice and capital of minoritized groups. As such, a deterministic Bourdieu would frame marginalized peoples and communities as mired in veritable cycles of deprivation indelibly tied to their own cultural patterns and make any association with a CRT platform incompatible.

Can Bourdieu do race?

One of my first introspective questions was if Bourdieu can do race. Bourdieu does not explicitly deal with race in his analyses, but as Jenkins (2002) confirms, many of his constructs are rather opaque and vague, perhaps deliberately, allowing for a measure of manoeuvre. Reay (2004, p. 436) suggests that habitus was designed as a method to analyse 'the dominance of dominant groups in society and the domination of subordinate groups', implying its suitability for analysis of racialized systems. With habitus, McClelland (1990, p. 105) argues that 'one of its strengths is that although it has been developed most extensively with respect to social origins, it can easily be applied to the analysis of gender (or racial and ethnic) disadvantage as well.' In a practical sense, habitus can be used as a conceptual tool in unpacking how race, class and gender are embodied and played out, not only in individuals' actions and attitudes, but also in a whole range of bodily gestures (Reay, 2004). This may prove very useful in interpreting what may appear to be mundane human behaviour within specific fields at specific junctures of time as expressions of domination or subordination. Habitus, in spite of its determinist critique, can also be regarded as a tool for social activism, where within the same repertoire of limited options for acting lies resistance for the oppressed, racially or otherwise.

Equally, when habitus is combined with other concepts of capital and field it has the potential for elucidating a fuller picture of practice as raced, classed and gendered. In this sense, human behaviour is arguably shaped by the potentialities engrained in the habitus as one navigates the system of societal competition for capital accumulation, within a certain field (Reay, 2004).

As for capital, Yosso (2006) regards its imbuement with significance as political in nature, as opposed to democratic and neutral. In reference to cultural capital, defined as 'an accumulation of cultural knowledge, skills and abilities possessed and inherited by privileged groups in society', Yosso (2006, p. 174) highlights that its political nature is stressed whereby only certain cultural products are constructed as legitimate and valuable as opposed to others. However, the pivotal nature of capital to status ensures that dominant groups guard access and imbuement of meaning jealously. Jenkins suggests that the familial habitus enables the upper classes to disguise what they have *learned* as what they are *born* with. So even with appropriate schooling, the primary school teacher or the clerk is unlikely to be able to 'bring it off': another case of 'manners maketh the man' (Jenkins, 2002, p. 139).

In a related sense, Yosso (2006) maintains that Bourdieu's concept of cultural capital has often been misappropriated in deficit models of why students of colour academically underachieve, claiming a lack of (normative) cultural capital, rather than appreciating the relative worth of their culture and how it comes to be denigrated and devalued. This is part of the process embodied in the 'new racism' where racialized discourse is disguised under the rubric of culture (Bonilla-Silva, 2005; Mirza, 2009). This becomes particularly pertinent in social research in Trinidad where much of the racialized discourse may actually be intra-group and where the discourse on failing Afro-Trinidadian boys centres on cultural deficiencies, such as the 'culture of poverty' arguments of Wilson and Fordham and Ogbu (Gould, 1999) constructed in: broken homes, a dearth of male role models, lack of communal educative aspirations, criminality and popular culture. For instance, in a newspaper article Fraser (2004) denies that his analysis of Afro-Trinidadian education and failure is part of a racial discourse as evident in his rejection of claims of genetic or biological inferiority. However, he then proceeds to channel his efforts towards cultural deficit, engaging in the new racist discourse, arguing that,

> it seems clear that quality family life, the values inculcated in our children (of all ethnic groups) and the ambitions we help them to develop are the major factors that create a class of achievers and separate them from this emerging underclass of young people, uninspired to positively exercise their minds in the classroom and outside of it.
>
> (Fraser, 2004)

Arguably, this is part of a new racist discourse because, while Fraser accurately acknowledges that equally large numbers of Indo-Trinidadians are indeed failing (see Jules, 1994a), he uses very simplistic methods to construct Afro-Trinidadians as the only ones emerging as the 'underclass', situating this fall in cultural traits unique to this group. His argument is premised on identifying the race of the top achievers in the 2004 secondary entrance examination by their surname; this is a rather futile exercise in a multicultural postcolonial population where there is a relatively large mixed category, suggesting that a person's Afro- or Indo-Trinidadian identity may not be easily surmised through a reading of their surname. Hence, 'like the genetic theories of intelligence that preceded them, cultural theories that attempt to explain the link between race and academic performance generally locate the cause of the problem within students (lack of motivation, devaluing academic pursuits, and others)' (Noguera, 2008, p. 132), effectively absolving the school system or societal structures.

Operationalizing Bourdieu

With the creation of a theoretical hybrid combining Bourdieu and CRT, the question turned to its practical application. This theoretical model was designed to be able to grasp both the micro and macro as the individual interacts with the surrounding environment and it with them. I will attempt to explain this through an examination of what I term racialized facilitative capital (RFC); for a full explanation of RFC see Rampersad, 2014. In interrogating issues in the achievement of Afro-Trinidadian boys the concept of RFC was developed as an analytical vehicle that uses both CRT and Bourdieu in appreciating how racialized structures are embedded and enacted in daily discourse (Rampersad, 2014). RFC focuses on the racialization process and positioning of social, economic and cultural capital as a facilitator of social progress or social stagnation for different groups in society. For the purposes of this chapter the focus on RFC will centre on the much debated issue of cultural capital (for a more in-depth view of the operationalization of social and economic capital within an RFC framework, see Rampersad, 2014).

Racialized facilitative capital

Bourdieu (1986, p. 46) understands capital to be the foundation of social order which imbues social accumulation and consumption of resources with meaning, stressing that

> capital, which, in its objectified or embodied forms, takes time to accumulate and which, as a potential capacity to produce profits and to reproduce itself in identical or expanded form, contains a tendency to persist in its being, is a force inscribed in the objectivity of things so that everything is not equally possible or impossible.

With this, capital in all its forms is framed as a 'facilitative' mechanism for social accumulation; this is so much so that access to the 'right' capital can position one to take advantage of pathways to social advancement as compared to social stagnation. This may initially appear in congruence with deficit thinking and cycle of deprivation models, which lay blame for the social position of minoritized groups on their cultural patterns (Valencia, 1997; Yosso, 2006). However, for this to be so would require capital to be structured as something intrinsically democratic and easily accessible by all. Bourdieu (1986, p. 46) proffers a different perspective, suggesting that access to capital is indelibly intertwined into a society's unequal structuring of power, whereby,

> the structure of the distribution of the different types and subtypes of capital at a given moment in time represents the immanent structure of the social world, i.e. the set of constraints, inscribed in the very reality of that world, which govern its functioning in a durable way, determining the chances of success for practices.

The use of Bourdieu's concepts of capital within a CRT framework allows for an understanding of capital as a pivotal part of the process of control and domination of minorities by hegemonic groups. This is a process where ownership and access to the 'right' type of capital (so defined) as a socially facilitative vehicle is limited and restricted in favour of dominant groups.

Whose culture has capital?

Cultural capital as an explanative platform for educational attainment has increasingly grown in popularity (Yosso, 2006). Bourdieu (1986, p. 243) sees cultural capital as

> a theoretical hypothesis which made it possible to explain the unequal scholastic achievement of children originating from the different social classes by relating academic success, i.e. the specific profits which children from the different classes and class fractions can obtain in the academic market, to the distribution of cultural capital between the classes and class fractions.

He goes on to add that this 'starting point implies a break with the presuppositions inherent both in the commonsense view, which sees academic success or failure as an effect of natural aptitudes, and in human capital theories' (Bourdieu, 1986, p. 243).

Bourdieu (1986) therefore uses social class and associated levels of cultural capital as a way to explain differential academic achievement. In this sense, Bourdieu (1986) rejects the scientific discourse, which centres on genetic racial difference as the cause of differential achievement. However, Yosso (2006) argues that, unaltered, this perspective also implies pathology at the core of why certain social groups perform poorly in education, namely, because they lack the requisite cultural capital.

Yosso (2006) suggests that Bourdieu's work on cultural capital has often been used in the privileging of white middle- and upper-class cultural patterns as normative and the basis on which cultural expressions of minoritized groups are judged and debased. These cultural 'norms' relate to 'specific forms of knowledge, skills and abilities that are *valued* by privileged groups in society' (Yosso, 2006, p. 175). Jenkins' (2002, p. 85) simple, but equally poignant definition of cultural capital as 'primarily legitimate knowledge of one kind or another' foregrounds the very political nature of capital in all its forms (Bourdieu, 1986). This is largely so as it raises a question of who determines what is legitimate knowledge and what is not. In ensuring that use of cultural capital does not render this analysis as pathologically focused and thus incompatible with CRT, there is a need to understand and account for the process which imbues certain cultural practices with a sense of normativity, and how this is tied into a pigmentocratic structuring of power and dominance in society. This section proceeds with an analysis of the cultural capital of teachers and parents at both schools through an adaptation of Diane Reay's (2005a) concept of the psychic landscape of social class. This concept is expanded to incorporate analysis of the psychic dimensions of racialized systems of social class, that is, pigmentocracy. The arguments that follow suggest that cultural capital as expressed in the views and embodiment of pigmentocracy is indeed an important aspect in the maintenance of such structures of dominance over minoritized groups.

The psychic landscape of pigmentocracy

In explaining her concept of psychic landscapes, Reay (2005a, p. 912) argues that 'it is class thinking and feeling that generates class practices. At the very least there is a generative dynamic between thinking, feeling and practices.' As such, this concept suggests that feelings and emotions are inseparably attached to and embodied within human behaviour. Reay (2005a, p. 912) continues that 'emotions and psychic responses to class and class inequalities contribute powerfully to the makings of class.' In the context of Trinidad, articulation of this concept would add that thinking and feeling about social class concomitantly implies pigmentocracy and that this would direct action. Reay (2005a) argues that there is an inherent complexity in these feelings and emotions and they should not be construed as simplistic or one dimensional. That said, action will vary from individual to individual based on personal and familial trajectories and resultant habitus. This will be explored by briefly comparing interview data from two parents with children at each of the two schools.

One aspect of the psychic landscape of pigmentocracy is confidence in navigating the education system. The level of confidence reflects the ease or unease with which an individual can effectively traverse the different sites of education and form 'profitable' relationships and networks. In Trinidad, this sense of confidence is ultimately manifested in a parent's capacity to access quality education of the dual system for their children through their knowledge of the system and engaged networks.

For instance, at St George's (the high achieving prestige school), one of the mothers, Mary, related how she removed her son from an earlier primary school because the class teacher was not meeting her standards and she felt that this affected her son, Adrian's performance. It was her knowledge of the education hierarchy and the dual system that allowed her to access a place for him at the much sought-after St George's and to quickly develop a close rapport with the class teacher. It is argued that Mary's knowledge of, and confidence within the system is premised on her social positioning within the lighter-skinned middle class (see Table 5.1 below). This is a position representative of normative cultural capital, which has facilitated access to university education, high status employment and residence in suburban Trinidad. As such, it can be argued that she engenders an emotional perspective of both entitlement and duty towards her status as lighter skinned and middle class. Her comments suggest the embodiment of such views, where she says,

> I don't really believe in incentive or bribes for school success . . . but rather pride in self . . . so I don't offer incentives, neither make threats . . . except for one . . . That's when [Adrian] jokes with me and says something like 'when I get big I will be a maxi conductor [bus conductor]' . . . I say to him . . . 'boy I will cut your tail so bad . . . after I spent all my money on books for you to be just a maxi conductor'.

Conversely, there is Sally, a mother at Pinehill (the failing, stereotyped community school). While she has an equal desire to Mary for her son to succeed, there is a differential in confidence in navigating the system. In my interview with her, she expressed a level of frustration at not being able to help Nicholas raise his academic achievement; this despite buying learning aids and actively engaging with the school. Unfortunately, her focus and dedication is not matched by confidence and knowledge of the system. Much like Mary, confidence is linked to social positioning; however, the socio-historical positioning of Sally within Pinehill and the darker-skinned working class (see Table 5.1 below) is reflected in a lack of confidence. This was highlighted in

Table 5.1 Characteristics of parents at both schools[1]

	Skin colour	Occupation	Residence	Education
St George's				
Mary	Light	White-collar worker	Middle-class suburb	University
Pinehill				
Sally	Very dark brown	Part-time shopkeeper and domestic worker	Pinehill, working class	Gov't secondary

1 The five skin colour categories used were: very dark brown, dark brown, medium brown, light and very light and is adapted to the local Trinidadian context from the seminal work of Keith and Herring (1991, p. 766) in the US.

one of my conversations with Ms John, Sally's son's class teacher. When I mentioned that I had spoken with Sally, her reaction spoke volumes; first, there was a sigh and a rolling of the eyes and then she proceeded to say in a demeaning tone, 'She's always here'.

Ms John's statement was uttered while shaking her head; her body language suggested a trivializing of this mother's concern and her dismissal as a nuisance as opposed to a legitimate partner and stakeholder in the educative process. This sort of reaction mirrors the idea that the capital Sally possesses, reflective of her status as darker-skinned working-class woman, is undervalued and derided by the teacher and the system as a whole. Alternatively, if she possessed sufficient knowledge of the system and, concomitantly, the requisite capital she could have orchestrated a move for her son to a better school. However, her sense of identity and place gives birth to emotions and feelings of helplessness, frustration, anger, shame and envy. These feelings are further manifested in her views of her son Nicholas' experiences of the school, expressing the opinion that:

> He has some problems with his classmates also . . . They have this mentality that because they come from [Pinehill], you know . . . they have this 'niggery'[2] attitude with them, because the teacher ask a question and [Nicholas] answered and apparently the answer was wrong and he say one of the classmates jump up and say, 'boy [Nicholas] boy, sit down nah boy . . . You ain't self know the answer, you ah dunce boy'.

In speaking with her, it was implicit that while she focused on Nicholas' education, she desperately wanted to get her family out of Pinehill and move Nicholas to another school, but lacked the capacity to do so.

It is not argued that cultural capital and the confidence to navigate the education system can solely explain the access to quality education that the lighter-skin middle and upper classes disproportionately enjoy (Jules, 1994b, p. 63). Rather it should be seen as part of a cumulative 'bag' of RFC (along with social and economic capital), which supports the disproportionate access to quality education within the dual system of those lighter-skin groups within a pigmentocracy, such as Trinidad. The comparative stories of Mary and Sally reflect the psychic impacts and embodiment in the daily discourse of pigmentocracy in a real and powerful way. The capacity for extracting analytical insights from these stories, from what on the surface may appear to be seemingly innocuous statements and narratives, speaks volumes for the application of Bourdieu in 'real world' research and methodologies.

Conclusion

While it has been a rewarding journey, the experience in using Bourdieu has been at times difficult or, probably better said, laboured. For instance, the concept of RFC did not initially present itself to me in a direct way but was painstakingly pieced together as I fought to see the 'forest for the trees'. This was particularly so as I first engaged with the issue of skin colour within the concept of pigmentocracy and a CRT framework. Within this trajectory my exposure to the key works of people like Margaret Hunter was crucial. The discourse on pigmentocracy and skin colour helped me to both conceptualize skin colour as a form of capital but, importantly as well, began the process of crafting the idea of capital in all its forms as racialized.

And while my initial steps along the way took me first to CRT, Bourdieu has become a central and inseparable part of my analytic gaze in understanding social phenomena. For me CRT is a discourse positioned to adequately interrogate the structural dimensions in the intersections of race, skin colour, social class and gender. Its strength lies in its ability to grasp the pernicious and persistent nature of race and the socio-historical imperatives, such as pigmentocracy, which underpin racialized processes and structures in the postcolonial world. However, this is only part of the equation. There is a need to fully comprehend the nuances and shades of human agency on the ground, to appreciate how the social world is evident in the individual as much as the individual is in the social world, to see the interplay between structure and agency (Reay, 2004). This is where Bourdieu's theoretical and methodological fortitude lies with adaptable concepts, such as habitus and capital and their constituent elements.

As such, Bourdieu's sociology has facilitated the development of a dynamic and innovative theoretical platform with the combination with CRT, giving birth to key concepts such as RFC. This is an important point to underscore as per theory and methodology in Trinidad, the Caribbean and other postcolonial settings. The nature of race and marginalization in the postcolonial world is neither static nor simplistic. Their systems are heavily intertwined with contemporary and socio-historic trajectories of multiple histories and experiences of slavery, indentureship, colonialism and neocolonialism. Likewise, analytical approaches engaging with these issues cannot be one dimensional and rigid, but rather ought to be flexible and adaptable to a changing landscape of race and society in the postcolonial world.

As for further applications of Bourdieu, the inherent flexibility in Bourdieu has also allowed me to re-imagine the question of male role models. This application looks to move the discourse away from traditional deficit thinking models, which lay blame for minority male underachievement and antisocial behaviour on a dearth of positive male role models (Cushman, 2008). Through the use of concepts of popular culture and the interplay of habitus, role models are re-imaged. With this approach they are seen more as an analytical tool to gain insight into the process of identity construction and relationship to education, as opposed to a prescriptive panacea for minority male delinquency. It is argued that unpacking the social consumption of popular icons has the potential to reveal the process of situational identity construction and internalization of the social world in the creation of a person's habitus.

Notes

1   Please note that in local dialogue 'Dougla' refers to a person of mixed Afro- and Indo-Trinidadian heritage. For an understanding of the term's genesis see England (2009).
2   Please note that the term 'niggery' is indicative of a racialized discourse of pigmentocracy in Trinidad and implies the stereotypical views of blackness and darkness.

References

Bonilla-Silva, E. (2005) ' "Racism" and "new racism": The contours of racial dynamics in contemporary America', in Z. Leonardo (ed.) *Critical pedagogy and race* (pp. 1–15). Malden, UK: Blackwell.

Bonilla-Silva, E. and Dietrich, D. R. (2008) 'The Latin Americanization of racial stratification in the US', in R. E. Hall (ed.), *Racism in the 21st century: An empirical analysis of skin colour* (pp. 151–70). New York: Springer.

Bourdieu, P. (1986) 'The forms of capital', in J. G. Richardson (ed.), *Handbook of theory and research for the sociology of education* (pp. 241–58). New York: Greenwood Press.

Bourdieu, P. (1990) *In other words: Essays towards a reflexive sociology.* Cambridge: Polity Press.

Bourdieu, P. and Nice, R. (1993) *Sociology in question.* London: Sage.

Braithwaite, L. (1953) 'Social stratification in Trinidad: A preliminary analysis', *Social and Economic Studies,* 2(2): 5–175.

Connolly, P. (2004) *Boys and schooling in the early years.* London: Routledge Falmer.

Coppin, A. (1997) 'Color in an English-speaking Caribbean labor market', *Journal of Developing Areas,* 31(3): 399–410.

Coppin, A. and Olsen, R. N. (1998) 'Earnings and ethnicity in Trinidad and Tobago', *Journal of Development Studies,* 34(3): 116–34.

Crossley, N. (2001) 'The phenomenological habitus and its construction', *Theory and Society,* 30: 81–120.

Cushman, P. (2008) 'So what exactly do you want? What principals mean when they say "male role model"', *Gender and Education,* 20(2): 123–36.

Delgado, R. and Stefancic, J. (2001) *Critical race theory: An introduction.* New York: New York University Press.

England, S. (2010) 'Mixed and multiracial in Trinidad and Honduras: Rethinking mixed-race identities in Latin America and the Caribbean', *Ethnic and Racial Studies,* 33(2): 195–213.

Fanon, F. (1967) *Black skin, white masks.* New York, Grove Press.

Fraser, T. (2004) 'The emerging underclass'. *Trinidad Publishing.* Retrieved from http://legacy.guardian.co.tt/archives/2004-07-15/Tonyfraser.html

Gould, M. (1999) 'Race and theory: Culture, poverty, and adaptation to discrimination in Wilson and Ogbu', *Sociological Theory,* 17(2): 171–200.

Hunter, M. L. (2002) ' "If you're light you're alright": Light skin color as social capital for women of color', *Gender and Society,* 16(2): 175–93.

Jenkins, R. (2002) *Pierre Bourdieu.* London: Routledge.

Johnson, T. A. (2004) 'The enduring function of caste: Colonial and modern Haiti, Jamaica, and Brazil – the economy of race, the social organization of caste, and the formulation of racial societies', *Comparative American Studies,* 2(1): 61–73.

Jules, V. (1994a) *A study of the secondary school population in Trinidad and Tobago: Placement patterns and practices.* St. Augustine: Centre for Ethnic Studies, University of the West Indies.

Jules, V. (1994b) *A study of the secondary school population in Trinidad and Tobago: Placement patterns and practices – A research report.* St. Augustine: Centre for Ethnic Studies, University of the West Indies.

Keith, V. M. and Herring, C. (1991) 'Skin tone and stratification in the Black community', *American Journal of Sociology, 97*(3): 760–78.

Ladson-Billings, G. (1999) 'Just what is critical race theory, and what's it doing in a nice field like education', in L. Parker, D. Deyhle and S. Villenas (eds) *Race is . . . race isn't: Critical race theory and qualitative studies in education* (pp. 7–30). Boulder, CO: Westview Press.

Lowenthal, D. (1967) 'Race and color in the West Indies', *Daedalus, 96*(2): 580–626.

Lynch, J. (2006) 'Race and radical renamings: Using cluster agon method to assess the radical potential of "European American" as a substitute for "white"', *KB Journal, 2*(2).

McClelland, K. (1990) 'Cumulative disadvantage among the highly ambitious', *Sociology of Education, 63*(2): 102–21.

Meighoo, K. (2003) *Politics in a half made society: Trinidad and Tobago 1925–2001.* Kingston, Jamaica: Ian Randle.

Miller, E. (1986) *Marginalization of the black male: Insights from the development of the teaching profession.* Mona, Jamaica: ISER.

Miller, E. (1991) *Men at risk.* Kingston, Jamaica: Jamaica Publishing House.

Mirza, H. S. (2009) *Race, gender and educational desire: Why black women succeed and fail.* London: Routledge.

Mohammed, P. (2000) '"But most of all mi love me browning": The emergence in eighteenth and nineteenth-century Jamaica of the mulatto woman as the desired', *Feminist Review, 65* (Summer): 22–48.

Noguera, P. (2008) *The trouble with black boys: And other reflections on race, equity, and the future of public education.* San Francisco, CA: Jossey-Bass.

Parker, L. and Lynn, M. (2002) 'What's race got to do with it? Critical race theory's conflicts with and connections to qualitative research methodology and epistemology', *Qualitative Inquiry, 8*(1): 7–22.

Rampersad, R. (2014) '"Racialised facilitative capital" and the paving of differential paths to achievement of Afro-Trinidadian boys', *British Journal of Sociology of Education, 35*(1): 73–93.

Reay, D. (2004) '"It's all becoming a habitus": Beyond the habitual use of habitus in educational research', *British Journal of Sociology of Education, 25*(4): 431–44.

Reay, D. (2005a) 'Beyond consciousness? The psychic landscape of social class', *Sociology, 39*(5): 911–28.

Reay, D. (2005b) 'Gendering Bourdieu's concepts of capitals? Emotional capital, women and social class', *Sociological Review, 52*(2): 57–74.

Taylor, E. (1998) 'A primer on critical race theory', *Journal of Blacks in Higher Education, 19:* 122–4.

Taylor, E. (2000) 'Critical race theory and interest convergence in the backlash against affirmative action: Washington State and Initiative 200', *Teachers College Record, 102*(3): 539–60.

Taylor, E. (2009) 'The foundations of critical race theory in education: An introduction', in E. Taylor, D. Gillborn and G. Ladson-Billings (eds), *Foundations of critical race theory in education* (pp. 1–13). New York: Routledge.

Tomlinson, S. (2008) *Race and education: Policy and politics in Britain.* Berkshire, UK: Open University Press.

Valencia, R. R. (ed.) (1997) *The evolution of deficit thinking: Educational thought and practice.* London: Falmer Press.

Wacquant, L. J. D. (1989) 'Towards a reflexive sociology: A workshop with Pierre Bourdieu', *Sociological Theory, 7*(1): 26–63.

Yosso, T. J. (2006) 'Whose culture has capital? A critical race theory discussion of community cultural wealth', in A. D. Dixson and C. K. Rousseau (eds), *Critical race theory in education: All God's children got a song* (pp. 69–91). New York: Routledge.

Chapter 6

Inequalities, parental social capital and children's education

Maria Papapolydorou

Parental social capital and Bourdieu's theory

Parental influences on students' educational achievements have been widely discussed by sociological and educational research on both sides of the Atlantic. Time and time again, research has demonstrated the advantageous position of middle-class parents compared to their working-class counterparts when it comes to successfully intervening and shaping their children's education (see for instance Ball, 2003; Lareau, 1989; Reay, 2005b). Likewise, research that explored parental educational influences through the lens of ethnicity found that parents' practices, related to their children's education, vary considerably among different ethnic groups (see Archer and Francis, 2007; Desimone, 1999; Qian and Blair, 1999). Following on from this research, this chapter employs social capital as a concept to explore further whether inequalities related to social class and ethnic background cut across parental involvement in their children's education.

The use of social capital can be traced to the nineteenth century[1] but it was not until the 1970s, after Bourdieu's and Coleman's writings, that it became more perceptible and influential. Bourdieu and Coleman worked at about the same time; yet, their conceptualization of social capital was inherently different and it influenced different strands of society. On the one hand, Coleman with his rational choice theory approach became well known among economists, and later influential to policy makers. On the other hand, Bourdieu was influential among sociological circles – mainly in Europe – and brought the notion of social capital into the focus of academics and researchers working in the field of sociology. Pierre Bourdieu's work maintains that social capital, alongside cultural, symbolic and economic capital, reflects societal inequalities. As such, the research upon which this chapter is based focuses on Bourdieu's theorization of social capital to make sense of parental practices across ethnic and social class groups and how these are informed by concomitant inequalities.

Nevertheless, the scope of this chapter is not only to elaborate on this study's findings but also to use this research as a case study that will enable discussion of the way Bourdieu's theoretical frameworks have been applied for the empirical exploration of the topic. Emphasis, then, is also placed on the relationship between Bourdieuian theory and the adopted methodology. The research findings are, of course, important too, in that they exemplify the way the adoption of Bourdieuian theory, through certain research processes, can produce important research outcomes that, in turn, have the potential to inform research and practice. In addition, the chapter discusses the strengths of Bourdieu's social capital theory and its contributions to the field of education, while at the same time reflecting on the challenges that Bourdieu's theory might imply in the context of educational research.

When Bourdieuian theory meets educational research

The French sociologist Pierre Bourdieu was the first scholar to use the term 'social capital' in a sociologically nuanced way and he is greatly responsible for its introduction to academic research, despite the fact that his work focuses more on cultural rather than social capital. Bourdieu's overall work drew on social class inequalities and social hierarchies. In the same vein, the strength of his social capital approach is that he emphasizes its role on the reproduction of power and inequalities, as opposed to other social capital theorists, such as Putnam (2000) and Coleman (1988), who largely overlook this aspect. Overall, Bourdieu's theory seems to be the only theory, compared to Coleman's and Putnam's, which addresses structural issues of inequality and highlights the constant significance of economic capital in both the generation of social capital and its subsequent utilization for economic advancement (Gamarnikow and Green, 1999, 2000). As such, Bourdieuian frameworks lend themselves to the exploration of the relationship of parental social capital with children's education and the possible ways this is mediated by axes of inequality, such as social class and ethnic background. In this light, this study can be seen as an empirical examination of Bourdieu's social capital tenets in the context of education.

A challenge in this endeavour, however, arose in relation to the operationalization of social capital for data collection purposes. Although Bourdieu discusses cultural capital's relationship with education (Bourdieu, 1977), his concept of social capital is not considered with reference to the field of education, and therefore his definition is not clear in this context. Bourdieu defined social capital as

> the aggregate of the actual or potential resources which are linked to ~session of a durable network of more or less institutionalized rela-
> 'ips of mutual acquaintance and recognition – or in other words, to
> hip in a group – which provides each of its members with the
> 'e tively-owned capital, a 'credential' which entitles them
>   us senses of the word.
>
> (Bourdieu, 1986: 248–9)

This generic definition of social capital, which is somewhat narrower than other social capital definitions (see for instance Coleman, 1988; Putnam, 2000), is put forward without elaboration as to how social capital might be operationalized for research purposes, let alone for research in the realm of education.

In this study, parental social capital, in relation to Bourdieu's framework, was seen as comprising the social networks possessed by parents and the participation and/or membership of parents in associations that might benefit their children's education, for example their educational achievements and opportunities. Parents' contacts with other parents and teachers (for example through the parent–teacher associations) can be argued to have a positive outcome on children's education. So the operationalization of the definition of social capital in this study was a result of an interpretation of Bourdieu's theory due to the absence of more specific elucidations by the theorist himself on this matter. Hence, the compatibility of the methodology of this study with Bourdieu's theory is partly subject to the right extrapolation of his definition of social capital in the context of educational research.

Another challenge related to the use of Bourdieu's approach was the relative paucity of his work on the topic of ethnicity. Bourdieu's work mainly focuses on power differentials across social class groups in the French context, yet, social capital's role and function in relation to ethnicity is not explicitly addressed. As a result, an extension has had to be made here whereby ethnically related issues of inequality, power and injustice were seen in the same vein as issues related to class. In other words, allowance was made for social capital to be informed and shaped by structurally generated ethnic inequalities. This stretching of Bourdieu's theoretical framework is seen as compatible with the overall spirit of his theory and germane to the purposes of this study's analysis, as issues of power are often implicated not only in social class issues but also in ethnicity related issues. For instance, the mobilization or absence of mobilization of social capital by people from minority ethnic groups, whose lives are influenced by racism (i.e. discrimination, ethnic stereotypes etc.), could be analysed through the prism of Bourdieu's theory due to the presence of power differentials.

Finally, an issue related to the use of Bourdieuian frameworks, ironically, stemmed from one of Bourdieuian theory's major strengths, namely, its emphasis on the reproduction of power. Bourdieu's elaboration of social capital has been criticized for being somewhat elitist (Field, 2003; Tolonen, 2007). For instance, Field (2003) argued that Bourdieu considers social capital as a benefit for those advantaged groups who acquire it but there is actually no discussion in his theory for the possibility that disadvantaged groups could also benefit from social capital. Indeed Bourdieu's research mainly focused on the processes through which already advantaged people are able to maintain and/or expand their status. In this study, Field's analysis is usefully expanded to examine how all social groups mobilize aspects of social capital. Accordingly, Bourdieu's framework, as employed here, maintains an interest in the crucial role of structural inequalities and power, and at the same time it explores the way social capital might work not only for already advantaged social groups (e.g. middle-class individuals) but also for other, less advantaged social groups (e.g. working-class individuals).

The study discussed here is based on data collected from Year 12 students, in four co-educational, state-secondary schools in London, United Kingdom. Mixed methods of collecting and analysing data were employed. A survey questionnaire was administered to 225 students and in-depth, semi-structured interviews were carried out with 75 students. The quantitative data was analysed with the statistical software SPSS. Before any statistical analyses were carried out with SPSS, all questionnaire data was reduced to a manageable set of new uncorrelated variables (Jolliffe, 2002) with a principal component analysis. The qualitative data was analysed with the aid of the Atlas.ti software using a thematic content analysis approach (Flick, 1998).

Research findings

Parental social capital and ethnicity

One-way ANOVA tests were used to explore the relationship between social capital dimensions and ethnicity as the latter variable was categorical and comprised more than two categories. The ANOVA results (see Table 6.1) suggest that ethnicity is strongly associated with a number of social capital items. Following each ANOVA, post hoc tests were carried out in order to identify a more precise relationship between ethnicity and social capital. Three different post hoc tests were carried out: (a) Hochberg's GT2 as the sample sizes of the ethnicity categories were not identical, (b) Games–Howell procedure in order to avoid any biases resulting from the homogeneity of variances problems (Field, 2009), and (c) Dunnett's test, which treats one group as a control and compares the rest against it. In this case the control group was White British students.

Table 6.1 ANOVA results investigating social capital differences by ethnic groups

Variable name	Label	F ratio degrees of freedom (df)	F
SC13disc.advis	Parents discuss and seek advice about their children's education	F (3, 203)	2.858*
mothpareven80	Mother attends parents' evenings in your school	F (3, 201)	5.621**

* p <.05, ** p <.01, *** p <.001

Table 6.2 Summary of ANOVA post hoc tests investigating the differences between ethnic groups in relation to social capital dimensions

Mother attends parents' evenings in your school: Black African and Caribbean students' mothers were reported to attend parents' evenings less than the mothers of all other ethnic backgrounds, namely, White British (p <.05), Indian (p <.001) and Other Ethnic Backgrounds (p <.05)

Parents discuss and seek advice about their children's education (Item SC13disc.advis): Indian students scored significantly higher than Black African and Caribbean students (p <.05).

The post hoc results (see Table 6.2) confirmed the significant relationship between ethnicity and social capital and demonstrated the way in which different ethnic groups varied with reference to each social capital item.

In particular, the mothers of Black African and Caribbean students appeared to attend school parents' evenings less often than mothers of all other ethnic backgrounds examined here, namely White British, Indians and Other Ethnic Backgrounds. This is consistent with existing literature that suggests lower levels of participation in the school community from Black African and Caribbean parents (Crozier, 1996). In addition, Indian students' parents seemed to be significantly more likely than Black African and Caribbean students' parents to discuss their children's education with their friends, colleagues and other parents as well as to seek advice about their children's education from people such as their relatives, friends, colleagues, other parents and their children's teachers.

A similar pattern was suggested by qualitative data. The Black African and Caribbean parents seemed to be less engaged in interacting with the school than parents of other ethnic backgrounds. In particular, Black African and Caribbean parents attended parents' meetings less frequently than White British parents and were less likely to participate in the parent–teacher association than White British parents. An explanation for that could be that schools, as White British middle-class institutions (Gillborn, 2008b), do not address the needs and interests of the Black African and Caribbean students and as a result Black African and Caribbean parents consider the mobilization of social capital difficult in this context. This gap between schools' culture and values on the one hand and Black African and Caribbean communities' needs on the other hand appears to hinder Black African and Caribbean empowerment and participation in the school community.

An exemption to this pattern was an event that took place in Chester Central School, one of the four schools that participated in the research. Chester Central School – a school with a significant number of Black African and Caribbean students – had organized an event in relation to Black students' achievement and educational opportunities. In the framework of this event, the school invited all the parents to attend and help with the organization. The invited speakers were Black African and Caribbean people (i.e. a social worker and a teacher) and allowed many opportunities for discussion and opinion exchange among the parents and the speakers. The interviewed students mentioned that the event was successful in that it was well attended by Black African and Caribbean parents, who were also actively engaged in its organization. For instance, the mum of one of the interviewed students was responsible for the catering of the event.

The success of this event suggests that Black African and Caribbean parents are not disengaged from and uninterested in their children's education but they are in fact willing, in certain contexts, to participate in the school community in order to get informed about issues pertinent to their children's education. Furthermore, the high attendance rates on behalf of Black African and Caribbean parents reveal the importance of the context in which parental participation takes place. In this case, the event was successful as it addressed issues that they were concerned with and that they were interested in discussing, namely, the educational opportunities and outcomes of Black children. The success of this event is in direct contrast to the lower overall rates of Black African and Caribbean parents' participation in the school community and suggests the potential that schools have to empower and engage parents from minority ethnic backgrounds in the school life.

Parental social capital and social class

Pearson correlations were carried out to statistically explore the relationship between parental social capital and social class. Table 6.3 in the Appendices summarizes the results of the correlations and reports the correlation coefficients for items that were significantly correlated, the level of significance and the sample size upon which each correlation was carried out. One of the most important findings that derived from this analysis was that high social class background was associated to more frequent and/or intense parental involvement in students' education at least in respect to some indicators. In relation to the latter, the higher the social class of the parents the more likely they were to discuss their children's education with their children's teachers. Furthermore, the mothers from a high social class background were more likely to attend parents' evenings in the school than mothers from a lower social class background. Finally, parents with a higher social class background were more likely to discuss their children's education with their friends, colleagues or other parents as well as to seek advice in relation to their children's education from other people, including colleagues, other parents and relatives.

These examples demonstrate that middle-class parents use their social networks to discuss their children's education more than working-class parents. This finding is interesting in that the types of social networks within which parents discuss educational issues, i.e. friends, colleagues, relatives, are generally available to all social class groups. Therefore, it is not a matter of possessing the actual networks or not, but it is rather about the nature of discussions that take place within these networks. In addition to discussing their children's education within their networks, parents with higher social class backgrounds are also more likely to mobilize these networks in order to seek advice and get information regarding a number of education related issues, such as school or university choices. Qualitative data analysis corroborated this.

In the case of school choice, upper-middle and middle-class parents mobilized their social networks in order to investigate the quality of education provided in a number of schools and thereafter decided which one suited their children's

---

Box 6.1

Researcher: How come you came to this school?

Punit: I just applied to many schools and I got accepted in two. And then ... I don't know I just checked Ofsted reports and I found this one was better ... so I came here.

Researcher: Right. So who checked Ofsted reports? Was it you?

Punit: My mum did.

Researcher: So she thought this school was better than the other one?

Punit: Yeah!

Researcher: Why did she think that?

Punit: Because it got generally better reviews and it got more students who passed their GCSEs with A*–C grades.

Researcher: Right. Did she ask anyone about this school?

Punit: Yes, she knew someone in her work whose son also came here and he is at Cambridge now so ... it seemed like a good idea.

(Punit, Indian, middle-class boy,
Kinderhook High School)

Researcher: Right. So how come you came to this school?

Malcolm: I had two options. I was going to go to either X school which is a boys' school, which is about 15 minutes from here, or Chester Central School. And I didn't get Chester Central High School so my parents had to contact the governors to let me in to this school.

Researcher: Right. So how did you apply? Did you have to sit for exams?

Malcolm: You just apply but my parents and I had to go to an interview as to why I should be let into this school.

(Malcolm, Black African, middle-class boy,
Chester Central School)

needs best. For this purpose, parents asked other parents, contacted the school, attended open days and looked at information available on the internet, such as Ofsted reports, in order to compare the results of various schools. Some of these strategies are evident from Malcolm's and Punit's extracts.

From these extracts it appears that both Punit's mum and Malcom's parents mobilized social capital in order to choose the best between two schools. Punit's mum drew on her cultural capital to investigate and interpret Ofsted results and subsequently drew on her social capital asking a colleague of hers whose son had previously studied in the same school and had been successful in going to university. Working in a middle-class environment, Punit's mum had access to middle-class networks and middle-class cultural capital on which she drew for assistance before she decided which school was the best for her son. This is in line with Ball and Vincent's findings about middle-class 'hot knowledge' acquired through middle-class people's social networks (Ball and Vincent, 1998). Malcolm's middle-class parents appeared to be aware of the way the educational system works and they did not hesitate to intervene and challenge this system when it did not meet their interests, by mobilizing their social networks. This is an expression of successfully mobilized social capital as Malcom's parents reached up to powerful and influential agents, namely, the school governors, in order to negotiate their son's access to what they perceived as the best school.

These kinds of interventions were very common among upper-middle and middle-class parents whose cultural capital provided them with the confidence to navigate the system through their social networks. Working-class parents did not employ similar strategies when choosing their children's school but they seemed to be abiding by the schools' or the Local Educational Authorities' decisions, without drawing on social capital to appeal those. Conversely, the criteria for working-class parents' choice of school were often the school's proximity to their house and the number of primary school friends of their children who would also go to the secondary school. From this, it seems again that working-class parents do not have the type of cultural and social capital resources that upper-middle and middle-class parents have to choose and negotiate their child's admission to the best among more than one school. And within this framework of scarce resources, the criteria employed are related to convenience (school's distance from home) and their children's happiness (an adequate number of primary school friends going to the same school).

Finally, social capital was deployed in relation to parents' participation in the school community. Parents participated in the school community on a number of occasions, such as parents' evenings, the parent–teacher association, other school events or even sometimes by directly contacting the teachers and the head teacher. This participation and the social networks they developed with the teachers and the head teacher of the school enabled them to acquire useful information about their children's education and/or intervene appropriately in what they thought better suited their children's educational interests. The expression of this kind of social capital, namely, the parental participation in the school community and their development of social networks with the school personnel, was both classed and ethnicized. It was mainly White British middle-class parents who drew on this kind of social capital in order to benefit from the educational opportunities available to their children. Working-class and Black African and Caribbean parents were the least likely to participate in this kind of activities.

The only event that working-class parents seemed to have attended as frequently as middle-class parents was the parents' evenings. Even on these occasions, the nature of the social networks that working-class parents developed with their children's teachers, was different from the ones developed by the upper-middle and middle-class parents. In particular, whereas middle-class parents would ask for additional information about their children's education and often guide the teachers as to how they would like them to deal with some related issues, the information provided by the teachers would suffice for working-class parents, who would then draw on this to deal with their children at home. For example, when a teacher informed a middle-class mother that her daughter was not paying adequate attention in class and that she was rather chatty with her best friend, the mother asked the teacher to change her daughter's seat and place her next to another student who was not a close friend. Working-class parents did not often draw on the social networks developed during parents' evenings to ask for special arrangements for their children's education. This does not mean that they did not take this seriously but merely that they did not feel as confident as middle/upper-middle-class parents to ask for further information and/or to intervene in what they thought was the teacher's responsibility by requesting special arrangements for their children. This could be seen in the framework of working-class parents' entrustment to the schools as institutions and their reluctance to occupy teachers with their concerns (Crozier, 1997). In view of this, working-class parents' participation in the school community is often limited to their attendance at parents' evenings.

In contrast to working-class parents, middle/upper-middle-class parents build on the social networks developed with the teachers and do not hesitate to request special arrangements for their children if they are unsatisfied with their educational experience. In the extract below, Isabella describes an incident where her mum intervened in order to negotiate better educational provision for her daughter.

Isabella's mum seems to be very familiar with the way the educational system operates and of the responsibilities of the teachers. So she has taken teachers' side on many occasions when Isabella was complaining by outlining their duties and explaining that what they did was part of their job. Yet in this instance, she thought that there was a fundamental mistake with the school's practices: namely, English teachers kept coming and going from her daughter's class and she was underachieving as a result of the lack of classroom stability. At this point, Isabella's mum decided to intervene, 'that needs to be sorted out'

Box 6.2

Researcher:	Has she [your mum] ever called [the school]?
Isabella:	I think she called up once [. . .] She called out because I was having problems with English. Because we didn't have a single teacher for a long time and she was worried. And I was getting bad grades and I was like 'no one else in my class is getting good grades' you know. And she was like 'oh well that needs to be sorted out'. So she phoned the head of English and I was 'oh my God this is so embarrassing'.
Researcher:	So what did she say?
Isabella:	To him she just said like 'What's happening with the teachers? Why is my daughter getting so bad grades? He [the teacher] should have been doing this and this and this'. And I was like 'this is not something you do' because my mum to an extent has a lot of sympathy for teachers and when I complain about them she is like 'but you know they've got this to do, and they've got this to do and they've got this to do' and I'm like 'yeah but they were mean' (Laughs) But sometimes I just hate it when she interferes.

(Isabella, White British, middle-class girl,
Kinderhook High School)

---

and she mobilized her social capital in this direction. Interestingly, she did not phone the English teacher but the head of English in the school by employing her social capital in order to reach a person in authority and negotiate better educational provision. The middle-class background and the cultural capital possessed by Isabella's mum equipped her with confidence to not only interact with the school authorities but also to interrogate their practices with determination – 'what's happening with the teachers?'. As Lareau (2008) argued, middle-class parents watch, wait and decide when to intervene. And indeed as suggested by Isabella's extract, middle-class parents do not act spasmodically in relation to their children's education. They rather constantly monitor their progress as well as the school processes and intervene strategically through deployment of social capital when they judge that their children's educational outcomes are at stake.

Results from regression analyses

Multiple linear regression results (see Table 6.4 in the Appendices) and binary logistic regression results (see Table 6.5 in the Appendices) seem to confirm the suggestions derived from Pearson correlations and ANOVAs that social capital can be predicted by contextual factors such as class and ethnicity. An important number of social capital items reflecting various dimensions of the concept, were predicted by one or both of the two factors (class, ethnicity). Gender was used as an additional indicator in the regression models. Interestingly, the simultaneous modelling of more than one indicator, which allowed for controls over each other's effects, sometimes resulted in outcomes that cancelled the previous results of correlations and the ANOVA. For instance, according to the ANOVA results, the item that represented the social networks parents possessed to discuss and seek advice about their children's education was associated with ethnicity and, according to the Pearson correlation, it was also associated with social class. Yet regression evidence suggests that when both factors are entered into the model along with gender then ethnicity is no longer a significant indicator whereas class is ($p < .05$). So all things being equal, the higher the social class background of the parents the higher the likelihood of them being engaged in discussions and seeking advice about their children's education. On the contrary, whereas ANOVA and the Pearson correlation showed mothers' attendance at parents' evenings to be informed by both class and ethnicity, regression evidence suggests that when both indicators are included in the model only ethnicity is significant ($p < .01$). In particular, *ceteris paribus*, Black African and Caribbean students' mothers were less likely than White British students' mothers to participate in parents' evenings in their child's school.

Similarly, in relation to people that parents knew who could help their child get a job in the future, class was not a significant indicator. On the contrary, being Indian as opposed to White British positively predicted this type of social capital ($p < .05$). This might be a reflection of the close knit relations within Indian families (Ballard, 1994) in light of which parents' active engagement in their children's welfare does not cease after children become adults. Consistently, as Bacon argues 'one of the central features of the Indian worldview is the emphasis on social relationships over autonomous and separate individuals as the fundamental building block of social life. Individuals have meaning only when they are embedded in the context of social relations' (1996, p. 30). As a result, the existence of these norms within Indian families might legitimize parents' mobilizing social capital in order to ensure their children's future career. An additional point in this model was that being female was negatively associated with the outcome variable; parents were less likely to mobilize their social capital for a female child than for a male one ($p < .05$). The opposite was the case when it came to parents' knowing the parents of their children's friends. This item represents theoretical concepts put forward by Coleman (1987, 1988), who suggested that when parents' knew other parents an intergenerational closure occurred that had a beneficial effect on students' education. Yet this very type of intergenerational closure was more likely to exist for girls than for boys ($p < .05$). It appears that parents were far more likely to know the parents of their female children rather than of their male children. A hypothetical explanation for this might lie in the gender constructs of our society according to which parents might feel the need to be more protective of their female than of their male children. Alternatively, girls' social networks might be more accessible to parents than boys' ones.

Furthermore, social class was positively associated with the extent to which parents discussed their children's education with their teachers ($p < .05$). The higher the social class background of the parents the more likely they were to do so. This finding, which is vividly mirrored in the qualitative data discussed above, is in accordance with previous research which demonstrated that middle-class parents are more involved in their children's education than working-class parents (Crozier, 1997; Lareau, 1989, 2008; Reay, 2005a). In the example of this study, middle- and upper-middle-class parents made use of their networks to derive useful information that would improve their children's educational opportunities/qualifications, and it could be argued that this is associated with their future class and status.

Concluding remarks

In conclusion, this chapter discussed the ways in which a piece of research was influenced and informed by Bourdieu's social capital research. Bourdieu's theoretical frameworks were very constructive for the understanding of social capital with reference to parental educational practices, especially regarding social hierarchies and associated inequalities. However, to draw on a theorist's framework is not to uncritically adopt it under all circumstances. On this occasion, Bourdieu's theory was helpfully expanded to overcome some of its limitations, such as its narrow definition and lack of elaboration on issues of ethnic inequality. Finally, the findings of this research can be used not only to enhance the validity of Bourdieu's theory in the empirical field of education but also to suggest its relevance in contemporary research and policy making.

This chapter presented evidence from statistical and qualitative analysis which proposes that social capital is an important mechanism through which parents attempt to maximize and improve the educational opportunities available to their children. Yet, as suggested by the data analysis, not all parents possess identical social capital reservoirs and, even if they do, they might not necessarily draw on these in the same way. Conversely, parents from different class and ethnic groups possess different types of social capital and/or they draw differentially on those. In particular, parental social capital that presupposes the existence of cultural capital and necessitates its deployment outside the household context, i.e. in the workplace or the school, is mainly a form of social capital employed by middle-class parents and less often by working-class parents. This might suggest the difficulty that working-class parents face to draw on or mobilize certain types of social capital in order to negotiate better educational provision for their children, not because of their lack of interest or motivation but mainly because of 'barriers' related to their working-class background. Hence, these findings provide an empirical confirmation of Bourdieu's work on social capital, which maintains that middle-class people draw on their social capital in order to reproduce their status and advantage their position in society (Bourdieu, 1986).

Moreover, this study provides an extension of Bourdieu's theoretical application to issues of ethnicity, as inequality pertaining to ethnic background is shown here to also shape the social capital possessed and mobilized by parents. Black African and Caribbean parents seemed to exhibit lower levels of social capital related to the school context (i.e. participation in the school community). This pattern might be seen in light of schools being White British institutions that do not often address the needs and interests of non-White British communities. Two different forms of racism that have been discussed by researchers might be relevant here. First, institutional racism, according to which Black African and Caribbean students are pathologized by schools and policies as non-academic, troublesome and lacking discipline (Cole, 2004; Gillborn, 2008a; Mirza, 2007) might implicitly or explicitly discourage parents from participating in the school community. Second, dysconscious racism might establish and exaggerate the effects of institutional racism in relation to parental participation in the school community. According to King, 'dysconsciousness is an uncritical habit of mind (including perceptions, attitudes, assumptions, and beliefs) that justifies inequity and exploitation by accepting the existing order of things as given' (1991, p. 135). So the possible acceptance of school staff that racism is no longer a problem in contemporary educational contexts could also contribute to the perpetuation of the problem by failing to tackle it.

An advance in Bourdieu's theory that stemmed from this study is in regard to the operationalization of social capital and the distinction of its different types. As has been suggested by the principal component analysis results, social capital is not a coherent entity but, on the contrary, comprises different dimensions that do not all relate to each other. This is indeed confirmed by the exploratory analysis of social capital items as well as by the regressions of social capital, which demonstrate that different social capital items are informed by different contextual factors – class, ethnicity, gender – or different combinations of those. The latter is also relevant in relation to the vulnerability of social capital as a concept since it is shown to be significantly influenced by other factors to an important degree.

Related to this is the evidence presented by this study that social capital works in a cumulative way regarding education. Both quantitative and qualitative results suggest that it is not merely one type of parental social capital that is employed with regard to education but rather a combination of various types mobilized in more than one context (i.e. school, home, community), which jointly work to inform students' education. This innovatively returns to Bourdieu's concept of 'aggregate', which is used in his definition of social capital. In particular, Bourdieu referred to social capital as 'the *aggregate* of the actual or potential resources' (my emphasis) (1986, p. 248). This study provides research evidence to support this notion of 'aggregate', in other words that social capital comprises many types and resides in many contexts. So a possible research and/or policy approach that focuses on certain types of social capital and/or on particular contexts without acknowledging the manifestations of social capital in other forms and occasions would inevitably miss out important information about the overall nature of social capital and its relationship with education.

All in all, it appears that whereas parental social capital is often drawn upon to advocate students' educational opportunities, its deployment is more often than not strongly informed by issues of ethnicity and class. Considering this, the results of this study highlight the crucial role that Bourdieu's social capital theory could exercise on policy making. So far, Bourdieu's theory has been rather disregarded in policy discussions and implementations which have involved social capital work, even though his work has been considered by some researchers as the most insightful and sophisticated theory of social capital (DeFilippis, 2001; Portes, 1998). In contrast, discounting Bourdieuian elaborations of social capital, policy making has often perceived social capital as a universal cure for several social ills. As this study proposes evidence that suggests that parental social capital related to children's education is importantly mediated by social class and ethnicity, the possibility of investing in social capital as a remedy for various social situations, or at least the possibility of success-fully investing in social capital as a 'panacea' (Healy, 2006) without taking into account the role of the context, is significantly compromised. This study's findings suggest that social capital should be treated with caution especially with regard to discourses of educational achievement, and should be understood in relation to its context rather than as a substitute for it. Bourdieu's theory, which acknowledges the role of structural inequalities and power differentials in the fabric of the society, can be helpful in this direction.

Note

1 A *New York Times* article published in 1883 used social capital in relation to the topic of husband-snatching.

References

Archer, L. and Francis, B. (2007) *Understanding minority ethnic achievement: Race, gender, class and 'success'*. New York: Routledge.

Bacon, J. (1996) *Life lines: Community, family and assmiliation among Asian Indian immigrants*. Oxford: Oxford University Press.

Ball, S. (2003) *Class strategies and the education market: The middle classes and social advantage*. London: Routledge Falmer.

Ball, S. and Vincent, C. (1998) '"I heard it on the grapevine": "Hot" knowledge and school choice', *British Journal of Sociology of Education*, *19*(3): 377–400.

Ballard, R. (ed.) (1994) *Desh Pardesh: The South Asian presence in Britain*. London: Hurst and Company.

Bourdieu, P. (1977) 'Cultural reproduction and social reproduction', in J. Karabel and A. H. Halsey (eds), *Power and Ideology in Education* (pp. 56–68). Oxford: Oxford University Press.

Bourdieu, P. (1986) 'The forms of capital' in J. Richardson (ed.), *Handbook for theory and research for the sociology of education*. New York: Greenwood Press.

Cole, M. (2004) '"Brutal and stinking" and "difficult to handle": The historical and contemporary manifestations of racialisation, institutional racism, and schooling in Britain', *Race Ethnicity and Education*, 7(10): 35–56.

Coleman, J. S. (1987) 'Families and schools', *Educational Researcher*, 16: 32–8.

Coleman, J. S. (1988) 'Social capital in the creation of human capital', *American Journal of Sociology*, 94: S95-S120.

Crozier, G. (1996) 'Black parents and school relationships: A case study', *Educational Review*, 48: 253–67.

Crozier, G. (1997) 'Empowering the powerful: A discussion of the interrelation of government policies and consumerism with social class factors and the impact of this upon parent interventions in their children's schooling', *British Journal of Sociology of Education*, 18(2): 187–200.

DeFilippis, J. (2001) 'The myth of social capital in community development', *Housing Policy Debate*, 12: 781–806.

Desimone, L. (1999) 'Linking parental involvement with student achievement: Do race and income matter?' *Journal of Educational Research*, 93(1): 11–30.

Field, A. (2009) *Discovering statistics using SPSS (and sex, drugs and rock 'n' roll)*, London: Sage.

Field, J. (2003) *Social capital*. London: Routledge.

Flick, U. (1998) *An introduction to qualitative research*. London: Sage.

Gamarnikow, E. and Green, A. (2000) 'Citizenship, education and social capital', in D. Lawton, J. Cairns and R. Gardner (eds), *Education for citizenship* (pp. 93–113). London: Continuum.

Gamarnikow, E. and Green, A. G. (1999) 'The third way and social capital: Education Action Zones and a new agenda for education, parents and community?' *International Studies in Sociology of Education*, 9(1): 3–22.

Gillborn, D. (2008a) 'Coincidence or conspiracy? Whiteness, policy and the persistence of the black/white achievement gap', *Educational Review*, 60(3): 229–48.

Gillborn, D. (2008b) *Racism and education: Coincidence or conspiracy?* London: Routledge.

Healy, T. 2006. 'Social capital: An educational panacea or a challenge to the way we do policy?', *European Educational Research Journal*, 5(2): 131–9.

Jolliffe, I. (2002) *Principal component analysis*. New York: Springer.

King, J. (1991) 'Dysconscious racism: Ideology, identity, and the miseducation of teachers', *The Journal of Negro Education*, 60(2): 133–46.

Lareau, A. (1989) *Home advantage: Social class and parental intervention in elementary education*. London: Falmer.

Lareau, A. (2008) 'Watching, waiting, and deciding when to intervene: Race, class, and the transmission of advantage' in L. Weis (ed.), *The way class works: Readings on school, family, and the economy* (pp. 117–33). London: Routledge.

Mirza, H. S. (2007) '"The more things change, the more they stay the same": Assessing black underachievement 35 years on' in B. Richardson, (ed.), *Tell it like it is: How our schools fail black children* (pp. 111–19). London: Bookmarks and Trentham.

Portes, A. (1998) 'Social capital: Its origins and applications in modern sociology', *Annual Review of Sociology*, 24(1): 1–24.

Putnam, R. (2000) *Bowling alone: The collapse and revival of American community*. New York: Simon and Schuster.

Qian, Z. and Blair, S. (1999) 'Racial/ethnic differences in educational aspirations of high school seniors', *Sociological Perspectives*, 42(4): 605–25.

Reay, D. (2005a) 'Beyond consciousness? The psychic landscape of social class', *Sociology*, 39(5): 911–28.

Reay, D. (2005b) 'Mothers' involvement in their children's schooling: Social reproduction in action?' in G. Crozier, D. Reay and C. Vincent (eds), *Activating participation: Parents and teachers working towards partnership* (pp. 23–33). Stoke-on-Trent, UK: Trentham.

Tolonen, T. (2007) 'Social and cultural capital meets youth research: A critical approach' in H. Helve and J. Bynner (eds), *Youth and social capital*. London: Tufnell Press.

Appendices

Table 6.3 Pearson correlations investigating social capital's relation with social class

Variable name	Label	Social class correlation coefficients (r)	N
SC13disc.advis	Parents discuss and seek advice about their child's education	.20**	201
mothpareven80	Attend parents' evenings in your school	.15*	200
Pardiscedu8.109	Parents discuss their child's education with teachers	.18*	201

* p <.05, ** p <.01, *** p <.001

Table 6.4 Results from multiple linear regressions of social class, ethnicity and gender on social capital items

Models with outcome variable (y)	Indicators (x)	B	SE B	β	R²
SC13disc.advis **(parents discuss and seek advice about their child's education)**					**.08**
	Constant	**0.11**			
	Social class	.043	0.02	.18*	
	Ethnicity – Black	–.090	0.05	–.15	
	Ethnicity – Indian	.014	0.05	.03	
	Ethnicity – Other	–.057	0.04	–.12	
	Gender	.039	0.03	.09	
SC14helpjob **(people whom parents know that can help their child get a job)**					**.05**
	Constant	**0.56**			
	Social class	.016	0.04	.03	
	Ethnicity – Black	.067	0.10	.06	
	Ethnicity – Indian	.174	0.09	.17*	
	Ethnicity – Other	.010	0.08	.01	
	Gender	–.152	0.07	–.17*	
mothpareven80 **(attend parents' evenings in your school)**					**.12**
	Constant	**2.14**			
	Social class	0.10	0.07	.10	
	Ethnicity – Black	–0.70	0.21	–.26**	
	Ethnicity – Indian	0.25	0.18	.11	
	Ethnicity – Other	0.00	0.17	.00	
	Gender	0.01	0.14	.00	
Parknowpar98 **(parents know children's friends' parents – intergenerational closure)**					**.04**
	Constant	**.82**			
	Social class	0.03	0.07	.03	
	Ethnicity – Black	0.05	0.21	.02	
	Ethnicity – Indian	0.08	0.18	.04	
	Ethnicity – Other	–0.16	0.17	–.08	
	Gender	0.30	0.14	.17*	

* p <.05, ** p <.01, *** p <.001

Table 6.5 Results from binary logistic regressions of social class, ethnicity and gender on social capital items

Models with outcome variable (y)	Indicators (x)	B (SE)	95% CI for odds ratio			χ^2 (df)	R^2		
			Lower	Odds ratio	Upper		Hosmer & Lemeshow	Cox & Snell	Nagelkerke
Pardiscedu8.109 (parents discuss their child's education with teachers)						**14.69 (5)**	.07	.07	.10
	Constant	**-2.02 (0.79)**							
	Social class	0.43* (0.21)	1.03	1.54	2.31				
	Ethnicity – Black	-1.44* (0.68)	0.06	0.24	0.90				
	Ethnicity – Indian	0.01 (0.43)	0.43	1.01	2.36				
	Ethnicity – Other	-0.61 (0.43)	0.23	0.54	1.27				
	Gender	-0.10 (0.35)	0.46	0.91	1.80				

* $p <.05$, ** $p <.01$, *** $p <.001$

Chapter 7

Doing critical educational ethnography with Bourdieu

Katie Fitzpatrick and Stephen May

Introduction

Critical ethnographers of education draw on a range of theoretical perspectives to work at the intersection of theory and method. Indeed, the relationship between theory and method is central to the kind of analyses that result from such studies. This tenet in many ways sets critical ethnographic work apart from other kinds of empirical education research. In our own critical ethnographic work, Bourdieu's generative sociological model and concepts have been integral in enabling us to bridge the theory–method gap and work our method in ways that are ontologically consistent with the theories applied (Fitzpatrick, 2013; May, 1994, 1998, 2011; see also Albright and Luke, 2008). One of the reasons this is possible is because Bourdieu himself was a methodologist who conceptualized theory *through* his empirical (often ethnographic) work. He pointed out that method requires as much theoretical insight and nuance as analysis, and he warned against what he called 'the mania for methodology', by which he meant a 'recipe' of method devoid of theory:

> As well as threatening to induce paralysis and even error, the mania for methodology also makes it possible not so much to achieve the economy of thought that all method permits, but rather to economize on thought about method.
>
> (Bourdieu, Chamboredon and Passeron, 1991, p. 62)

Bourdieu is essentially arguing here that we cannot dislocate the *how* of method from the *where* and *why* of context, culture and politics. Indeed, what is possible to do in research is bounded and defined by the very field of research and the disciplinary field of practice in which it is situated – its conventions, its parameters, what is methodologically 'acceptable' and what is not (May, 2011). Likewise, the way we research reproduces the field in particular ways. As Dillabough (2008) argues, we need to 'uncover the degree to which . . . representations and their associated methodological approaches . . . may be seen as processes at work in shaping the cultural field' (p. 203).

The theoretical lens via which we define the 'problems' and questions that frame our research will thus also necessarily define the possibilities for methodological actions. Grenfell and James (1998) argue that a Bourdieuian approach to ethnography has particular methodological emphases that are consistent with the theoretical framework his ideas provide. We argue that these ideas are overtly political, and thus 'critical', and that putting Bourdieu's ideas to work methodologically, as he himself did, enables theory and method to work productively together in a critical, and reflexive, manner. This echoes Bourdieu's own view that ethnography is an epistemological issue. As Blommaert (2005) observes of this: 'It is a mature position; [Bourdieu] accepts ethnography in its fullest sense, including the inevitable quagmires of subjectivity, bias and "doing-as-if" in the field, and in that sense prefigures what later came to be known as Critical Ethnography' (p. 228). The advent of many notable examples of Bourdieuian-informed critical ethnographies (for example, Fine, 1991; Jones, 1991; Thrupp, 1999; Willis, 1977), including our own work (Fitzpatrick, 2013; May, 1994), are testament to this claim.

In the first part of this chapter, we overview the key tenets of critical ethnography, how they differ from conventional ethnography, and how Bourdieu's theory articulates with and drives this methodology in particular ways. In the second part, we then explore specifically how Bourdieuian theory and method are connected in critical ethnographic research; in so doing, we draw on a range of examples from various educationally focused studies.

Critical ethnography

A key problem with conventional ethnography, including those conducted in educational settings, is its lack of attendance to wider socio-historical and sociopolitical contexts, and associated power relations (Carspecken, 1996; Fine, 1991). This is demonstrated in many school-based ethnographic accounts by an overly descriptive tendency – trying to present the context 'as it really is' – at the expense of critical, contextual analysis. These descriptive accounts are also inevitably framed by the 'ethnographer's gaze' (May, 1997), or what Bourdieu (1990b) describes as 'the epistemological privilege of the observer' (p. 14). The subjects of the research, with all the lack of agency that this term implies, are 'interpreted' and refracted by the researcher, through whom the reader gains access. In so doing, there is also little, if any, forethought to the asymmetrical relationship between the researcher and the researched. Nor is there any active accounting of the researcher's own positionality – their background, their experiences, their theoretical influences – and its inevitable impact on the ethnographic research and related interpretative schema employed within it (Madison, 2012).

Critical ethnographic approaches to educational research are the response to these perceived limitations. They have never been dominant in the field, inhabiting its margins, but this methodology has been employed since the late 1970s to highlight the workings of capital in education (although, of course, various theoretical perspectives are used). Beginning with Paul Willis' (1977) account of working-class boys in Birmingham, critical ethnographies have interwoven the subjective with politics, and theory with method, to ask questions about power relations in education settings. This is, indeed, what sets critical ethnography apart from other kinds of ethnographic research: the explicit focus on power relations and political issues such as social class, gender, racism, sexuality, ability and the like. Thomas (1993, p. vii) notes that:

> Critical ethnography is a way of applying a subversive worldview to the conventional logic of cultural inquiry. It does not stand in opposition to conventional ethnography. Rather, it offers a more direct style of thinking about the relationships among knowledge, society and political action.

Like all ethnography, critical ethnography requires the researcher to gain deep, lived understandings of a context and to reflect on the meanings of cultures within that context. This requires significant time in the field trying to understand what Willis (1977) refers to as 'the social creativity of a culture' (p. 121). Ethnographers employ a range of actual methods depending on the focus and the site; these can include field notes, visual artefacts (such as photos and artwork), interviews, observations and video recordings. Documents such as official policies and email conversations, statutes, newsletters and the like can also be included. Contemporary ethnographers are increasingly using participant-generated research methods and engaging participants as co-researchers, videographers, diarists and interviewers (Cammarota and Fine, 2008; Pink, 2012). Ethnography in this sense is not bounded by any rigid methodological rules. It rather draws on a range of methods and is flexible, dependent on practicality, the research foci, and relationships between participants and researchers. Interestingly, Bourdieu advocated methodological openness and abhorred rigid and prescribed methodological approaches, which he viewed as enabling researchers to 'see more and more in less and less' (Bourdieu, Chamboredon and Passeron, 1991). Instead, he advocated for researchers to 'mobilise all the techniques that are relevant and practically useable, given the definition of the object and the practical conditions of data collection' (Bourdieu and Wacquant, 1992, p. 227). This is possible in ethnography as a range of methodological tools can be used within a broad framework and, crucially, wider social and political contexts can be analysed alongside and in relation to specific contextual incidences.

What sets critical ethnography apart from more conventional ethnographic approaches is the specific and overt focus on the politics of the cultures under study, the positioning of the site of research with respect to other sites, and the overt positionality of the researcher(s) which, in turn, requires the latter's reflexivity (Foley, 2002). In this sense, critical ethnography extends conventional ethnography by attending directly to issues of ethics, power and representation

(Madison, 2012). Critical ethnography thus aligns well with Bourdieu's insistence that all research should attend to the relations between the objects of study, rather than just the objects themselves. He argued that only via the relations between and within fields can we understand the wider significance of our research and overcome the 'common sense' assumptions which are inevitable when we are ourselves immersed in any particular field of practice (Bourdieu and Wacquant, 1992). There are a number of (almost unlimited) ethnographic considerations, given the complexity of political concerns and their divergence across sites, but we touch on a few key considerations here and how these align with Bourdieu's theoretical tools.

Positionality

Critical ethnographers are specifically interested in the positionality of the researcher within both wider politics and the study itself. Bourdieu argued for sociologists to remain reflexive, not only with regard to their positionality in terms of gender, social class and the like, but also as pertains to their positioning in the field of academia: their academic habitus which enables them to 'see' certain things and not others (Bourdieu and Wacquant, 1992; May, 2011). The researcher then is implicated in the study in ways that require reflexivity and an orientation to the wider contexts of the research and the relations between their own and other contexts. For example, researchers in a school are implicated in the relations of power they experience within the school but also with regard to their place in academic hierarchies, subject disciplines, and the interrelationship between those and the school and community. As Madison (2012) argues, critical ethnography should 'further its goals from simply politics to the politics of positionality' (p. 7). In order to do this, she explains, a focus on politics must include both self-reflection and a rigorous critique of one's own implication in the related relations of power and social hierarchies. Within such a framework then 'we are accountable for our own research paradigms, our own positions of authority, and our own moral responsibility relative to representation and interpretation' (Madison, 2012, p. 9). This focus on the politics of representation, interpretation and positionality also concerns the research methods and the relationships between researchers and participants. Several scholars have labelled this concern with positionality 'post critical' (Noblit et al., 2004) but critical ethnographers have long examined their own positioning within wider political concerns. For example, in her study of students dropping out of school in New York City, Fine (1991) examined her own privilege, as a white, middle-class academic, as a counterpoint to the lives of the African American school 'drop outs', and their lived experiences, that her study foregrounds. We have similarly tried to situate ourselves contextually, biographically and relationally in relation to the ethnographic work that we do. For example, May (1998) revisits the origins of his critical ethnography of a progressive multicultural school (May, 1994), via a personal reflective and reflexive exploration of his own schooling experiences, and their influence on the development of his commitment to social justice. Fitzpatrick (2013) likewise begins her critical ethnographic account of a school in a low socio-economic, culturally diverse community in South Auckland, New Zealand, with the juxtaposition of the very different cultural and class milieu of her own early life and the journey that led her to end up teaching in the school in question. Furthermore, in both studies, we maintain a reflexive awareness throughout about how our own habitus affects the way we 'see' the research site and our own experience of the field. We each employed a range of strategies to 'unpick' and expose our assumptions when analysing empirical materials and, crucially, sought to understand the research site in its relations with other sites socially, politically and historically.

Reflecting on positionality also extends to understanding how individuals in the field of practice are themselves positioned within wider fields. Bourdieu provides a wonderful example in *An invitation to reflexive sociology* (Bourdieu and Wacquant, 1992), which shows the importance of understanding localized, embodied experience within the wider politics of the field and related doxa. While in any particular study of gender, for example, the individual (ethnographic) stories of women and girls will be varied, there is no doubting that across fields, particular gendered relations of power persist. We are all implicated in these and, at least partially, blind to them because they form such a fundamental part of the fields we all exist within, and which form our habitus. If we look at this issue ethnographically, we will, no doubt, see a range of women and men interrelating in a wide range of ways, some of which may (or not) reinforce these gender relations. If we were to interview women some may insist that gendered forms of power do not affect them and others may describe how they personally enact forms of resistance. All of these stories will be authentic and may both contravene and support theories of gender. What is missed in such an analysis, however, is how gendered relations of power are so inscribed in our bodies as to seem naturalized, to the extent that we no longer feel any kind of injustice at the outcomes. This necessitates the researcher to draw on wider evidence and theory in order to locate their ethnographic experiences in relation to other fields and over time. Bourdieu explains it thus:

> But the best illustration of the political import of doxa is arguably the symbolic violence exercised upon women. I think in particular of the sort of socially constituted agoraphobia that leads women to exclude themselves from a whole range of public activities and ceremonies from which they are structurally excluded (in accordance with the dichotomies public/male versus private/female), especially in the realm of formal politics. Or which explains that they can confront these situations, at the cost of an extreme tension, only in proportion to the effort necessary for them to overcome the recognition of their exclusion inscribed deep in their own bodies. Thus, what comes with a narrowly phenomenological or ethnomethodological analysis is the neglect of the historical underpinnings of this relation of immediate fit between subjective and objective structures and the elision of its political significance, that is, depoliticization.
>
> (Bourdieu and Wacquant, 1992, p. 74)

Critical ethnographic approaches aim to unearth and name these depoliticizing processes and our place within them.

Politics and theory

In order to attend to positionality, the research site and participants (and the researcher) must be understood relationally within wider sociopolitical and historical contexts. Drawing on Bourdieu, Willis (1977) explained this as attending to 'the logic of living', which he noted 'always concerns, at some level, a recognition of, and action upon, the particularity of its place within a determinate social structure' (p. 121). Bourdieu and Wacquant (1992) note that any site of research (and the objects within) can only be fully understood sociologically in their relation to other sites and spaces. In this, the fields of practice within and across which research sites are situated provide a meaningful starting point in terms of analysis. Bourdieu notes, however, that the politics of field/s are, of course, inscribed within the bodies of individuals, and therein can also be read the social history of the site:

> Because practice is the product of a habitus that is itself a product of the embodiment of the immanent regularities and tendencies of the world, it contains within itself an anticipation of these tendencies and regularities, that is, a nonthetic reference to a future inscribed in the immediacy of the present. Time is engendered in the actualization of the act, or the thought, which is by definition presentification and de-presentification, that is the 'passing' of time according to common sense. . . . Habitus, adjusted to the immanent tendencies of the field, is an act of temporalisation through which the agent transcends the immediate present via practical mobilization of the past and practical anticipation of the future.
>
> (Bourdieu and Wacquant, 1992, p. 138)

A study of habitus is, by necessity, a study of social history and how the field (a product itself of historical politics and relations of power) is inscribed in and expressed by the body. Social theory then is central to the methodology of critical ethnography and, indeed, critical ethnography is not possible without social theory. The theory, however, needs to be put to work at all levels of the study and articulated via practice (such as in the example of habitus above). Grenfell and James (1998) observe that, for Bourdieu,

> theory is not something to be gained 'out there' . . . . Rather, it is a developed understanding, sometimes grasped empathetically, gained as part of a practical engagement with empirical situations and the problems they present. Bourdieu's theory is one *of* practice and *for* practice.
>
> (p. 155, emphases in original)

In critical ethnographic research, theory and practice actively co-constitute each other throughout the study. Theoretical understandings necessarily inform the researcher before s/he enters the field but are then challenged, extended, re-thought, reinforced and rejected in relation to the experience of doing the research with people in a particular place and time. How the researcher experiences the site is an articulation of their own habitus in relation to social class, gender, ethnicity, cultural background, age and a multitude of other factors. But the site is also informed by doxa about place, community, location and so forth. A clear example of this can be found in Fitzpatrick's (2013) critical ethnography with young people in South Auckland (the southern suburbs of New Zealand's largest city). In popular and media discourse, South Auckland is positioned as a culturally diverse but also dangerous place. Local news media frequently report on criminal activity in the area and it is 'known' as a place of gangs, crime and unemployment (Loto *et al.*, 2006). The dominant doxa of place then positions South Auckland in a particular way that informs the habitus of those who live there, along with the forms of capital associated with places and the location of people. The geographical 'reality' that South Auckland is not a homogeneous or even singular community, that the boundaries of place are less than clear, and that these communities are more diverse (both ethnically and socio-economically) than is presumed, is masked by the doxa. Being able to unearth the doxa and its consequences for the field of practice was thus central to understanding how the young people in the study understood themselves and how their embodied dispositions reflected the place *in relation* with other places.

Relationships

A third underlying principle of critical ethnography is the importance of ethical and reciprocal relationships within research settings. Relationships in ethnographic research are necessarily complex and exist relative to social hierarchies and forms of capital in the field. So while researchers may hold significant social and cultural capital relative to their position in the academy, they may or may not hold forms of capital recognized in the specific field of research. If the researcher's habitus aligns with the field of practice, then s/he may 'naturally' fit in with others in that space, lessening the distance between all participants in the research site. But this also has its challenges, requiring the researcher to specifically attend to and detail the arbitrary cultural practices, or doxa, in that research site, rather than just accepting them as part of, or seamlessly articulated with, their own habitus. If the habitus of the researcher is not in alignment with the field, or aspects of the field and forms of capital therein, he or she is likely to be more obviously 'different'. On the one hand, the novel nature of the research site is likely to allow the researcher to better notice the cultural arbitrary and the logic of practice of the field, and how it differs from other fields. On the other hand, this researcher may have more difficulty in connecting, gaining trust and communicating because of his/her embodied cultural difference. Relationships can then be awkward and misunderstandings common. In this sense, the researcher also risks misrepresenting participants and misreading cultural nuances. Understanding one's own positioning in the field then requires significant, ongoing reflection and greatly influences how the researcher might go about gaining (and keeping) trust, understanding the relationships within the context, and working towards reciprocity. This requires developing consciousness of the doxa of the fields one hails from as well as the field of research (and the connections and disjunctures between the two).

According to Bourdieu, the researcher must engage with a reflexivity of self in order to see where the gaps between theory and practice in the research, and thus the limitations of the research, lie. Bourdieu and Wacquant (1992) note that 'an adequate science of society must construct theories which contain within themselves a theory of the gap between theory and practice' (p. 70). As Grenfell and James (1998) insist,

> practice and theorizing are not regarded as separate activities, displaced in time and place during the research process, but mutually generative of the ways and means of collecting data, analyzing it and developing explanations which lead to an understanding of the object being investigated.
>
> (p. 155)

Of course, Bourdieu's theoretical tools are by no means the only ones of use in this sense. We have both productively employed a multiplicity of theoretical tools – including those of Foucault, Bhabha, Deleuze (Fitzpatrick), Bernstein, Gramsci (May) and others – in addition to Bourdieu's. The advantage, however, of employing a Bourdieuian lens is the overt focus in this work, as discussed above, on the relations between: theory and method, overlapping fields, and theory/practice.

Physical capital: A Bourdieuian tool at work in critical educational ethnography

Let us finish with the application of one of Bourdieu's theoretical concepts as an analytical (and methodological) frame in critical ethnography. This is drawn from the work of Hills (2006, 2007) and Fitzpatrick (2013) and their focus, in the field of health and physical education, on the notion of 'physical capital'.

Bourdieu did not separate out 'physical capital' from other types of capital (lisahunter, Smith, and emerald, 2015). However, the turn to the body in sociology has highlighted the importance of the value of bodily movement, shape, size and embodied dispositions, and physical capital is one analytical framework that is useful for understanding this (Shilling, 2012). According to Shilling (2012):

The production of physical capital refers to the development of bodies in ways recognized as possessing value in social fields, while the conversion of physical capital refers to the translation of bodily participation in work, leisure and other fields into contrasting resources. Physical capital is most usually converted into economic capital (money, goods, services), cultural capital (e.g. education) and social capital (social networks which enable reciprocal calls to be made on the services of its members).

(p. 135)

Young people in schools, for example, arrive with certain forms of physical capital 'formed through their participation in social life' (Shilling, 2012, p. 136). These are expressed by the body and 'read' by others in relation to what is valued. Physical capital can be developed and employed strategically within a social field, according to the boundaries of that field and the possibilities for development. Skeggs (2004) argues that 'embodiment is the product of the composition and volumes of capital that can be accrued and carried by the body and the fit between the habitus (the disposition organizing mechanism) and the field' (p. 22) and she notes that 'embodiment also provides us with a way of recognising authority in its physical dispositions'(p. 22). This is partly in the control of the person but, as a function of habitus, is largely unconscious and strongly related to social class positioning and other factors (gender, obviously, as well as ethnicity, culture etc.). A clear example of this is the historical muscularity of the working-class body, a bodily form that held lower capital value in the past in other non-working-class fields. In recent times, with the rise of gyms and an overt focus on the 'healthy and fit' body, the muscular body now holds high capital value across fields in the western world. Indeed, the fat body is now routinely and almost universally vilified.

[P]hysical capital is not only an embodied capacity to use the body, but the appearance of the body, the body as evidence of particular work on the body. . . . "Ability" here could arguably be equated with the appearance of the body as an indicator of "fitness" . . . The value of such ability in this context seems, however, less to do with what the body can do than with what the body looks like it can do.

(Wright and Burrows, 2006, pp. 278–9)

In education, the body and physical capital have been explored ethno-graphically in at least two studies. We draw on these here to highlight how the physical can productively be analysed at the intersection of theory and method.

The first study we draw on here is Laura Hills' research (2006; 2007) into girls in physical education classes in the north of England. Hills drew upon Bourdieu's notion of habitus to explain how embodied discourses of gender and sexuality among the girls affected their engagement in classes and how this was ultimately linked to physical capital. Hills spent a year with 12- and 13-year-old girls and used interviews, focus groups and observations of physical education lessons. Several of the girls in Hills' study identified a tension between their feminine/heterosexual identities and physical pursuits, perceiving the latter as masculine. Following this, Hills (2006) argues that the habitus of these girls prevented them from accessing physical and sporting identities, and capital. In this sense, she concluded that forms of physical capital were a result of 'the field of female peer relations' at work in this school. She used the example of student perceptions and actions apropos of girls' involvement in football, which was viewed as inappropriate for girls within the field of the school. The advantage of her critical ethnographic methodology here was twofold. First, she was able to invest significant time in the setting in order to get beneath the surface level of the students' statements and contrast these with their actions within the wider cultural setting. (For example, she noted that some girls actually did play football despite their insistence that it wasn't an appropriate activity for girls in PE classes.) Second, the methodology required her to locate the experiences of these girls within wider societal gender relations and to contrast the field in question with other fields of practice and so, consistent with Bourdieu, analyse the relational nature of the specific site of cultural practice, in her case school PE lessons. In so doing, she was able to conclude that 'girls' self-repression in relation to physical activity participation constitutes a form of symbolic violence.' She notes that 'constructing a potentially positive corporeal experience as outside the field of feminine peer relations implicates the body in its own subjugation by removing the potential for benefiting from an activity' (p. 548). In Hills' study, theory and method thus work together to show how girls are positioned in relation to physical capital in physical education classes (a site in which physical capital is central to practice). The Bourdieuian theoretical framework in this sense worked with the critical ethnographical methodology and drove the questions, methodological actions and analyses that resulted.

The second study is Fitzpatrick's (2013) critical ethnography of 16–18-year-old health and physical education students, and their understanding of the intersections of social class, ethnicity, culture and gender/sexuality in their lived school experiences. Here we offer a few reflections on how theory and method intersected in the analysis of physical capital, and its interconnections with ethnicity and racialization, in the students' low socio-economic, culturally diverse South Auckland high school.

Ethnicity was a central concern in this ethnographic account. The researcher is Pakeha (New Zealand European) and the students in the study are predominantly Māori (New Zealand's indigenous peoples) and/or Pasifika (first, second or third generation migrants from the Pacific Islands). Fitzpatrick was able to write about her own embodied experience of participating in the health and PE classes (and in outdoor education) with the students and how her body was 'read' in terms of physical capital. White and brown bodies then became a productive point of analysis and Fitzpatrick was able to draw links between the students' chosen involvement in physical education classes and their embodied identities as 'physical beings'. This identity position was contrasted with ability and achievement in so-called 'academic' subjects, which some students insisted were 'not for them'. Physical capital was therefore highly valued in the field of school physical education and as a form of social capital linked with health and beauty. However, hierarchies inherent in the wider field of education specifically pitted physical capital against academic ability, forming the students' habitus in relation to the physical, at a cost of the academic. This could then be further understood and analysed along Cartesian lines in relation to wider social hierarchies positioning the black and brown body as inherently physical rather than intellectual, itself a highly racialized construction (see also Fitzpatrick, 2010, 2011).

Again, theory and method worked in this study to require the researcher to analyse her own embodiment and physical capital, while also researching the students' experiences within and in relation to other fields of practice and wider politics. Bourdieu's sociology was critical to the articulation between theory and method in understanding how the body and habitus exist in relationship with the field and forms of capital operating in the field. With respect to social hierarchies, a Bourdieuian analysis 'rejects the sociological opposition between "rational"and "normative" action by viewing all action as interested in relation to particular fields' (Shilling, 2004, p. 473). This means that situated action is a result of both the cultural context and the person's strategic involvement in that context, and therefore the researcher is implicitly a part of the contexts s/he is researching.

Final thoughts

Bourdieu was, and continues to be, (mis)interpreted as a 'grand' theorist, a label he rejected, insisting that his work was deeply located in practice (Bourdieu, 1990a). While his writing continues to be enormously sociologically productive, it is located deeply in both his empirical research and his own reflexive accounts of practice, including those of the academic and sociological fields within which he was immersed. In many ways, Bourdieu lived his research-writing as a kind of ongoing critical ethnography, in the sense that he was constantly reflecting on the limitations of the field/s in which he practised, and seeking to expose and extend them. This can be seen in the way his work reached across different fields: from education to the arts, from the academy and language to the media and popular culture. In all he sought to expose the cultural arbitrary of practice by analysing relations between and within fields, and extending the realms of possibility. In so doing, he challenged the distinction between theory and method, arguing that 'operations of practice are only as good as the theory in which they are grounded' (Bourdieu, Chamboredon and Passeron, 1991, p. 63). Bourdieu also constantly revisited, critiqued and extended his own analyses and, in so doing, furnished his ideas with case studies and reflections taken from his own and others' research practice (for example, Bourdieu, 1990a). In this, he exposed his own processes of theory and method by commenting explicitly on the possibilities of thought rendered by doxa, his own habitus and the limitations of the fields of practice. His work then contains layers of, not only spatial, but also temporal reflexivity. Albright and Luke (2008) argue that 'Bourdieuian reflexivity cuts through forms of misrecognition at the heart of fields to ignore how questions are typically asked and pursue lines of inquiry thought unthinkable in those fields' (p. 23). His methods of inquiry have thus extended the fields of practice because of his attention to the theoretical and epistemological within.

It is no surprise that those interested in issues of social justice, reproduction and the politics of education have found Bourdieuian analyses so very productive for informing both theory and method. Critical ethnographic research demands attention to these very issues and requires in-depth engagement with the relational nature of all research and the need for reflexive accounts. In this sense, critical ethnographic research overcomes the distinction between theory and method and the associated problems of ontological inconsistency. This allows particularly cogent educational insights to emerge, ones that both expose injustice in the field of education and extend the boundaries of possibility in the field.

References

Albright, J. (2008) 'Problematics and generative possibilities', in J. Albright and A. Luke (eds), *Pierre Bourdieu and literacy education* (pp. 11–32). New York and London: Routledge.

Blommaert, J. (2005) 'Bourdieu the ethnographer', *The Translator*, 11(2): 219–36. doi: 10.1080/13556509.2005.10799199.

Bourdieu, P. (1990a) *In other words: Essays towards a reflexive sociology*. Stanford, CA: Stanford University Press.

Bourdieu, P. (1990b) *The logic of practice*. Cambridge: Polity Press.

Bourdieu, P. and Wacquant, L. (1992) *An invitation to reflexive sociology*. Cambridge: Polity Press.

Bourdieu, P., Chamboredon, J. C. and Passeron, J. C. (1991) *The craft of sociology: Epistemological preliminaries*. Berlin: Walter de Gruyter.

Cammarota, J. and Fine, M. (2008) 'Youth participatory action research: A pedagogy for transformational resistance', in J. Cammarota, and M. Fine (eds), *Revolutionizing education: Youth participatory action research in motion* (pp. 1–12). New York: Routledge.

Carspecken, P. (1996) *Critical ethnography in educational research: A theoretical and practical guide*. New York: Routledge.

Dillabough, J. (2008) 'Exploring historicity and temporality in social science methodology: A case for methodological and analytical justice', in K. Gallagher (ed.), *The methodological dilemma: Creative, critical, and collaborative approaches to qualitative research* (pp. 185–218). London: Routledge.

Fine, M. (1991) *Framing dropouts: Notes on the politics of an urban public high school.* Albany, NY: State University of New York Press.

Fitzpatrick, K. (2010) 'A critical multicultural approach to physical education: Challenging discourses of physicality and building resistant practices in schools', in S. May, and C. Sleeter (eds), *Critical multiculturalism: Theory and praxis* (pp. 177–90). New York: Routledge.

Fitzpatrick, K. (2011) 'Brown bodies, racialisation and physical education', *Sport, Education and Society, 18(2)*: 1–19.

Fitzpatrick, K. (2013) *Critical pedagogy, physical education and urban schooling.* New York: Peter Lang.

Foley, D. E. (2002) 'Critical ethnography: The reflexive turn', *International Journal of Qualitative Studies in Education, 15(4)*: 469–90.

Grenfell, M. and James, D. (1998) *Bourdieu and education: Acts of practical theory.* London: Falmer Press.

Hills, L. (2006) 'Playing the field(s): An exploration of change, conformity and conflict in girls' understandings of gendered physicality in physical education', *Gender and Education, 18(5)*: 539–56.

Hills, L. (2007) 'Friendship, physicality, and physical education: An exploration of the social and embodied dynamics of girls' physical education experiences', *Sport, Education and Society, 12(3)*: 317–36.

Jones, A. (1991) *'At school I've got a chance': Culture/privilege: Pacific Islands and Pakeha girls at school.* Palmerston North, NZ: Dunmore Press.

lisahunter, Smith, W. and emerald, e. (2015) 'Pierre Bourdieu and his conceptual tools', in lisahunter, W. Smith and e. emerald (eds), *Pierre Bourdieu and physical culture* (pp. 3–24). London and New York: Routledge.

Loto, R., Hodgetts, D., Chamberlain, K., Nikora, L. W., Karapu, R. and Barnett, A. (2006) 'Pasifika in the news: The portrayal of Pacific peoples in the New Zealand press', *Journal of Community and Applied Social Psychology, 16(2)*: 100–18.

Madison, D. S. (2012) *Critical ethnography: Method, ethics, and performance.* Thousand Oaks, CA: Sage.

May, S. (1994) *Making multicultural education work.* Bristol, UK: Multilingual Matters.

May, S. (1997) 'Critical ethnography', in N. Hornberger (ed.), *Research methods and education. The encyclopedia of language and education*, Vol. 8 (pp. 197–206). Dordrecht: Kluwer.

May, S. (1998) 'On what might have been: Some reflections on critical multi-culturalism', in G. Shacklock, and J. Smyth (eds), *Being reflexive in critical educational and social research* (pp. 159–70). London: Falmer Press.

May, S. (2011) 'The disciplinary constraints of SLA and TESOL: Additive bilingualism and second language acquisition, teaching and learning', *Linguistics and Education, 22(3)*: 233–47.

Noblit, G. W., Flores, S. Y. and Murillo, E., Jr (eds), (2004) *Postcritical ethnography: Reinscribing critique.* Cresskill, NJ: Hampton Press.

Pink, S. (2012) *Advances in visual methodology.* London: Sage.

Shilling, C. (2004) Physical capital and situated action: A new direction for corporeal sociology. *British Journal of Sociology of Education, 25(4)*: 473–87.

Shilling, C. (2012) *The body and social theory.* London: Sage.

Skeggs, B. (2004) *Class, self, culture.* London: Routledge.

Thomas, J. (1993) *Doing critical ethnography*. Newbury Park, CA: Sage.

Thrupp, M. (1999) *Schools making a difference: Let's be realistic! School mix, school effectiveness and the social limits of reform*. Buckingham, UK: Open University Press.

Willis, P. (1977) *Learning to labor: How working class kids get working class jobs*. New York: Columbia University Press.

Wright, J. and Burrows, L. (2006) Reconceiving ability in physical education: A social analysis. *Sport, Education and Society, 11*(3): 275–91.

Part 3

Researching educational leadership and management

Chapter 8

Mobilizing Bourdieu to think anew about educational leadership research

Scott Eacott

Mobilizing the work of Pierre Bourdieu in my scholarship has led me to ask questions of the canons of my disciplinary space (educational leadership, management and administration) and pose serious methodological inquiry around the construction and ongoing maintenance of central research objects (e.g. leadership). Significantly, it has eroded the somewhat arbitrary division between theory and method and sustained a generative research programme concerned with the ongoing legitimation of the social world and its empirical manifestation in the organizing of education and educational labour. Engaging with, rather than necessarily overcoming, the methodological challenges in Bourdieu's work provides the basis for a rigorous and robust social 'science'.

While I have mobilized Bourdieu's key thinking tools of *habitus*, *fields* and *capitals*, and the lesser used *strategies*, my path to Bourdieuian thinking was not through the usual routes. My initial engagement was as a methodological – as in the coming together of theory and method – resource more so than a conceptual toolkit. As a result, when engaging with thinking through my usage of Bourdieuian thought and analysis in constructing method, my attention shifts mostly to what Bourdieuian thinking offers as a way of thinking about research and the research object.

The *relational* approach to scholarship in educational leadership, management and administration that I am advancing (see Eacott, 2015) is very much rooted in Bourdieuian thinking. However, my use of Bourdieuian theorizing is neither with utmost loyalty nor reverence. I take Bourdieu seriously in his claim that his work is constantly updated through ongoing scholarship. My interest in the theoretical problem of the legitimation of the social world and its empirical manifestation in the organizing of education and educational labour draws heavily on my reading of Bourdieu, yet at the same time the challenges of mobilizing Bourdieu in a new space have led to me thinking it anew.

Bourdieu's work on epistemological preliminaries, in particular the breaking with ordinary language (following Gaston Bachelard, 1984[1934]) and epistemic/empirical objects, casts doubt over the canonical 'leadership'. In bringing Bourdieu into a different time and space, as he never explicitly wrote about educational administration per se, has required a rethinking of temporality and spatial politics. Engaging with these conceptual problems leads to work at the forefront of contemporary thought and analysis through contributions that stimulate dialogue and debate in the interest of advancing scholarship. This chapter outlines the various ways in which Bourdieuian thinking has forced me to think anew the construction of my research object and how I can methodologically capture matters of temporality and space.

Finding Bourdieu

As with many doctoral candidates (and faculty, I might add) working in the intellectual space that is educational leadership, management and administration during the early stages of my doctorate, I was primarily working in an instrumental (almost atheoretical) analytical framework. However, as my candidature progressed I reached a point where the (a)theoretical resources I had engaged with during my master's (also in educational leadership) and that populated many of the journals of the discipline were not enabling me to do the sort of work I wanted to do in relation to how school leaders thought and acted strategically. That is, I needed an analytical lens that could engage with the theoretical problem of the legitimation of practices and its empirical manifestation rather than just the latter.

As a result of the work of, and engaging with, other doctoral candidates in the department, I began reading Michel Foucault, particularly around governmentality, the panopticon and strategy. I also revisited some of the key thinkers I came across during my master's programme, notably those from Deakin University (Victoria, Australia) during the 1980s–1990s such as Richard Bates, Jill Blackmore and John Smyth, whose work was built upon a foundation of critical social theory (see Tinning and Sirna, 2011). It was, however, during a conversation with James Ladwig (who ended up supervising my doctorate) that he suggested Bourdieu's work on strategy might be what I was after. He gave me a copy of *From rules to strategies* – an interview between Bourdieu and Pierre Lamaison (1986) published in *Cultural Anthropology* – and then later in the collection, *In other words* (Bourdieu, 1990). It was at this point I was hooked.

This path to Bourdieu is significant. Unlike many education researchers who come to Bourdieu through *Reproduction in education, society and culture* (Bourdieu and Passeron, 1990[1970]), *The state nobility* (Bourdieu, 1996 [1989]), or for those in higher education, *Homo academicus* (Bourdieu, 1988[1984]), and in doing so frequently equate Bourdieu with reproduction, I came to him as a theoretical, or more precisely, a methodological resource. My reading of Bourdieu as a resource came less from *An invitation to reflexive sociology* (Bourdieu and Wacquant, 1992), and more from *Pascalian meditations* (Bourdieu, 2000[1997]), *The social structures of the economy* (Bourdieu, 2005 [2000]) and, arguably most important, *The craft of sociology: Epistemological preliminaries* (Bourdieu et al., 1991[1968]). The distinction, to think with

Bourdieu, was that my initial engagement with Bourdieuian thinking was not to mobilize a key set of thinking tools but to think *with* Bourdieu. This is not to say I have not played with *habitus, capital* and *fields* – doing so is something of a rite of passage for Bourdieuian scholars – but that this mobilization of Bourdieu did not enable me to push my thought and analysis to where I wanted it to go. This also meant that my engagement with scholars working with Bourdieuian thinking was important. Using Elizabeth Silva and Alan Warde's (2010) classification system of Bourdieuian scholars, I was less intrigued by the 'defenders of the legacy' (e.g. Michael Grenfell) or the 'partial appropriators', (which Will Atkinson (2012) labels as a 'British speciality' (p. 170)), and more interested in the 'critical revisers' and 'repudiators'. This is not surprising given that what I sought was a rigorous and robust approach to social science, but not one that simply replaced one master narrative with another, rather an approach to scholarship that enabled me to think anew. Therefore, despite Bourdieu writing in a different time and space, it is in bringing his approach to scholarship face to face with the challenges of the here and now that was attractive. As James Ladwig (1996) argues, built within the very French Durkheimian sociological tradition, Bourdieu's methodological stance begins from the epistemological presumption that (in Poincaré's words) 'facts do not speak'. My mobilization of Bourdieuian thinking is guided by my singular (theoretical and empirical) task of trying to describe what I see happening in the scholarship of educational leadership, management and administration, the disciplinary space to which I pledge allegiance. This means I pay as much attention to the field of knowledge production as I do the field of practice.

Despite earlier claims about the minimal use of Bourdieu in educational leadership studies (Lingard and Christie, 2003), there is an increasing corpus of work based on Bourdieuian thinking. It has been the basis of works on school reform/policy (Gunter, 2012), leadership preparation and development (Eacott, 2011), leadership standards (English, 2012), strategy (Eacott, 2010), autonomy (Thomson, 2010), educational leadership at large (Thomson, 2015), and the intellectual *field* of educational administration (Gunter, 2002). Consistent with the re-emergence of a strong sociological tradition in educational leadership studies (Eacott, 2015; Gunter, 2010) and the critical social theory strength of Australia and New Zealand (Bates, 2010; Eacott, 2013), it is defensible to argue that there is a group of scholars on an international scale thinking with Bourdieu. Herein lies a challenge for those new to Bourdieu in educational leadership, management and administration. First, there is the temptation to simply grab Bourdieu's thinking tools and build research around that. This is problematic as Atkinson (2012) argues, Bourdieu is not to be ransacked, selectively applied, mashed with other ideas and twisted as empirical findings dictate. Similarly, Grenfell (2010) notes that Bourdieu's concepts are 'epistemologically charged' (p. 26), bounded by a set of philosophical assumptions and disregard for this limits them to meaningless descriptive vocabulary. This is central to Karl Maton's (2008) argument against adjectival *habitus*, claiming that the need for the adjective is evidence of the lack of work around context.

It is my original engagement with Bourdieu and Bourdieuian thinking that has enabled me to overcome the novelty of the great thinker. As Lisa Adkins (2011) argues, overlaying a theory or mapping a terrain with Bourdieu leaves the existing theorization intact, even if explained differently. What I sought was the theoretical resources to not only challenge the hegemonic discourse but to provide an alternate, one that would engage with blind spots in existing theorizations and open up new directions and frontiers for thought and analysis. This I found in tracing the logic of Bourdieu's analysis of classification struggles and thinking relationally rather than looking at his substantive findings. That is, Bourdieu provided me with the foundations of an approach to scholarship. Most importantly, my rather unorthodox coming to Bourdieu – at least for my area – has meant that Bourdieuian thinking has inspired me to think anew the educational leadership, management and administration project. It forced me to think of the organizing of education and educational labour not in the sense of improving productivity and practice, something rooted in Frederick Winslow Taylor's (1911) *Principles of scientific management* and reinforced through the systems thinking that dominates educational administration, but as one concerned with legitimation. This subtle shift gives charge to the underlying generative principles of practice, those which are shaping and shaped by how we come to know, do and be educational labour.

Thinking with Bourdieu

My unorthodox coming to Bourdieu led me to believe that in Bourdieuian thinking we can find important resources for understanding the contemporary organizing of education and educational labour. However, unlike common uses which privilege *habitus*, *field*, and *capital*, I argue that the theoretical resources of greatest potency are those which may need certain refinement and modifications, even if at first sight, those resources appear to have minimal if any connection to, or resonance with contemporary dialogue and debates. In particular, I contend that thinking with Bourdieu has enabled me to engage with some of the enduring critiques of educational leadership, management and administration studies.

While reading Bourdieu's (2005[2000]) *The social structures of the economy* an argument that caught my attention was the notion of 'native theories'. Bourdieu uses the example of management theory where a literature produced by business schools for business schools was likened to the writing of European jurists in the sixteenth and seventeenth centuries who, in the guise of describing the state, contributed to building it. This led me to ask, are the literatures of educational leadership, management and administration any different? Historically, had educational administration not sought to distance itself from education with the establishment of departments in the early 1900s? Had it not further legitimized itself through specialist journals, separate conferences, associations and networks? Asking these questions forced me to ponder Bourdieu's contention that an important element in scholarship is to *take as one's object the social work of construction of the pre-constructed object* (Bourdieu and Wacquant, 1992). As with Bourdieu, I seek to cast doubt on orthodoxy, or to make the familiar strange. This is a necessary and important task when working in the social world in which the researcher is involved. It is about getting beyond the confirmation of a pre-scientific orientation to the social world. As Bourdieu (2000[1997]) notes:

> it is clear that, to secure some chance of really knowing what one is doing, one has to unfold what is inscribed in the various relations of implication in which the thinker and his thought are caught up, that is, the pre-suppositions he engages and the inclusions or exclusions he unwittingly performs.
>
> (p. 99)

This epistemological vigilance is particularly necessary in the social sciences, where the separation between the everyday language and opinion of the spontaneous sociologist and the scientific discourse of the researcher is more blurred than elsewhere (Bourdieu *et al.*, 1991[1968]). It is familiarity with the social world, the ongoing struggle with the spontaneous understanding of the everyday that is the central epistemological obstacle for educational admin-istration as it continuously produces conceptualizations (e.g. organizational structures, leadership) and at the same time, the conditions which serve to legitimize and sustain them – native theories. The choice of problem, the elaboration of concepts and analytical categories function as a ratification of the everyday experience of organizing unless the crucial operation of scientific construction breaks with the social world *as it is* (Bourdieu and Wacquant, 1992, p. 248). Therefore, thinking with Bourdieu forces me to submit to scientific scrutiny everything that makes the everyday experience of the world possible. This includes not only the pre-scientific representation of the social but also the cognitive schemata that underlie the construction of the image (Eacott, 2014).

The challenge Bourdieu *et al.* (1991[1968]) raise, following Gaston Bachelard (1984[1934]) around epistemological vigilance, or the epistemological break, centres on Bachelard denying science the certainties of a definitive heritage and reminding us that it (science) can only progress by perpetually calling into question the very principles of its own constructs. As an intellectual space, educational administration has morphed into educational management and now educational leadership. While it is possible to map these against temporal and spatial markers, I am not going to do that for reasons which will become clear shortly; these shifts are marked through a demonizing of the previous label in some form of evolutionary track. What has always struck me about these shifting titles has been that while the labels or fads have changed, I am not as convinced the empirical focus of study has. That is, no one has yet to convince me of why if I were to use educational administration as my preferred label that I am wrong. I do get told by editors and reviewers that my work cannot be published until I update it to reflect contemporary times, but no one has been able to provide a definitive response as to why administration, or management, are wrong and 'leadership' is right. As Klaus Weber argues, we should study fads and fashions and not chase them (Birkinshaw *et al.*, 2014). Bourdieu's work provides a variety of resources for engaging in this space. Notably, work around the epistemological break in *The craft of sociology* provides ways of thinking about the construction of the research object. In doing so, it opens ups analysis to the *doxic* modality in which we come to understand the pre-scientific world and that without paying attention to such matters, it is possible, if not likely, that we remain within the pre-scientific and further legitimate the *doxa*. In many ways, a similar argument, but not as nuanced, is raised by Fenwick English (2006) who contends that advancing educational administration requires criticism of it, philosophically, empirically and logically, suggesting that we do not search for core pillars but the contested grounds on which educational leadership is defined moment to moment. Building from this attention to the break with the everyday, Bourdieuian thinking has also forced me to engage with the notion of science and scientific inquiry.

The labels of 'science' and 'scientific' have a long association with educational administration as a field of knowledge production and practice. The establishment of departments of educational administration in US universities loosely aligns with the publication of Taylor's (1911) classic, which was central to early programmes. Taylor, like other classic administration/management thinkers such as Lyall Urwick and Henri Fayol, were practice-based inquirers rather than scholars. That is, the mobilization of science was about rationalization and logic of process rather than an epistemological or ontological perspective on understanding the world. They were about chasing the latest 'what works', or to use Taylor's language 'one right method', rather than asking questions about under what conditions it is possible to think such things. Bourdieu offers a way of sustaining, if not advancing, scientific inquiry without submitting to the notion of objectivity and distance between the researcher and researched, or remaining within the ordinary language of the pre-scientific. This is because Bourdieu's belief in science is not the science of mainstream Anglophone employment, that which is mostly tied to logical empiricism and displays an 'exhibitionism of data and procedures'. Rather he believes, as noted earlier, 'one would be better advised to display the conditions of construction and analysis of these data' (Bourdieu and Wacquant, 1992, p. 65). Bourdieu's view of science, or more specifically scientific inquiry, sees it as an act of distinction from ordinary language and the under-problematized view of the social world. This way of thinking led me to explicitly ask questions of the contemporarily popular construct of educational administration – 'leadership'

(Eacott, 2013). In focusing less on trying to capture and measure 'leadership' I asked questions as to what exactly is it we mean when we mobilize the label 'leadership', and how do we bring it into being through method. This was not about operational definitions that create boundaries for inquiry prior to commencing, rather it is about the very construction of the research object. Thinking with Bourdieu enabled me to identify 'leadership' as an epistemic construct, or methodological artefact, whose criteria of existence is defined a priori yet whose identification of presence is done post-event. That is, Bourdieuian thinking facilitated me thinking anew the core research object of my disciplinary space and, in doing so, generated more questions about what it means to know or empirically ground my scholarship.

Taking such a stance in my scholarship has been somewhat problematic. As a disciplinary space, educational leadership, management and administration has clung very tightly to notions of being an applied field and needing to have actionable outcomes from research. An integral feature of this professional-ization of knowledge production is the discrediting of intellectual work (such as the critique and analysis of the construction, deconstruction and recon-struction of research objects) as exotic, indulgent and not in the public interest (Gunter, 2013). Yet herein lays a tension. There is a hegemonic position that context matters in educational administration – this is despite the search for a universal 'leadership' to resolve all issues, but that is another matter – however, as Jill Blackmore (2004) argues, to understand how educational leadership, management and administration are 'perceived, understood and enacted, one has to have a sense of the broader social, economic and political relations shaping educational work' (p. 267). This is where once again I found Bourdieu to offer the theoretical resources to engage.

To think with Bourdieu, practice is shaped by and shaping of contemporary conditions. As a result, any practice which we may come to know as 'leadership' is grounded in a particular time and space. Assumptions regarding its utility across space or its stability through time are cast into radical doubt. This is an area with which educational leadership, management and administration has not seriously engaged at scale. A key exception is Eugenie Samier (2006). She argues that, consistent with its parent discipline of public administration, educational administration exhibits a propensity for ahistorical accounts of practice whereas these accounts should be thought of as administration under historical conditions.

As an intellectual space, educational leadership, management and admin-istration has an interesting engagement with notions of time or temporality. For the most part, the leadership industry has built itself on a conceptualization of time that is focused on the present and a desired future, where the distance between the two entities is measured in clock time. Bourdieuian notions of temporality are contrary to such a conceptualization. Bourdieu gives greater privilege to the present, but this is grounded in historicizing practice. All of the Bourdieuian concepts mobilize history. This is not the causal claim of rational action theory, but one of conditioning what is and is not possible. This is what makes reproduction-based accounts of institutional arrangements a relatively easy case to make. However, this is not to be mistaken for essentialist accounts where the realm of possible outcomes is already decided. Much as Bourdieu was against the artificial partitioning of the social world in ways which serve the classifiers' purposes more than they reflect an empirical reality, the partitioning of historical periods is counter to Bourdieuian thinking. The historicizing of practice is more about why, under these conditions, such actions are taking place. As Michael Savage (2009) notes, it is not about understanding why someone is doing something, rather to relate actions to other actions, rather than causal relations, this is about unfolding an elaborated description of the ongoing politic work of organizations.

The shift in temporal thinking here is from clock time – that which is reducible to units of the clock, an external narrative of time overlaid *on* practice – to event time, one grounded in action and unfolding *with* practice. Lisa Adkins (2011) provides an account of this shifting temporal thought in relation to the global financial crisis building from Bourdieu's (2000[1997]) writings on time in *Pascalian meditations*. The shift in thinking makes the comparison of objects (e.g. schools) across space as though they exist in the same temporal conditions a flawed pursuit. It is a place-based trajectory and the configuration of actors (both material and symbolic) that is privileged.

Place as a notion is far from static. At the time of his death, Bourdieu argued that globalization was *doxic*. This is an important move in a conceptualization of space. Notions of the nation state, those somewhat arbitrary boundaries constructed by people to divide the terrain in ways that served their purposes more so than anything else, have become increasingly blurred with global discourses of policy borrowing – or even plagiarizing – as part of a larger comparative turn in global public (and especially, education) policy. A key shift in thinking here, and one pivotal to working with Bourdieu, is from an entity to a relational ontology. This serves to break down binaries at all levels of the analysis. The entity-based ontology that is hegemonic in educational leadership, management and administration, with roots in systems thinking, has arguably reached its limits. Partitions based on individual and collective, and structure and agency, become redundant when working relationally. It is important to note that not all uses of the relational are ontological, and that there are multiple schools of thought with relational ontologies. Both the entity and the relational ontologies are based on relations/relationships; it is the interplay that creates distinctions. From an entity perspective, the social world is made up of a series of independent, even if related, entities. These entities can be mapped against one another, often in two-dimensional diagrams with arrows, some double-headed, representing the various relationships and their strengths. In contrast, in a relational ontology, and consistent with Bourdieuian thinking, we come to know the world relationally. The constitution of particular objects is only made possible in relation to other objects. That is, we cannot have one without the other. To remove one object, as would be possible with an entity perspective, would reconfigure the other, therefore rendering the need for a new description of the object and its constitution. This is one reason why the artificial partitioning of *habitus*, *field* and *capital* in studies is somewhat counter to Bourdieuian thinking. While this may sound confusing, this onto-epistemological positioning is central to working with Bourdieu and arguably the underlying generative principle of Bourdieuian thinking.

Before moving to discuss some challenges of working with Bourdieuian thinking, I want to articulate, albeit briefly, the notion of Bourdieu as a 'critical' scholar. As an educational administration scholar, irrespective of my preference for rigorous and robust scholarship, an ongoing tension is the matter of criticality in the mobilization of social theory (Eacott, 2014). In his concluding commentary for the edited collection *Radicalising educational leadership* (Bogotch *et al.*, 2008), Jonathan Jansen (pp. 147–55) argues:

> But show me a theoretical framework particularly in the critical tradition that begins to grapple with this imperfect practice. There is none, for what critical theory does is to stand self-righteously at the other end of this struggle and declare the impossible ideals that real practising teachers and principals – the ordinary ones – must but simply cannot attain without working through the ruins of a troubled past, a testing present, and a future from which the lifeblood of hope is drained by the burden of the everyday.
>
> (p. 155)

For the most part, Bourdieu is identified as a critical sociologist – this is very much based on most education researchers coming to him via *Reproduction*. But I argue that this labelling is a straw man. It plays into the rhetoric of rigorous scholarship as exotic, and the caricature of the theory and practice divide. More importantly, it demonstrates a particular reading of Bourdieu, one which I argue is focused on specificity and missing the larger argument. It is based on an application of Bourdieuian thinking tools, which leaves the existing theorization intact. Jansen's critique of the critical in educational administration is legitimate. The utopia of equality and equity are far removed from the lived experience of the contemporary capitalist condition. But before labelling, for evermore, Bourdieu as a critical sociologist, I feel that this mistakenly misrepresents his research programme. What I contend Bourdieu achieves across this oeuvre, is the notion that we cannot change the world without creating new ways of seeing and knowing the world. Over his body of work, this is embodied in his methodological approach to scholarship. Assuming that Bourdieuian thinking is a vocabulary for labelling practices is to miss the epistemologically charged nature of his work. In doing so, while acknowledging the messiness that is the social, this also problematizes the scholarly exercise.

Enduring struggles

Working with Bourdieuian thinking creates a series of enduring struggles. As someone who would openly admit to still finding my way through these struggles, it seems somewhat premature (but when would it not be?) to claim any victory. Therefore, what I am going to offer here is some insights into the enduring struggles in which I engage. Building directly from my above mentioned grounding, the most substantive struggle I continue to encounter is epistemological vigilance. This is specifically as my identity is at stake in my own work. As with just about all educational administration faculty, I am a former school administrator (and a cursory glance at recruitment advertisements will demonstrate the privileging of such). Additionally, I hold, or have held, a number of administrative roles in the academy. This blurs the boundaries between the native perception of the spontaneous sociologist and the research object constructed through 'scientific' method. Therefore, the *doxic* modality through which the social world is perceived is the result of the internalization of the objective structures of the social world in the cognitive schema through which one apprehends the world. Not to mention that there exists a belief, or *illusio*, in administration and, most importantly, the stakes of the task at hand. That is, administration functions only so far as it produces a belief in the value of its product (e.g. policy, security, order) and means of production (e.g. governance).

Seriously engaging with my own ontological complicity led me to recognize the epistemic that is 'leadership' and how much of my work to that point had advanced the *doxa*. In particular, it enabled me to see how the construct of 'leadership' was a methodological artefact. Asking questions of the object from which one comes to focus makes it difficult to propose studies which are recognizable to those trained in the logical empiricist tradition. The absence of operational definitions and the thoughts of research programmes as opposed to projects – long-term thinking that is not about 'scaling-up', that canonical managerialist pursuit, but increasing depth and sophistication for the purpose of understanding – are unrecognizable to conservatives. Having a broader view means a shifting focus from the leader, teacher, school to leading, teaching and schooling. It is less about traits and behaviours, as a psychological or particular form of sociological perspective would seek, and more about situated practice. The focus on situated practice, or judgement, is evidenced in the increasing attention to the work of Luc Boltanski – a former collaborator with Bourdieu. From a situated practice perspective, the research object comes into being through relations with others rather than as separate entities. For me, this has meant a shift from seeking out school leadership to pursuing the organizing of education and educational labour. Therefore the stream of scholarship on policy, sociology of education, philosophy and history are not competitors encroaching on an intellectual space, but rather complementary.

Unlike many research training programmes which separate methods, working with Bourdieu blurs the boundaries between theory and method. This sounds simple, but the implications are substantive. It is less about paradigms – such as the quantitative and qualitative binary taught in introductory methods courses – and more about what is most appropriate at a point in time. As with the Savage quote earlier, it is not about causation but rather description. This description is not without explanatory power, but its genesis matters. Causation is the basis for intervention and consistent with a pre-existing normative orientation. Importantly, it also leaves the existing theorization intact, even if overlaid with a new master narrative. Description provides an avenue to explain, potentially in new ways, what is taking place. This approach to scholarship is a cumulative endeavour, a generative project. It is not defined by the problems it solves, but rather the questions it asks. It is not possible to map out a static and linear trajectory, as understanding unravels as the scholastic endeavour continues.

Thinking programmatically, instead of project to project, means the scholastic enterprise embodies and is embedded in the social world, as much as any research object. The generative nature of the research programme creates a new temporality for research. Unlike a focus on projects, those based in clock time, and linear rationality, thinking with Bourdieu privileges event time, a trajectory that historicizes scholarship – the present questions, methods, samples and the like – where choices are the enactment of the position of the researcher within a research tradition and intellectual journey. This journey is neither individual nor collective. It is not about building on where others have been, but delving deeper with more sophisticated methods and understandings. It is also about locating the work in place.

What I have outlined may seem vague or fuzzy on details. Despite this being somewhat frustrating for the reader, it is deliberate. If we are to take epistemological vigilance seriously, then it is very difficult, if not impossible, to articulate design and methods in advance. This is counter to conservative training in research, but it does bring knowledge production into alignment with the dynamics of the social world. Comfort with this onto-epistemological stance does not come easy. If anything, it requires unlearning much of the research training we have been exposed to, and definitely requires breaking with the spontaneous understanding of research advanced through everyday language. In short, working with Bourdieu requires a willingness to not accept the world, or the scholastic endeavour, at face value and to ask questions of everything.

An ongoing programme

With an intellectual heritage very much grounded in my engagement with Bourdieuian thinking, but also calling upon critical management studies and, understandably, educational administration scholarship, I am currently advancing a *relational* research programme in educational leadership, management and administration (see Eacott, 2015). In particular, I am seeking to bring Bourdieu into direct conversation and debate with contemporary issues in the organizing of education and educational labour. With a theoretical and empirical focus, the *relational* approach investigates how the production of knowledge of the legitimacy, effectiveness, efficiency and morality of organizing connects with the practices of organizing. In doing so, questions are raised regarding the extent to which existing ways of thinking are generative or limiting of alternate ways of being. A *relational* focus enables scholarship to move beyond internal tensions and external pressures by opening up institutions, those which constantly redefine their very existence. As a means of articulating the defining features of this *relational* approach to scholarship, below I list five key features.

- The centrality of 'organizing' in the social world creates an ontological complicity in researchers that makes it difficult to epistemologically break from our spontaneous understanding of the social world.
- Rigorous social 'scientific' scholarship would therefore call into question the very foundations on which the contemporarily popular discourses of 'leadership', 'management' and 'administration' in education are constructed.
- The contemporary social condition cannot be separated from the ongoing, and inexhaustible, recasting of organizing labour.
- Studying educational administration 'relationally' enables the overcoming of the contemporary, and arguably enduring, tensions of individualism and collectivism, and structure and agency.
- In doing so, there is a productive – rather than merely critical – space to theorize educational administration.

The *relational* perspective focuses on temporally and socio-spatially situated actions. This represents a significant shift from content specific issues (e.g. strategic planning, improving outcomes), as such content is not 'facts' of an objective reality but epistemic constructs, to social practices. The move to a focus on situated practice is not consistent with traditional theory-building approaches and requires new standards for validity, reliability and trustworthiness that are often uncomfortable within entity-based perspectives. Stability and certainty are not the goal nor conceivable. Conservative notions of validity are challenged when the idea of an independent scientific observer is rejected and the lines between subject and object blurred. Generalizability, which is of quintessential scientific value, is de-emphasized in a temporally and socio-spatially grounded description. Not to mention that such scholarly practice may be difficult to operationalize. It is messy, dynamic and situated in time and space. But if the social world of which we inquire is similar, should we expect any different?

Thinking anew

Will Atkinson (2012) argues that the incredible breadth of Bourdieu's influence on global sociology is not contested, yet the precise character and utility of it certainly is. What you will notice throughout this chapter is a distinct lack of attention to the big three thinking tools of Bourdieu. Here lies a key distinction, and the core of my research programme, the greatest potential in thinking with a great thinker (e.g. Bourdieu, Foucault, Derrida, Deleuze and so on) is not the direct application of their work, but the revitalizing of it for a different time and space. While I have no problems with those mobilizing Bourdieuian thinking tools in their scholarship, I contend that the greatest potency of social theory is arguably its generative nature.

As social theorists we pursue research objects that are always in motion. Ways of knowing, being and doing are not static. Numerous technological advances have made various aspects of field and desk research more efficient. Powerful processors have enabled large amounts of data to be analysed with the clicks of buttons. The expansion of research training has led to a proliferation of textbooks on 'how to' do Bourdieu (or any theorist) and countless chapters and articles outline how to mobilize particular thinking tools. What gets lost in much of this corpus is that the social world is messy. Why should we expect scholarship of it to be any different? Across my career thus far – and I have no intention of this changing – is that the most frustrating part is also the most rewarding. Getting one's hands dirty by engaging with the construction of the research object and challenging our own ontological complicity with the world as it is, is intellectually challenging, time consuming yet illuminating.

The intellectual project is an ongoing one. Any particular project is neither the beginning nor end of a line of inquiry. At risk of getting too normative, social theory should arguably seek to offer theoretical interventions that enable one to see the research object and/or process in new ways, ways which are not limited to any one specific socio-geographic location, but rather are theoretically charged. Theory travels far better across boundaries, both geographic and cultural, than empirical research. Offering scholarship that questions the status quo of knowledge production and practice, sketches areas of possible relevance and possible theoretical development that serve to extend current debates in fruitful directions. What quickly becomes clear though is that such scholarship is invitational. It warrants a generative reading, one that goes beyond the words on a page, but if done well, it requires a response. Therefore, as always, I encourage the reader to think with, beyond, and where necessary, against what I have argued in the spirit of the intellectual enterprise.

References

Adkins, L. (2011) 'Practice as temporalisation: Bourdieu and economic crisis', in S. Susen and B. S. Turner (eds), *The legacy of Pierre Bourdieu: Critical essays* (pp. 347–65). London: Anthem Press.

Atkinson, W. (2012) 'Where now for Bourdieu-inspired sociology?', *Sociology*, 46(1): 167–73.

Bachelard, G. (1984[1934]) *The new scientific spirit* (P. A. Heelan, trans.). Boston, MA: Beacon Press. [Originally published as *Le nouvel esprit scientifique* (Paris: Presses Universitaires de France).]

Bates, R. J. (2010) 'History of educational leadership/management', in P. Peterson, E. Baker and B. McGraw (eds), *International encyclopedia of education*, 3rd edn, (pp. 724–30). Oxford: Elsevier.

Birkinshaw, J., Healey, M. P., Suddaby, R. and Weber, K. (2014) 'Debating the future of management research', *Journal of Management Studies*, 51(1): 38–55.

Blackmore, J. (2004) 'Restructuring educational leadership in changing contexts: a local/global account of restructuring in Australia', *Journal of Educational Change*, 5(3), 267-88.

Bogotch, I. E., Beachum, F., Blount, J., Brooks, J. S., English, F. W. and Jansen, J. (eds). (2008) *Radicalizing educational leadership*. Rotterdam, Netherlands: Sense.

Bourdieu, P. (1988[1984]) *Homo academicus* (P. Collier, trans.). Cambridge: Polity Press. [Originally published as *Homo academicus* (Paris: Les Éditions de Minuit).]

Bourdieu, P. (1990) *In other words: Essays towards a reflexive sociology* (M. Adamson, trans.). Stanford, CA: Stanford University Press.

Bourdieu, P. (1996[1989]) *The state nobility* (L. C. Clough, trans.). Stanford, CA: Stanford University Press. [Originally published as *La noblesse d'état: Grandes écoles et esprit de corps* (Paris: Les Éditions de Minuit).]

Bourdieu, P. (2000[1997]) *Pascalian meditations* (R. Nice, trans.). Cambridge, UK: Polity Press. [Originally published as *Méditations pascaliennes* (Paris: Éditions du Seuil).]

Bourdieu, P. (2005[2000]) *The social structures of the economy* (C. Turner, trans.). Cambridge: Polity Press. [Originally published as *Les structures sociales de l'économie* (Paris: Éditions du Seuil).]

Bourdieu, P. and Passeron, J. C. (1990[1979]) *Reproduction in education, society and culture* (R. Nice, trans.). London: Sage. [Originally published as *La reproduction* (Paris: Les Éditions de Minuit).]

Bourdieu, P., Chamboredon, J. C. and Passeron, J. C. (1991[1968]) *The craft of sociology: Epistemological preliminaries* (R. Nice, trans.). Berlin, Germany: Walter de Gruyter. [Originally published as *Le métier de sociologue: Préalables épistémologiques* (Paris: Mouton).]

Bourdieu, P. and Wacquant, L. (1992[1992]) *An invitation to reflexive sociology*. Cambridge: Blackwell. [Originally published as *Résponses: pour une anthropologie réflexive* (Paris: Seuil).]

Eacott, S. (2010) 'Bourdieu's strategies and the challenge for educational leadership', *International Journal of Leadership in Education*, 13(3), 265–81.

Eacott, S. (2011) 'Preparing "educational" leaders in managerialist times: An Australian story', *Journal of Educational Administration and History*, 43(1): 43–59.

Eacott, S. (2013) 'Towards a theory of school leadership practice: A Bourdieusian perspective', *Journal of Educational Administration and History*, 45(2), 174–88.

Eacott, S. (2014) 'Sociological approaches to scholarship in educational leadership, management and administration', in D. Burgess and P. Newton (eds), *Theoretical foundations of educational administration and leadership* (pp. 173–85). London: Routledge.

Eacott, S. (2015) *Educational leadership relationally: A theory and methodology for educational leadership, management and administration*. Rotterdam, Netherlands: Sense.

English, F. W. (2012) 'Bourdieu's misrecognition: Why educational leadership standards will not reform schools or leadership', *Journal of Educational Administration and History*, 44(2): 155–70.

Grenfell, M. (2010) 'Being critical: the practical logic of Bourdieu's metanoia', *Critical Studies in Education*, 51(1), 85–99.

Gunter, H. (2002) 'Purposes and positions in the field of education management: Putting Bourdieu to work', *Educational Management and Administration*, 30(1): 7–26.

Gunter, H. (2010) 'A sociological approach to educational leadership', *British Journal of Sociology of Education*, 31(4): 519–27.

Gunter, H. (2012) *Leadership and the reform of education*. Bristol: Policy Press.

Gunter, H. (2013) 'Researching and conceptualising the field', *Journal of Educational Administration and History*, 45(2): 201–12.

Ladwig, J. G. (1996) *Academic distinctions: Theory and methodology in the sociology of school knowledge*. New York: Routledge.

Lamaison, P. and Bourdieu, P. (1986) 'From rules to strategies: an interview with Pierre Bourdieu', *Cultural Anthropology*, 1(1): 110–20.

Lingard, B. and Christie, P. (2003) 'Leading theory – Bourdieu and the field of educational leadership: An introduction and overview of this special issue', *International Journal of Leadership in Education*, 6(4): 317–33.

Maton, K. (2008) 'Habitus', in M. Grenfell (ed.), *Pierre Bourdieu: Key concepts* (pp. 49–65). Durham: Acumen.

Samier, E. (2006) 'Educational administration as a historical discipline: an *apologia pro vita historia*', *Journal of Educational Administration and History*, 38(2), 125–39.

Savage, M. (2009) 'Contemporary sociology and the challenge of descriptive assemblage', *European Journal of Social Theory*, 12(1), 155–74.

Silva, E. B. and Warde, A. (eds). (2010) *Cultural analysis and Bourdieu's legacy: Settling accounts and developing alternatives*. London: Routledge.

Taylor, F. W. (1911) *The principles of scientific management*. New York: W.W. Norton.

Thomson, P. (2010) 'Headteacher autonomy: A sketch of a Bourdieuan field analysis of position and practice', *Critical Studies in Education*, 51(1): 5–20.

Thomson, P. (2015) *Bourdieu and educational leadership*. London: Routledge.

Tinning, R. and Sirna, K. (eds). (2011) *Education, social justice and the legacy of Deakin University: Reflections of the Deakin diaspora*. Rotterdam, Netherlands: Sense.

Chapter 9

Narrative inquiry as a method for embedding Bourdieu's tools

Bruce Kloot

Introduction

I became interested in Bourdieu's ideas when teaching on a foundation programme in 2007. In the UK, foundation degrees generally refer to qualifications designed with the help of employers to combine academic study with workplace learning degrees (Harvey, 2009). However, in the South African context, foundation programmes are curriculum interventions aimed at assisting educationally disadvantaged students to make the transition to higher education. As such, they are entry-level, credit-bearing programmes catering for full-time students, most of whom are experiencing tertiary study for the first time.

It is important to note that the history of racial discrimination still looms large in South African education and the term 'educationally disadvantaged' refers to students who have been disadvantaged by apartheid education. In other words, foundation programmes specifically target students who would have been categorized as black[1] under apartheid.

The institution where I was working had launched its programme in the academic department in which I was teaching with the help of government funding a few years prior to my arrival. While I enjoyed my work and was glad to be able to make a contribution to the broader project of redress, a number of things intrigued me about the programme of which I had become a part. I realized that my colleagues, including the programme coordinator, did not know much more than I did about this type of initiative in terms of its origin and strategy. There was clearly a lack of understanding of what we were trying to do beyond simply teaching students who, in general, had experienced poor schooling.

I was also surprised to encounter hostility from some of the staff who were teaching in the 'mainstream', the term used to describe the traditional programme offering. In principle, the students passing my course were supposed to be more prepared for the mainstream curriculum, having had more time to adjust to the workload and pace of university. However, some mainstream staff felt that we were setting the bar too low and were concerned that the students coming into their courses from the foundation programme would negatively affect their pass rates. I realized that, despite the status accorded foundation programmes in the institution and support from the state in terms of funding, there were powerful forces within the university that were pitted against the entire foundation programme strategy.

At this time, I enrolled for my PhD and began to investigate whether something to do with foundation programmes might be an appropriate focus for my doctoral study. With the encouragement of my supervisor, I began to explore the relevant literature and was amazed to discover two articles, a decade apart and both written by advocates of the foundation programme approach that contained identical recommendations about how higher education needed to change. It appeared as if these programmes, as social entities, were somehow 'stuck'. As a strategy to change the system they seemed to be somewhat ineffective.

A significant development at the time was a call by the Ministry of Education for all higher education institutions in South Africa to develop and 'roll out' foundation programmes (DoE, 2006). Prior to this, the foundation programme initiative was described as 'small in scale and ad hoc in nature' (Kotecha *et al.*, 1997), but this was about to change. A recent adjustment to the higher education funding framework also meant that substantial funds from the Ministry were earmarked for these interventions. Given their marginal history and the impending roll-out, it seemed an opportune moment to focus on the impact of these programmes on the higher education sector.

In my reading I came across an article by Robbins (1993) about the practical importance of Bourdieu's work. I was struck by his description of Bourdieu's notion of how social spaces – 'fields' – strategically assimilate discourses from other fields in order to maintain their autonomy. This provided a means of characterizing the reaction of South African higher education to the foundation programme strategy. My personal experience and the reading I had done suggested that foundation programmes were stuck because the system was resisting more fundamental kinds of change. While ostensibly accepting the responsibility to assist underprepared students, higher education was also somehow keeping foundation programmes 'at arm's length'.

I decided to explore Bourdieu's work in more detail and was attracted by his persistent concern with the role of education in the reproduction of inequality in society. After reading some commentaries on his work and struggling through some of his original prose, I decided that his framework would be useful in understanding how the impending policy of rolling out foundation programmes would influence South African higher education.

Field, capital and habitus

Having sketched the empirical context, it is to Bourdieu's theoretical framework that this chapter now turns. This requires some clarification since Bourdieu insists that it was never his intention to develop a theoretical framework as such:

> There is no doubt a theory to my work, or better, a set of *thinking tools*
> visible through the results they yield, but it is not built as such . . . It is a
> *temporary construct which takes shape for and by empirical work.*
>
> (Wacquant, 1989, p. 50, original emphasis)

This focus on the empirical must be kept in mind in the discussion that follows.
Bourdieu's constructs are not to be taken as a set of hypotheses to account for
the particularities and functioning of an object of study (Grenfell, 2012) but
rather as thinking tools to illuminate social practice, in this case an instance of
policy intervention in the South African tertiary sector.

It must be acknowledged that Bourdieu derived his concepts from other
thinkers, adapting them as he saw fit. His use of the term '*cultural* capital', for
example, signals a break with a Marxist analysis to contend that both material
and non-material resources are efficacious in the struggle for domination within
society. Habitus and field were also adopted from other thinkers and adapted
in various ways (see Bourdieu, 1985; Nash, 1999; Maton, 2012). Whatever their
origins – and bearing in mind that these ideas also evolved within Bourdieu's
own corpus – it is crucial that the connection between these concepts and their
integrity within Bourdieu's broader frame is maintained. There is ample
evidence in the literature of the dangers of a single tool being 'operationalized'
in a common sense way. As a result of the confusion created by the multitude
of ways in which cultural capital had been operationalized – and this was in 1988
– Lamont and Lareau wrote 'We are now reaching a point where the concept
could become obsolete' (1988, p. 153). The same could probably be said for
the notion of habitus (Reay, 2004; Atkinson, 2011). Indeed, Maton (2012)
warns against stripping habitus from 'its crucial relationship with field in
generating practices and its dynamics qualities' (p. 62), a common tendency in
educational research. When used alone, Bourdieu's concepts are 'often little
more than theoretical icing on an empirical cake' (ibid.).

The thinking tools alluded to thus far – field, capital and habitus – form a
coherent triad that encapsulates Bourdieu's theoretical framework:

> A field consists of a set of objective, historical relations between positions
> anchored in certain forms of power (or capital), while habitus consists of
> a set of historical relations 'deposited' within individual bodies in the form
> of mental and corporeal schemata of perception, appreciation, and action.
>
> (Bourdieu and Wacquant, 1992, p. 16)

According to Bourdieu, social practice arises from the meeting of two
evolving logics or histories (Bourdieu, 1993a, p. 46), one in objective social
structures and the other deposited in individual bodies in the form of habitus.
Neither field nor habitus unilaterally determines social practice but it emerges
from the meeting of 'history incarnate in bodies as dispositions and history
objectified in things in the form of systems of positions' (Wacquant, 2008,

p. 269). These positions, as mentioned above, are anchored in certain forms of power and it is the struggle for these species of capital that Bourdieu considers to be the 'fundamental dynamic of all social life' (Swartz, 1997, p. 136).

A field can be thought of as a system of positions in social space but also as a *relatively autonomous* sphere of play that prescribes its own values and regulative principles (Bourdieu and Wacquant, 1992). The logic that governs a field hinges on the maintenance of autonomy and the necessity to distinguish itself from other fields. For example, in the artistic field, the maxim 'art for art's sake' describes the ideal pursuit of art without any immediate concern for economic profit. The university field is underpinned by the principle 'knowledge for its own sake' (Maton, 2005). This autonomy is *relative* because fields are constantly under threat from heteronomous influences and discourses from adjacent fields. Maton (2005) explains this notion in his application of Bourdieu to higher education policy:

> A field's autonomy is illustrated by the way it generates its own values and markers of achievement, but the relative nature of this autonomy means these values are not alone in shaping the field; economic and political power also play a role, albeit in a form specific to each field.
>
> (pp. 689–90)

As mentioned in the discussion of the empirical context, fields maintain their autonomy by strategically assimilating discourses impinging on them from other fields.

The reference above to a 'sphere of play' draws attention to Bourdieu's likening of social practice to a game. As already mentioned, conflict over the forms of capital that are active in a field drives social action. In this sense, a field is a 'space of conflict and competition' (Bourdieu and Wacquant, 1992, p. 17) between opponents who are taken in by the game and strive to accumulate and wield power in their struggle for domination. Bourdieu refers to the notion of *illusio* to describe actors' *investment in the game* (ibid., p. 98). The extent to which actors become invested depends on their trajectory and their initial exposure to the workings of the field. As they begin to appreciate the forms of power on offer and begin to perceive the implicit rules of the game, they are taken in, almost unconsciously, and become invested in the stakes of the field. Even if two agents oppose one another bitterly, the very fact that they are playing the game indicates their implicit agreement that the stakes are worth fighting for (ibid., p. 98). The opposite of *illusio* is indifference – agents are not only uninterested in the stakes of a field, they are 'unmoved by the game' (Bourdieu and Wacquant, 1992, p. 116). Bourdieu borrows the term '*ataraxy*' from the Stoic philosophers, whose aim it was to reach an untroubled state of mind, as an antonym for *illusio*. It is important here to distinguish between participation in a field as a space of power, and belonging to an organizational structure or an institution. Although an individual might be employed at a university, for example, he or she might be indifferent to the games that are played in the field and the forms of power that are on offer.

Understanding the properties of the field and how actors become invested in the game or whether they are excluded – or exclude themselves – is crucial in the development of an *empirical understanding* of the specific forms of capital operating within any field.

> People are at once founded and legitimized to enter the field by their possessing a definite configuration of properties. One of the goals of research is to identify the active properties, these efficient characteristics, that is, these forms of *specific capital.* Thus there is a sort of hermeneutic circle: in order to construct the field, one must identify the forms of specific capital that operate within it, and to construct the forms of specific capital, one must know the specific logic of the field. There is an endless to and fro movement in the research process that is quite lengthy and arduous.
>
> To say that the structure of the field – note that I am progressively building a *working* definition of the concept – is defined by the structure of the distribution of the specific forms of capital that are active in it means that when my knowledge of forms of capital is sound, I can differentiate everything that I need to differentiate.
>
> (Bourdieu and Wacquant, 1992, pp. 108–9, original emphasis)

In the present study, this process was made considerably easier by the work done in *Homo Academicus* in which Bourdieu (1988) identifies the two forms of power operating in the university field – intellectual (or scientific) capital which corresponds with the inward-looking, autonomous principle of 'knowledge for its own sake' – and academic capital, which corresponds with the heteronomous principle. These forms of power are simply cultural and economic capital, respectively, which have been *reinterpreted* in the university field (see Figure 9.1 below). Intellectual capital is linked to 'scientific renown' and is governed by the 'logic of research' (Bourdieu, 1988, p. 74) while academic capital, which is more temporal, is linked to the instruments of reproduction and corresponds with position in the institutional hierarchy (ibid., p. 84).

The university field (rectangle no. 3) lies towards the pole of cultural capital (Bourdieu, 1996) as it is closer to the artistic field (Swartz, 1997) than the economic (or political) field. It occupies a dominant position within the broader field of class relations (rectangle no. 1) but a *dominated* position within the field of power (rectangle no. 2). The ways in which economic and cultural capital are distributed in society as a whole – at a maximum at the poles and decreasing as one moves across the field – results in a chiasmatic ('X') arrangement. The distribution of intellectual and academic capital in the university field follows the same pattern. Bourdieu gives a hint of how these forms of power appear empirically:

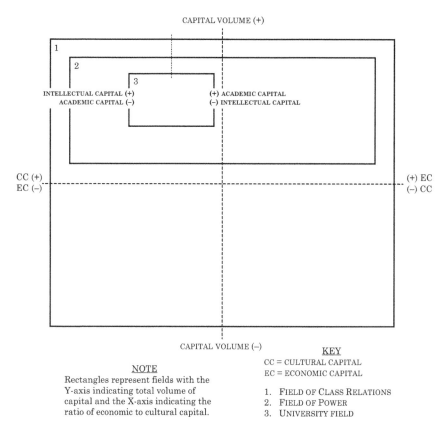

CAPITAL VOLUME (+)

1

2

3

INTELLECTUAL CAPITAL (+)   (+) ACADEMIC CAPITAL
ACADEMIC CAPITAL (–)   (–) INTELLECTUAL CAPITAL

CC (+)   (+) EC
EC (–)   (–) CC

CAPITAL VOLUME (–)

KEY
CC = CULTURAL CAPITAL
EC = ECONOMIC CAPITAL

NOTE
Rectangles represent fields with the
Y-axis indicating total volume of
capital and the X-axis indicating the
ratio of economic to cultural capital.

1. FIELD OF CLASS RELATIONS
2. FIELD OF POWER
3. UNIVERSITY FIELD

Figure 9.1 The location of the university field and associated forms of capital – adapted
from Bourdieu (1993b, p. 38)

It is understandable that academic power is so often independent of
specifically scientific [intellectual] capital and the recognition that it attracts.
As a temporal power in a world which is neither actually nor statutorily
destined for that sort of power, it always tends to appear, even in the eyes
of its most confident possessors, as a substitute, or a consolation prize. We
can understand too, the profound ambivalence of the academics who
devote themselves to administration towards those who devote themselves,
successfully, to research – especially in a university system where institutional
loyalty is weak and largely unrewarded.

(Bourdieu, 1988, p. 99)

A proper grasp of the logic governing the forms of capital active in the
field is obtained only once the empirical context has been engaged and the
data analysed. As mentioned above, this is a gradual process and is 'tightly

interconnected' (Bourdieu and Wacquant, 1992, p. 99) with the comprehension of the structure of the field. The discussion thus far has focused on the relationship between field and capital within the relatively autonomous social space of higher education and how this space is located within broader society. What follows is a discussion of how the systems of positions that make up the field are incarnated in individual agents in the form of habitus.

As mentioned already, the struggle over capital drives social practice. The outcome of a contest between two agents within a field depends on three factors: the *structure* of their capital, that is, both the volume and type of capital that an agent has access to; the *evolution* of the structure of capital over time; and the *ability* to wield capital and the skill and strategy by which an agent is able to 'play the game'. Importantly, it is not only the stakes *of* the field – the forms of capital – that agents struggle over but also the structure of the field itself. In other words, everything is a stake in the struggle of the game including what counts as capital, their relative strengths in a specific field, the tacit rules of the game, the boundary of the field and so forth. All of these properties are contestable and are part of the game. In reference to the boundary of the field, Bourdieu for example notes that the *right of admission* is a universal property of fields: 'There is a struggle within the object over who is part of the game, who in fact deserves the title' (Bourdieu and Wacquant, 1992, p. 245).

These struggles point to a deeper conflict over *legitimation* and are governed by two competing 'principles of hierarchisation' (Bourdieu, 1996, p. 270). On the one hand is the principle that corresponds with the cultural hierarchy, intellectual capital and the defence of the autonomy of the field; on the other hand is the principle corresponding with the social hierarchy and academic capital, and the introduction of heteronomous influences: 'Every field is thus the site of an ongoing clash between those who defend autonomous principles of judgement proper to that field and those who seek to introduce heteronomous standards because they need the support of external forces' (Wacquant, 2008, p. 269).

Just as a field can be likened to a game, so habitus can be thought of as the 'sense of the game' (Bourdieu, 1990a), an appreciation for the social structures that agents inhabit. Once a social actor is taken in by the game, she develops skills and learns strategies appropriate for the game in terms of its struggles and rewards, and learns to wield the forms of power on offer. As her sense of the game develops through perception and action, the structure of the field becomes inscribed on her being as 'mental and corporeal schemata', as mentioned on page 134. The struggles and conflicts that an agent encounters as he traverses any number of fields shape the habitus, which can be thought of as 'embodied history, internalized as a second nature and so forgotten as history – the active presence of the whole past of which it is the product' (Bourdieu, 1990b, p. 56).

This returns us to the idea of field and habitus as evolving histories, as 'two distinct social logics [that] are interpenetrating and mutually generating' (Grenfell, 2012, p. 214). The power structure of a field, as a set of objective

historical relations, is embodied by individuals as mental and corporeal schemata
– the habitus. However, the habitus also acts as a 'structuring structure'
(Bourdieu, 1990b, p. 53) in that agents are able to transform or reinforce the
structure of the field as they struggle over its rules, limits, recognized forms of
capital and so on. Perhaps the relationship between field and habitus is best
described in terms of the 'ontological complicity'

> between the agent (who is neither a subject or a consciousness, nor the
> mere executant of a role . . .) and the social world (which is never a mere
> 'thing' even if it must be constructed as such in the objectivist phase of
> research). Social reality exists, so to speak, twice, in things and in minds,
> in fields and in habitus, outside and inside of agents. And when habitus
> encounters a social world of which it is the product, it finds itself 'as [a]
> fish in water,' it does not feel the weight of the water and takes the world
> about itself for granted.
>
> (Wacquant, 1989, p. 43)

This characteristic complicity between habitus and field is what makes it
possible to use narrative inquiry to illuminate social structure. While narrative
accounts normally provide a *subjective* reading of the social world, analysing the
'habitus constituents and life trajectories' (Grenfell and James, 1998, p. 173)
may be used to reveal the contours of *objective* social structures.

> To speak of habitus is to include in the object the knowledge which the
> agents, who are part of the object, have of the object, and the contribution
> this knowledge makes to the reality of the object. But it is not only a matter
> of putting back into the real world that one is endeavouring to know . . .
> It means conferring on this knowledge a genuinely constitutive power.
>
> (Bourdieu, 1984, p. 467)

Used in this way, narrative inquiry can be thought of as a method for
embedding of Bourdieu's theoretical tools. The following section returns to the
empirical context to explicate the contribution of narrative analysis to the
mapping of the field of higher education.

Constructing the research object: empirical groundwork

As mentioned in the introduction, the intention of using Bourdieu's framework
was to understand how a policy to roll out a foundation programme would
influence South African higher education. In order to do this, it was necessary
to establish the site for empirical work. Naidoo's (2004) analysis of the field of
higher education in South Africa at the time of the democratic transition was
useful in this regard. Her observation that the field was divided into distinct

tiers resulted in an English-medium and another predominantly Afrikaans-medium university being chosen as institutional case studies. Both of these institutions are well established and may be described as research-intensive in the South African context. The aim was to construct the field as a trans-institutional space of power but also to explore how language, culture and, indeed, 'race', continue to mark the field despite two decades of democracy at the time of the investigation. To this end, a historical analysis of these institutions was conducted with particular attention being paid to their relationship to the political sphere.

Because of the author's background in engineering as well as the involvement of various industrial companies in the establishment of foundation programmes in South Africa – the role of the mining giant Anglo American is especially relevant here – engineering was chosen as the disciplinary context for the study. The context of engineering had an influence on the field but this was found to be relatively minor and is not explicitly considered in the discussion of method that follows. This decision meant that the foundation programmes within the engineering faculties at the two case study institutions were the specific locations for the investigation into the impact of the foundation programme policy on higher education. The history and structure of these programmes was documented, and a quantitative analysis was undertaken of the students who had passed through these programmes since their inception. Finally, in order to contextualize the foundation programme policy initiative that was the focus of the study, a review of higher education policy since the democratic transition was undertaken.

These sources – a historical analysis of the case study institutions, the documentation of the engineering foundation programmes and the policy analysis – are crucial groundwork for the construction of the research object. While these data sets did not explicitly refer to Bourdieu's theoretical framework, the final level of analysis specifically employed narrative inquiry to mobilize Bourdieu's theoretical tools. Semi-structured interviews were performed with 21 individuals from various sectors of the field. These included interviews with seven mainstream professors from a range of the traditional engineering sub-disciplines, interviews with seven 'academic development managers' who were involved in administering or organizing foundation programmes, and seven more interviews, mainly with foundation programme staff.

The first set of interviews, consisting of those conducted with mainstream engineering professors, were used to map the field. This is the focus of the section that follows the discussion of method below. The other interviews were used to theorize academic development[2] as a field phenomenon (see Kloot, 2014), which is the focus of the subsequent section that highlights the dangers of using narrative inquiry. The other interviews were used to determine the location of foundation programmes within the field of higher education that are not part of this discussion (but see Kloot, 2015).

Method of the current study

Narrative inquiry is a powerful tool by which to understand the subjective motivations of agents. According to Polkinghorne (1995), narrative 'preserves the complexity of human action with its interrelationship of temporal sequence, human motivation, chance happenings, and changing personal and environmental contexts' (p. 7). Clandinin and Connelly (2000) echo the notion of habitus in saying that in 'narrative inquiry, people are looked upon as embodiments of lived stories' (p. 43). Thus, in order to understand why agents act in the way that they do, we need to understand their perspective and subjective motivations. Polkinghorne's (1995) notion of *narrative analysis* was drawn on as a particular mode of inquiry for the empirical study under consideration. He defines this methodology as one that 'gathers events and happenings as its data and uses narrative analytic procedures to produce explanatory stories' (p. 5). This is similar to Kvale's (1996) notion of 'narrative structuring' (p. 192).

In the study under consideration, semi-structured interviews were used as the primary – but not the only – means of generating narrative data. Crucially, the interview schedule was constructed and conducted with Bourdieu's theoretical framework in mind. For example, at the start of the interview, respondents were asked to describe how they 'got into' higher education. The resulting narrative generally revealed respondents' *illusio* in terms of how they were 'taken in' by the game. This framed the rest of the interview and naturally led to a description of what was valorized and thus the agent's trajectory within the field in terms of the structure and evolution of capital. This included, for example, positions within the academic hierarchy and on boards and committees, postgraduate qualifications, publications, citations and research accolades, etc. These all contributed to a qualitative measure of agents' habitus in terms of the *structure and evolution of capital*.

After this, the interview was guided towards a discussion about foundation programmes *from the perspective of the respondent*. Care was taken to avoid imposing any rhetorical or common sense ideas in the interview situation as to why these programmes had been devised or what they were supposed to do. Respondents were invited, on the basis of the momentum of their narrative, to share their views on how these programmes came about and their interpretation of their purpose within the institution or in terms of their alignment with the government's efforts to transform higher education (DoE, 1997, for example). If the respondent was involved in managing or teaching on a foundation programme, the nature of this relationship was also explored.

The contested nature of foundation programmes meant that struggles or conflict were inevitably part of respondents' stories. This was not only true for those who were working or had worked on foundation programmes but also for mainstream academics who often had strong views about the role of foundation programmes in the institution or in the broader context of post-

Table 9.1 Coding categories used to organize the interview transcriptions

Code category	Reason
industry	These categories were included in order to identify the sections of the interview that dealt with the relationship of power between the university field and these realms.
political research	Care was taken not to set research and teaching up against each other in the interview situation but discussion often revolved around tensions between these activities.
teaching	This category was included mainly for respondents from the
foundation	mainstream in order to flag their references to the foundation programme.
conflict	Since conflict, according to Bourdieu, is the motor cause of all social activity, this category was included to flag instances of struggle. These instances often provided insight into characteristics of the field.

Source: (Kloot, 2011)

apartheid society. Given the importance of conflict in Bourdieu's framework, such issues were explored in order to help refine the contours of the field.

The interviews were audio-recorded (after consent was obtained) and transcribed. The transcription was then colour-coded according to six categories. The purpose of this 'loose' coding was simply to organize the data for the next stage of analysis. The categories employed in the coding process are listed in Table 9.1 with a description of the reason for including the coding category. As can be seen, these categories are related to Bourdieu's framework but are deliberately generalized so as to avoid imposing a rigid scheme on the data.

After this coding, the transcription was used to write up a separate document, termed the 'interview narrative', which encapsulated respondents' social trajectories. The audio recording was retained in order to ascertain meaning when representative excerpts were later chosen to document the research process.

As mentioned above, semi-structured interviews were not the only means of generating narrative data. Information from curricula vitae, National Research Foundation submissions or follow-up emails was used to substantiate the narratives generated in the interview context. There were even occasions on which these sources revealed crucial omissions in the interview data that were extremely useful in determining the structure of the field.

Mapping the field of higher education

To illustrate how narrative analysis enables the mapping of the field, the interview narratives of three professors from the English-medium university,

Emerston,[3] will be considered. The first two, Andrew Edmund and Steven Williams, occupy extreme positions in the field since they valorize different types of capital. The third, Sebastian Nicholls, combines intellectual and academic capital and thus occupies a powerful position in the centre of the field.

After a brilliant undergraduate career, Prof. Andrew Edmund worked in industry for a few years to fulfil his bursary obligations. For a number of reasons, including the fact that he did not find it intellectually stimulating, he was dissatisfied and returned to Emerston University. He did his master's degree and then his PhD and worked as a research officer for 15 years before being appointed to a research chair. In the excerpt below, Andrew demonstrates how his trajectory into higher education has a bearing on his position and disposition in the field:

> So I grew up in a very strong, very focused research-minded environment and it is that strong-minded which I perceive Emerston to mean when it says that it's a research-led university. So I will cling to the name 'research-led university' even when it comes to impacting undergraduate teaching, for example. Because if we're a research-led university, we should be led by research and we teach undergraduates second. Now I know there is a huge tension in that issue, massive tension, and those tensions are intensifying and have been over the last 10 years.

It is quite clear that Andrew's position is strongly anchored in the form of power that Bourdieu calls intellectual capital. The logic of research governs his 'time-economy' (Bourdieu, 1988), which means that he resists spending any extra time on undergraduate teaching. Elsewhere in the interview he reveals that he is quite prepared to be a 'crusty old professor' in the eyes of his undergraduate students because of his commitment to Emerston as a 'research-led university'. This allowed him to accumulate vast quantities of intellectual capital: he is one of the most cited engineering professors in the world. On the other hand, the form of power connected to the heteronomous principle of the field, academic capital, does not appear to be important to Andrew. It is interesting to note, for example, that he had occupied the position of Head of Department for five years but did not mention this at all in the interview.

Associate Professor Steven Williams studied engineering and was on such good terms with the Head of Department that he was effectively promised a post if he decided to return. This he did after seven years of working for the family business, a general dealership in the town where he grew up. Once back at Emerston, he began working in the engineering department from which he had graduated. Steven became a dedicated teacher and an efficient administrator, and grew to enjoy his work, especially in terms of his interactions with students and staff.

> So I was happy as Larry, I mean, I really was enjoying my work . . . I knew what I was doing and so I got to the stage where I said, 'To hell with

research! I'm happy as I am and provided I can go on doing what I'm doing, and nobody's going to shout at me, I'm very happy.' And nobody did, I mean, [the Dean], as I said, then started fighting for me on other fronts to get me an associate professorship.

This excerpt reveals a great deal about the field. Without any pressure to do research, Steven would not have felt the need to take some sort of position against this activity. However, safe in the knowledge that no one was going to 'shout at him' for not doing research, he was able to exclaim, 'To hell with research!', and focus his energies on management and governance. The reason that he was able to take such a stance was that he had found favour with the Dean of the Faculty, who appointed him Assistant Dean of Undergraduate Affairs, the first such appointment in the faculty. This suggests that the capital underpinning Steven's position is almost wholly academic capital.

The choice not to conduct any research meant that it was unlikely that Steven would be promoted to the level of Associate Professor by conventional means. This also reveals how the university field, like the field of cultural production, functions like the 'economic world reversed' (Bourdieu, 1993b). The production of research outputs is associated with intellectual capital, which is derived from the pole of cultural power in society. Rewarding this activity through promotion – and thus by economic means – serves to entrench the autonomy of the field. However, the fact that Steven says the Dean 'started fighting' to have him promoted shows that the rules of the game are contestable.

While Steven was eventually promoted, it is significant that he did not achieve a full professorship but remained at the level of Associate Professor until he retired after working at Emerston for 34 years.

The third professor whose narrative will be considered here demonstrates that 'doubling up' (Bourdieu, 1988, p. 104) the two forms of capital available in the field is possible. Prof. Sebastian Nicholls studied engineering at a respected university in the United States and continued to study his master's at another institution in that country. On occasion, he lectured for his supervisor and it was here that the academic bug 'got him'. When he first mentioned this phrase I asked him what he meant and he explained:

The academic bug, to become an academic: it's the look you get from the students when you're watching them when you're teaching and you can see their eyes light up or you can see their eyes go sleepy and you know where you're doing well or you're doing badly and I got excited.

This delightful phrase suggests the notion of *illusio*, but we must be careful to link what appears to be a love for teaching too closely to investment in the game. Interestingly, Sebastian goes on to describe how the academic bug evolves into the 'research bug' once one realizes that 'being a teacher is not enough'. However, rather than dedicating himself to research like Andrew or occupying himself with administration like Steven, Sebastian managed to accumulate significant quantities of both intellectual and academic capital. The result was a solid research career and a steady climb up the ladder of the institutional hierarchy until he was promoted to professor. He was also a departmental head for a total of nine years and became involved in a number of management and administration tasks within the university. Here Sebastian discusses what it takes to be a Head of Department.

> To begin with I think the Head of Department requires to be a person who represents a good, all-around profile. I mean, you can't just be a good teacher because then he hasn't got the bug of the research and then he can't stimulate the research part of the department. He won't have the same affinity to some researcher coming along and telling him, 'Look, please, get me off these 10 lectures . . .'

For Sebastian, the academic bug, through all of its stages and with all of its facets, results in the formation of an 'all-around' academic, someone who is able to teach, consult, take on administrative responsibilities and do academic research.

At the end of his career he occupied a powerful position in the centre of field. Although he is now an Emeritus Professor, Sebastian still does research and continues to teach the occasional course in the department in which he served. In fact, at the time of writing he is enjoying his 50th year at Emerston!

These excerpts from the interview narratives of Andrew, Steven and Sebastian give a hint of how useful narrative inquiry can be as a method for embedding a Bourdieuian perspective. It is not difficult to imagine how a fuller analysis of these narratives would allow a more fine-grained mapping of the field. Although it is not possible to go into the details here, offsetting these narratives against the four narratives of professors from the Afrikaans-medium university reveals the influence of the institutional context and illuminates how the struggle over language, culture and 'race' at a national level moulds the field. The positions of all of these agents within the university field are illustrated below.

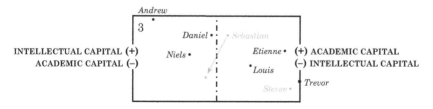

Figure 9.2 The positions of eight respondents in the university field
Note: Sebastian and Steven are coloured grey since they were retired at the time of the interviews

At this stage it is possible to reflect on some of the benefits of using narrative analysis. First, narratives are relatively straightforward to document. People generally enjoy talking about themselves and what matters to them in the interview situation and, if guided through appropriate questions, are ready to engage in discussion about the struggles that they are facing. Second, the resulting narrative provides a means of characterizing the habitus although care must be taken not to conflate these. If the researcher is mindful of the particular field under consideration and the forms of capital that are active within that field, the narrative *can reveal an agent's social trajectory* through the lens of Bourdieu. This begins with their investment in the field, various markers which indicate the accumulation of capital and, once the agent has become established, provides insight into the struggles for the stakes of the field. Third, narrative inquiry can provide keen insights and elucidate details about the field that are difficult to obtain through other means. Of course, personal accounts of the workings of power must be treated with care as the following section demonstrates. However, the multiple perspectives afforded by narrative inquiry provide a robust means of constructing the field, as long as the empirical groundwork has been done and the interviews are performed with Bourdieu's framework in mind.

The dangers of using narrative accounts

In order to demonstrate the dangers of using narrative inquiry, data from an interview with Prof. Trevor Norfolk will be drawn on. This was a particularly rich interview that was carried out on two separate occasions, the total interview time adding up to about three hours.

Trevor had been involved with foundation programmes since the mid-1980s and was (and still is, even though he is now retired) a strong advocate for them as a strategy to assist educationally disadvantaged students. He has been instrumental in the formulation and drafting of government policy for foundation programmes over many years and was thus well aware of the impending policy that was the focus of my investigation. As such, Prof. Norfolk is an influential figure in the sphere of academic development in South Africa.

When asked about how he entered higher education, Trevor spoke about getting 'really hooked' on education when he started teaching in a 'coloured' school during the apartheid years:

> Education was something that seemed to be an area that I felt I could make some kind of contribution. It was politically very relevant at the time and I think what truly interested me and – the taste – and what gripped me about it was that it was a mixture of the political and the social. I mean, education being something that is a crucial element of political and social development but at the same time something that was very concrete.

I didn't want to be a politician, you know, or anything of that sort, I was not a military activist or anything but there was an area here . . . I think what grabbed me was the possibility of real change.

After working for some years in education publishing, Trevor was appointed Director of Academic Support Programmes (ASP) at Emerston University. This small inter-faculty unit was established in the 1980s as cracks began to appear in the apartheid edifice. While Emerston had always been – rhetorically at least – opposed to separate education, as the prospect of democratic elections became more and more likely it began to prepare for the inevitable. Although it was still officially a 'white' university at the time, the ASP was tasked with finding ways to assist the small number of black students who had managed to gain admission by special permission from the Ministry of Education.

Driven by a strong personal desire to contribute to change through education in South Africa, Trevor took his job very seriously. He was, however, surprised to discover that not everyone was in favour of what he was trying to do. His efforts to seek assistance for students that were struggling were met with resistance by some 'established heads of department and other power brokers' at Emerston:

Prof. Norfolk: What really struck me, and what still interests me about this area, was that I came in as a lecturer with a BA Honours and heading this funny thing called the ASP so I found it extremely puzzling that established heads of department and other power brokers in the place would get really angry with me. You know, I'd be sitting across the desk from them and asking for some concession or whatever and I would find fierce hostility going on. People frothing at the mouth, you know . . . I began to think, 'How can I, or what I stand for be so threatening?' because, of course, it took me aback completely, and it was very disturbing to get yelled at in that way. But I began to think, 'Oh well, there's something more in this than meets the eye because there must be something that is inherently threatening to people and therefore it's got some kind of power.'

BK: What is that?

Prof. Norfolk: I think to a large extent it was the threat to established ways of doing things. It was the barbarians at the gates. So I say that while many people would have espoused a non-racial viewpoint, they actually still saw black people as the enemy of standards and if you let them in, you were going to go down the tubes.

The final quotation has to do with foundation programmes, initiatives that Trevor and his colleagues from the ASP in the early days were instrumental in developing.

So we, you know, we had to do something systemic about it and yet, how could we against this massive monolith like Emerston? . . . These impressions grew on us more and more and the understanding became that you can't just leave this to individual will and, you know, willingness to co-operate. You actually have to bring about systemic changes . . . Hence what came about with what we now call extended programmes, we would have called them foundation – we still use the term – we would have called them foundation programmes at the time . . . I think the key thing about them was that they were trying to address one of the fundamental systemic problems by creating an introductory curriculum that was closer to meeting the students where they were at. So it was trying to deal, systemically, with what was fundamentally a systemic problem.

These three excerpts reveal Trevor's deeply personal investment in higher education, the motivations governing his career trajectory, the struggles that he encountered in his role as Director of the ASP and his confrontations with racism, and the relevance of his narrative to a study of foundation programmes in South African higher education. Given his intimate involvement in the development and establishment of foundation programmes, and his ongoing work in foundation programme policy, Prof. Norfolk's coherent and persuasive narrative is directly relevant to the study at hand.

However, there are real dangers in approaching this narrative armed with Bourdieu's theoretical tools. For example, Trevor's reference to being 'hooked' by education seems to fit with the notion of *illusio* and his subsequent employment as Director of the ASP at Emerston suggests that he quickly gained access to the field of higher education. It is tempting, in line with other voices in the literature (Clegg, 2009a, 2009b), to construe the space of academic development as a sub-field within the field of higher education, or even a field in its own right, and situate Trevor's actions within this space of play.

Such a move requires parallel assumptions about the type of capital that he wields. This seems logical given the vitriolic reaction of various 'power brokers' at Emerston to his challenge to the 'established ways of doing things', according to his account. This form of power might be named *academic development capital*, defined in terms of its opposition to conservative ways of being in higher education. This is not incompatible with the ways in which the notion of capital has been adopted and adapted in the literature (see Bathmaker *et al.*, 2013; Wood, 2014).[4] From this position it would not be difficult to argue that Trevor embodies a particular disposition, a habitus that is characterized by sympathy to student concerns, advocates equality in education and is inclined towards the promotion of teaching and learning. While some might argue that this is a perfectly valid 'heterodox' reading of Bourdieu (Burke *et al.*, 2013), the result is in fact 'little more than a *metaphorizing* of data using Bourdieuian language' (Grenfell, 2012, p. 224).

In the light of the empirical groundwork described above, with a sound knowledge of the forms of capital that are active in the field and building on the structure of the field as developed in the previous section, the real value of this narrative to the study can be grasped. First of all, it is evident that Trevor possesses very small volumes of the forms of capital active in the university field as defined by Bourdieu. Although his position as Director of the ASP suggests a measure of academic capital, this was not accrued in the usual way (see Kloot, 2009) and thus does not give much leverage in the field; the volume of intellectual capital that he possessed at the time was similarly small. This leads to the inevitable conclusion that Trevor is not part of the field of higher education or at least occupies a peripheral position in it (see Figure 9.2).

It is here that the notion of autonomy becomes critical to understanding the contribution of Trevor's narrative to the study under consideration. The struggle in which he became so deeply engaged, in Bourdieu's terms, was for the transformation of the structure of the field. Whereas the 'power brokers' at Emerston – a profile that comfortably fits Sebastian, for example – would naturally be led to defend the autonomous principles underpinning the field, Trevor was obliged to draw on forces external to the field in order to accomplish his mission. The power he wields, so clearly evident in the second excerpt above, is not the fictitious 'academic development capital' but a form of power emanating from the political sphere, which he was able to bring to bear on the university field. Such an analysis fits with Trevor's narrative of why he entered higher education and his being 'grabbed . . . [by the] . . . possibility of real change'. From his peripheral position in the field, Trevor was able to contest the rules of the game, challenge what counts as capital and dispute the traditional boundary of the field in terms of who is part of the game.

The point is that agents tend to represent the social world in accordance with their interests. Although it might not be readily apparent for someone involved in the academic development project in South Africa, Trevor's account of the workings of power in higher education is convincing. His experiences in confronting what he perceived to be an academically conservative (Kloot, 2011) 'system' and how foundation programmes arose in this context is particularly persuasive. His narrative thus serves to legitimate the academic development project and portrays foundation programmes as the solution to what he has constructed as a 'systemic problem'. The policy initiative under investigation in this study in fact rests on such a paradigm.

Without a sound understanding of the empirical context, it would not be easy to distinguish between the structure of the field and Trevor's competing representation. The temptation is to tailor Bourdieu's tools to foreground his representation in the ways suggested above. The 'findings' would then con- tribute to the promotion of foundation programmes and serve to further the noble causes of access, equality and redress in what remains a deeply divided sector (Wangenge-Ouma, 2013). Ironically, such an approach would also be to decline Bourdieu's invitation to reflexive sociology (Bourdieu and Wacquant, 1992), the central principle around which his theoretical tools were developed.

Conclusion

In this chapter, the empirical context of foundation programmes in South African higher education was used to illustrate both the advantages and the dangers of using narrative inquiry as a method for embedding Bourdieu's theoretical tools. It was demonstrated that, because narratives are relatively easy to document, they provide an accessible, qualitative representation of habitus and provide insights that are not easy to obtain by other means. Furthermore, the ontological complicity between field and habitus in Bourdieu's framework means that the structure of the field can be unveiled through an analysis of multiple narratives. This is provided, of course, that the narratives represent an agent's trajectory within the field in terms of the structure and evolution of capital.

Such a mapping of the field provided a basis for analysing the contested nature of foundation programmes. While anecdotal evidence suggested that these programmes were somehow constrained by the higher education system, it was not clear what was constraining them or how this 'system' might be characterized. Bourdieu's tools were invaluable in this sense and his notion of autonomy provided the means to understand the deep-seated contestations by the advocates of foundation programmes and those involved in academic development generally. As a method of embedding Bourdieu's theoretical concepts, narrative inquiry brought alive these competing discourses and also provided a very tangible sense of the structure and contours of the field and the different ways in which it was embodied by agents.

Notes

1 This includes those classified as black African, 'coloured' and Indian. It is acknowledged here that 'race' was used as a construct to institutionalize oppression in South Africa and such references are not intended to entrench racial classifications.
2 Also commonly known as 'educational development'.
3 The names of individuals and the institution are all pseudonyms.
4 My personal favourite is the form of 'bush capital' accumulated 'through hunting and shooting feral pig and kangaroos' (Funnell, 2008, p. 19) in the Australian outback!

References

Atkinson, W. (2011) 'From sociological fictions to social fictions: Some Bourdieusian reflections on the concepts of "institutional habitus" and "family habitus"', *British Journal of Sociology of Education* 32(3): 331–47.

Bathmaker, A. M., Ingram N. and Waller, R. (2013) 'Higher education, social class and the mobilisation of capitals: Recognising and playing the game', *British Journal of Sociology of Education* 34(5–6): 723–43.

Bourdieu, P. (1984) *Distinction: A social critique of the judgement of taste.* Cambridge MA: Harvard University Press.

Bourdieu, P. (1985) 'The genesis of the concepts of "habitus" and "field"', *Sociocriticism*, 2(2): 11–24.

Bourdieu, P. (1988) *Homo academicus*. Cambridge: Polity Press.

Bourdieu, P. (1990a) *In other words: Essays towards a reflexive sociology*. Stanford, CA: Stanford University Press.

Bourdieu, P. (1990b) *The logic of practice*. Cambridge: Polity Press.

Bourdieu, P. (1993a) *Sociology in question*. London, Sage.

Bourdieu, P. (1993b) *The field of cultural production: Essays on art and literature*. Columbia, NY: Columbia University Press.

Bourdieu, P. (1996) *The state nobility: Elite schools in the field of power*. Cambridge: Polity Press.

Bourdieu, P. and Wacquant, L. (1992) *An invitation to reflexive sociology*. Chicago, IL: University of Chicago Press.

Burke, C.T., Emmerich N. and Ingram, N. (2013) 'Well-founded social fictions: A defence of the concepts of institutional and familial habitus', *British Journal of Sociology of Education*, 34(2): 165–82.

Clandinin, D. J. and Connelly, F. (2000) *Narrative inquiry: Experience and story in qualitative research*. San Francisco, CA: Jossey-Bass.

Clegg, S. (2009a) 'Forms of knowing and academic development practice', *Studies in Higher Education*, 34(4): 403–16.

Clegg, S. (2009b) 'Histories and institutional change: Understanding academic development practices in the global "North and South"', *International Studies in Sociology of Education*, 19(1): 53–65.

DoE. (2006) *Funding for foundational provision in formally approved programmes: 2007/8 to 2009/10*. Pretoria, South Africa: Department of Education.

Funnell, R. (2008) 'Tracing variations within "rural habitus": An explanation of why young men stay or leave isolated rural towns in southwest Queensland', *British Journal of Sociology of Education*, 29(1): 15–24.

Grenfell, M. (2012) *Pierre Bourdieu: Key concepts*. London: Routledge.

Grenfell, M. and James, D. (eds). (1998) *Bourdieu and education: Acts of practical theory*. Oxon, England: Routledge Falmer.

Harvey, L. (2009) *Review of research literature focussed on foundation degrees*. Review done on behalf of Foundation Degrees Forward. Lichfield, Staffordshire, UK.

Kloot, B. (2009) 'Exploring the value of Bourdieu's framework in the context of institutional change', *Studies in Higher Education*, 34(4): 469–81.

Kloot, B. (2011) 'A Bourdieuian analysis of foundation programmes in the field of engineering education: Two South African case studies'. PhD thesis. University of Cape Town, Capetown, South Africa.

Kloot, B. (2014) 'A historical analysis of academic development using the theoretical lens of Pierre Bourdieu', *British Journal of Sociology of Education*. First online doi: 10.1080/01425692.2013.868785.

Kloot, B. (forthcoming) 'Curriculum modification as a driver for change in higher education: The case of South Africa', *Journal of Education*.

Kotecha, P., Allie, S. and Volmink, J. (1997) *Narset report: Issues relating to access and retention in science, engineering and technology in higher education*. Pretoria, South Africa: Department of Arts, Culture, Science and Technology.

Kvale, S. (1996) *InterViews: An introduction to qualitative research interviewing*. Thousand Oaks, CA: Sage.

Lamont, M. and Lareau, A. (1988) 'Cultural capital: Allusions, gaps and glissandos in recent theoretical developments', *Sociological Theory*, 6 (Fall): 153–68.

Maton, K. (2005) 'A question of autonomy: Bourdieu's field approach and higher education policy', *Journal of Education Policy*, 20(6): 687–704.

Maton, K. (2012) 'Habitus', in M. Grenfell, (ed.), *Pierre Bourdieu: Key concepts* (pp. 48–64). London: Routledge.

Nash, N. (1999) 'Bourdieu, "habitus", and educational research: Is it all worth the candle?', *British Journal of Sociology of Education*, 20(2): 175–87.

Naidoo, R. (2004) 'Fields and institutional strategy: Bourdieu on the relationship between higher education, inequality and society', *British Journal of Sociology of Education*, 25(4): 457–71.

Polkinghorne, D. (1995) 'Narrative configuration in qualitative analysis', in J. A. Hatch and R. Wisniewski (eds), *Life history and narrative: Influences of feminism and culture* (pp. 5–24). London: Falmer.

Reay, D. (2004) '"It's all becoming a habitus": Beyond the habitual use of habitus in educational research', *British Journal of Sociology of Education*, 25(4): 431–44.

Robbins, D. (1993) 'The practical importance of Bourdieu's analyses of higher education', *Studies in Higher Education*, 18(2): 151–63.

Swartz, D. (1997) *Culture and power: The sociology of Pierre Bourdieu*. Chicago, IL: University of Chicago Press.

Wacquant, L. (1989) 'Towards a reflexive sociology: A workshop with Pierre Bourdieu', *Sociological Theory* 7(1): 26–63.

Wacquant, L. (2008) 'Pierre Bourdieu', in R. Stones (ed.), *Key sociological thinkers* (pp. 261–77). London: Palgrave Macmillan.

Wangenge-Ouma G. (2013) 'Widening participation in South Africa', in Higher Education Funding Council for England, *International research on the effectiveness of widening participation* (pp. 1–51). Bristol, England: HEFCE.

Wood, B. E. (2014) 'Participatory capital: Bourdieu and citizenship education in diverse school communities', *British Journal of Sociology of Education*, 35(4): 578–97.

Part 4

Researching teacher education

Chapter 10

Turning a Bourdieuian lens on English teaching in primary schools

Linguistic field, linguistic habitus and linguistic capital

Naomi Flynn

The research project used to frame discussion in this chapter was a doctoral study of the experiences of English primary school teachers teaching pupils whose home language was not English in their previously monolingual classrooms. They taught in a region in the south of England which experienced a significant rise in the population of non-native English speakers following eastern European member states' accession to the EU in 2004 and 2007. The study focused principally on the teachers' responses to their newly arrived Polish children because Polish families were arriving in far greater numbers than those from other countries. The research aims focused on exploring and analysing the pedagogical experiences of teachers managing the acquisition of English language for their Polish children. Critical engagement with their experiences and the ways in which they did or did not adapt their pedagogy for teaching English was channelled through Bourdieuian constructs of linguistic field, capital and habitus. The following sections explore my reasons for adopting Bourdieu's work as a theoretical lens, the practicalities and challenges of incorporating Bourdieu's tools for thinking in data analysis, and the subsequent impact on my research activity.

Bourdieu as method for exploring the teaching of English

Bourdieuian constructs of field, habitus and capital have been used in analysis for the teaching of language and literacy perhaps primarily because of his work *Language and symbolic power* (Bourdieu, 1991) that theorizes the power relationships inherent in the promotion of standardized forms of language in classrooms. This work takes the notions of field, capital and habitus introduced in *The logic of practice* (Bourdieu, 1990b) and applies them to both the nature of language use of itself and to the nature of language use in the classroom. Bourdieu found fault with the view of linguists like Saussure and Chomsky, who put forward an image of language as coming from a store to which we all have equal access (Bourdieu, 1991, p. 43). Rather, he surmised, nations create a dominant form of language which transcends accent and dialect and which is potentially capable of unifying citizens from a range of linguistic backgrounds; in reality, however, it more commonly divides citizens into those who know the rules and those who do not (Luke, 2008). Inherent in this establishment of a dominant form of the language is an understanding that it becomes the one against which all other forms of language are measured (Bourdieu, 1991, p. 45). Thus, by default, those who are able to understand and use the dominant form of the language are able to gain access to employment and other aspects of the social and economic marketplace by virtue of their ownership of linguistic capital (Goldstein, 2008).

Grenfell (2012a) draws our attention to Bourdieu's view of language as a special kind of field in that language transcends all fields because it is the medium for communication (Bourdieu, 1977). Bourdieu identified the notion of the linguistic marketplace as a way of describing how language exchanges of themselves are a structuring feature through which agents are able to gain social and economic capital. Thus ownership of linguistic capital is pivotal as a bargaining chip whether that be fluency in a language that is valued over other languages, or sociocultural understanding of the rules relating to language use in any field. The position of language use as a key player in interaction in any field means that 'All language has a value ... and at every linguistic level' (Grenfell, 2012a, p. 51). Education as a field is therefore potentially instrumental in 'construction, legitimation and imposition of an official language' (Bourdieu, 1991, p. 47) and therefore something of a broker in terms of facilitating or inhibiting the flow of linguistic capital between teachers and children.

Education as 'field' is a broad construct and one that has been subdivided by researchers in order to explore the interrelationships of fields within fields. This subdivision has the useful potential to highlight the conflicting pressures on classroom practitioners in ways that are not necessarily apparent without the layers of analysis afforded by a Bourdieuian lens. Hardy (2012) explores the relationship of the field of education to the field of power; more specifically, she examines how teachers in the field of education are related to the expectations of policy for the curriculum which is generated by central government (field of power). Interestingly in her study she found that teachers are more likely to relate to their local field – their local authority or their school and their head teacher – in terms of who they wish to please, than to national expectations for the teaching of a subject. Thus, Hardy surmises, teachers' habitus appears more likely to be shaped by the local field than by the national field, despite successive governments' desire to shape practice from the top down. Nevertheless, there are those who recognize the social and political embeddedness of language policy in the field of power in particular and urge researchers to seek ways of highlighting how policy for language may foster symbolic violence through inequality (May, 2012).

In my own work Bourdieu's view of language as a form of embodied cultural capital, and the accompanying notion of a linguistic field or fields, had a natural match with analysis of primary school teachers working with children who did not speak English for several reasons: these related to the power inherent in English as a language and to the very particular nature of the curriculum and policy for the teaching of English in England. First, the position of English as a language that dominates discourse on a global scale imbues the English language with an immeasurable weighting of symbolic capital. This potentially generates a linguistic habitus among English language users that assumes without question the superior and desirable position of the language they use. The classroom has a linguistic 'sense of place' in which those lacking capital may be constrained, possibly silenced, by specific expectations of discourse (Bourdieu, 1991, p. 82). Luke, using a Bourdieuian interpretation of the pedagogy for literacy, proffers that reading and writing are gifts given by teachers to prospective literates (Luke, 2008, p. 71). Through this metaphor he likens teaching and learning to a commodity exchange which entails unspoken rules relating to obligation and responsibility. The teacher might see it as their role to modify and impose expectations of a code that will allow access to 'appropriate' forms of spoken English and standardized forms of written English. Furthermore they may be unaware of the extent to which their pedagogical choices for the teaching of English will support or inhibit the development of English in both their native-born and foreign-born pupils. In this way they have the potential to enact what Bourdieu identifies as the illusion ('illusio') of buying in to the game that is prescribed by the curriculum by reproducing values generated by government (Bourdieu, 1991, 1999).

Second, an important feature of the curriculum for the teaching of English in England is that it has been prescribed at national level since 1989. The curriculum is framed in overview through the National Curriculum programme of study for English, and during the years 1998–2010 was further defined through the guidance in the ambitious national strategies for teaching English (DfES, 1998, 2006) that sought to raise standards in reading and writing by dictating both the curriculum and the practical pedagogy for teaching language and literacy. At the time of data collection for my own research, teachers were working with a National Curriculum that had been in place since 2000 (QCA/DfES, 1999) and with the additional guidance provided by *The primary national strategy for English* (DfES, 2006) which gave detailed advice on how to plan and deliver the objectives for teaching English in both paper-based and online guidance. The fact that teachers were expected to use this documentation as the starting point for their teaching meant that the linguistic field for the teaching of English was, and remains, very clearly marked out for teachers in England. Something that became particularly apparent from the data was the way in which the linguistic field – and the sub-fields within the overarching linguistic field – unconsciously dominated teachers' classroom practice. The fact that teachers had become assimilated into a national framework that governed the decisions they made for their teaching had already been examined in broad terms (Moore *et al.*, 2002), and the ways in which linguistic field became important in data analysis of teachers talking about their practice for English teaching is explored in the next section.

Applying practical logic to data analysis: the position of subjectivity

Methodologically this project was framed within an interpretive paradigm and used interview as the principal research instrument. Interpretivist enquiry assumes that what we imagine is knowledge and truth is not an objective reality but is the result of our perceptions. Furthermore the interpretivist researcher sees a duality between objectivity and subjectivity that means the one is partnered by the other, and that the two are not necessarily separable as ways of either seeing or interpreting (Schwandt, 2000). Such a stance is closely matched to a Bourdieuian view that social scientists can only construct meaning when they take account of all levels of context for their participants and when they acknowledge their own habitus in both seeking and interpreting their data (Bourdieu, 1990b). It was particularly important during data collection and analysis that I acknowledged my own background, that of a researcher with practical-professional experience of the field of second language learning in inner-city classrooms, in order that I addressed the likelihood that I would make various evidence-free assumptions about my participants whose experiences were very different from my own.

The use of interview to gather data relating to language teaching was also matched to a Bourdieuian view of the world because I was exploring the nature of language teaching through a language-focused research method. That said, the Bourdieuian view of language as 'value laden' made analysing the nature of what teachers said about their language teaching, the ways in which they said it, and taking account of the context in which they were expressing their thinking, sometimes impenetrable and seemingly over-complex. Nevertheless, the fact that Bourdieu gives the researcher a clear account of his world view without defining a methodological prescription for the researcher allowed for flexibility in interpreting teachers' fields, habitus and capital that engaged my own linguistic habitus on a reflexive journey of enquiry. To deepen further the challenge of working with a Bourdieuian approach, it was also necessary to engage with his criticism of the academic who assumes that association with the practical field she is researching means that she shares an affinity with her participants (Bourdieu, 1990a). The difficulties of interviewing teachers, with whom I felt a professional fellowship, when I was positioned as 'the expert' in their eyes, took me by surprise. I had to work hard at openly exploring my erroneous sense of shared game playing that was based on an assumption that teachers and 'teacher as researcher' inhabit the same field.

Conceding the relationship between objectivity and subjectivity was made manifest in the adoption of a constructivist grounded theory approach to data analysis that merged Bourdieuian practical logic with the process of coding.

Within my research, the Bourdieuian constructs of field, habitus, doxa and capital were used to frame the generation of coding in the practice of constructivist grounded theory. Grenfell and James (1998) are critical of grounded theory as an approach because, in their view, it is precisely the kind of pseudo-scientific method despised by Bourdieu as attempting to create logic where there is none (Bourdieu, 1990b, p. 82). However, significantly, their criticism is related to Glaserian grounded theory and they may think differently of the more recent work of Charmaz (2000, 2014) in devising a form of grounded theory that matches the interpretive turn. Consistent with Bourdieuian theory, constructivist grounded theory respects the nature of research as presenting *a* reality – not *the* reality – that is grounded in a specific context of social and political history. For analysis of education in particular, with its complex fields within fields and the centrality of language to its operation, the match of Bourdieuian theory to constructivist grounded theory allowed for theory generation in a way that Bourdieu might recognize as logical practice.

The need to structure a coding framework of overarching node[1] families emerged after several iterations in the coding process. Initially I was subject to the belief that codes would somehow emerge from the data (Glaser and Strauss, 1967; Strauss and Corbin, 1998) and this resulted in a somewhat descriptive set of themes that principally reflected my own subjective and personally contextualized account of what I was 'reading' in the transcripts (Table 10.1). It was also true at this early coding stage that I had not intended using Bourdieuian constructs in the coding process, planning instead to layer on a Bourdieuian analysis post-coding.

The nodes in Table 10.1 show some move towards identifying node families, but they are arguably surface-level descriptors that have been generated largely through an informed but subjective practitioner-researcher lens. This was unsatisfactory because the value of simply reporting what I could 'see' was neither going to push any boundaries methodologically nor offer something new to the academy.

In order to bind some notion of objectivity, or perhaps reflexivity, to this subjectivity I chose to use Bourdieuian constructs explicitly to name node families. This construction of a framework for analysis grew from my understanding of the Charmazian view that 'we *construct* our grounded theories through our involvement with people, perspectives and research practices' (Charmaz, 2014, p. 17). The work of other researchers using what is described as Bourdieuian three-level analysis also influenced this choice. As noted in an earlier part of this chapter, field analysis supports the revelation of fields within fields and the embedded nature of policy with field (Hardy, 2012; May, 2012). Taking this further, three-level analysis encourages the researcher to seek explanations for the nature of agents' actions within fields through examination of their habitus and what is valued as capital within their social or professional field (Grenfell, 1996, 2012c). Coding of interview data using Bourdieuian constructs allowed for the possibility of researching the interrelationship

Table 10.1 Node titles from early coding

Nodes

Age of arrival makes a difference	Pedagogy – props or visual
Attainment – lack of English problem	Pedagogy – different from monolingual
Attainment – language development	Pedagogy – modelling
Attitude – other children	Pedagogy – no different
Attitude – cultural difference	Pedagogy – reading
Attitude – nurturing self esteem	Pedagogy – talk
Attitude to Polish – positive	Pedagogy – word level
Attitudes – teachers to EAL children	Pedagogy – writing
Confidence – training related	Polish children arrival circumstances
Confidence – feeling supported	Polish children early experience in school
Confidence – lack of	Polish children individual difference
Confidence – liaison inter-staff	Polish children settling in
Confidence – providing for EAL	Polish families and school
Experience of teaching EAL – teacher	Polish families and speaking English
Interview response – anxious	Research engaged
Metalinguistic awareness	Rise in number of EAL children
School anxiety about EAL	
School involvement EMAS	
School managing support for English language acquisition	
School prior experience of EAL	
Subject knowledge – limited	
Subject knowledge – understanding EAL issues	
Support EMAS – effective and how or not	
Tension – curriculum relevance for EAL	
Tension – PC	
Tension – role and time management	
Tension – streaming	
Tensions – age of arrival	
Tensions – funding support	
Tensions (class management)	

*EAL – English as an additional language; EMAS – Ethnic Minority Achievement Service between linguistic field and habitus for the possibility of 'mapping the field' and for identifying the role of linguistic capital in that field. The terms could inform the coding, but the codes were free to find their own homes as part of a reflexive process common to both Bourdieu and a Charmazian world view. This was not without its difficulties and the barriers to clarity in interpretation are discussed later in this chapter.

As coding generated nodes it became quickly apparent that there were two main stories emerging from the data: those of how policy and habits of practice worked to dominate teachers' classroom decisions, and of how their responses and the response of policy to the impact of migration in schools further influenced these decisions. Mapping the field involved mapping two seemingly separate fields – pedagogical and cultural – and tracking relationships across habitus, doxa and capital. Thus the way in which Bourdieu encourages the researcher to see data as relational (Grenfell, 2012b; Pahl, 2012) was apparent from the outset. I developed nodes according to the four constructs of field,

Table 10.2 Nodes related to field

PARENT NODE	1st-level child node	2nd-level child node	3rd-level child node
FIELD	Tensions	limited resources limited funding limited time leadership challenges philosophical difference	
	Curriculum influences	age-related policy-related school-related attainment-driven	

	Learning communities	teachers supporting
		  teachers
		beyond school
		teachers supporting
		  children
		children supporting
		  children and teachers	

	School philosophy	caring ethos other children accepting	
	Migration impact		
	EAL training limited		

habitus, capital and doxa and the following tables show examples from field and capital to make clear for the reader where analysis intersects across these notions (Tables 10.2 and 10.3). Note that in these later rounds of coding, node families generated subsets and thus became more complex than the single level titles in the early coding stage.

Exploring the examples of field-related nodes in the table above, the ways in which teachers' wider working communities impacted on their responses to their Polish children pedagogically and culturally became clear. There was a sense in which their decisions to change their classroom practice to accommodate their English language learners rested on notions of inclusivity that were common to their practice and the ethos of their schools. Similarly, their capacity to embrace cultural difference was nested within the same professional outlook. Thus their lives appeared governed by several fields: that of the nature of the curriculum and the nature of funding for schools which presented tensions for them, and that of their sense of moral purpose to support each other and their children which was generated by personal and group-related beliefs. This professional conflict between what policy demanded of them in relation to pupil attainment and what they believed they should be doing for their pupils was a key finding from the project (Flynn, 2013b), and one that might have remained invisible without Bourdieuian analysis. The reader may have already noted that within this paragraph my commentary moves towards discussion of habitus and doxa, and this fluidity between nodes was central to the marriage of Bourdieu with constructivist grounded theory.

Different forms of capital emerged from the coding process (Table 10.3), partly in response to their revelation of fields within fields and partly in response to the necessary exploration of both pedagogical and cultural responses in the teachers. The notion of linguistic capital was one already coined by Bourdieuian researchers such as Luke and Grenfell, and in Bourdieu's own writings, but within this project it came to mean several different things: the use of third-level child nodes was particularly important in revealing its complexity. Linguistic capital was apparent in teachers in the form of their own fluency in English, their responses to lack of fluency in English and their equating fluency in English to attainment. Finally, the notion of professional capital emerged in terms of the teachers' own subject knowledge about teaching either monolingual or second language learners, and this appeared to impact on their confidence or lack of confidence as practitioners facing linguistic difference in their classrooms.

Taking the nodes for field and capital together, within field it was necessary only to code comments as relating to 'migration impact', but recognition of this field encouraged the formation of nodes around social and cultural capital. Furthermore, within the coding related to doxa, nodes about teachers' responses to Polish parents and Polish children dominated analysis with much greater prevalence than coding of beliefs about teaching English. Thus, a study that had set out to explore teachers' pedagogy for teaching English to non-native

Table 10.3 Nodes related to capital

PARENT NODE	1st-level child node	2nd-level child node	3rd-level child node
CAPITAL	Linguistic capital	relative value of languages teachers' sense of capital use of Polish English fluency	*impact on attainment* *parents' level of* *children more fluent* *children less fluent* *confidence to speak* *English* *Polish better than native* *English*
	Professional capital (Experience)	research oriented inexperienced in L2 inexperienced	
	Professional capital (Subject knowledge)	L1 development L2 generic subject knowledge	*L1[1] writing* *phonics teaching* *L1 spoken* *L2 spoken* *L2 writing* *L1 SK is L2 SK* *relationship to English lessons* *L2 reading*
	Social capital	migrant parents in school attributed to Polish children social deprivation	
	Cultural capital	teacher perceptions of national differences difference celebrated difference generalized Polish culture and faith travel experience	

1 L1 refers to first language, which in this context means the teachers' first language of English, and L2 to second language, which in this context means the teachers' understanding of second language acquisition

speakers evolved into a study that also explored teachers' responses to the children of migrant families. It became impossible to separate the one from the other, and this development was fostered explicitly by the Bourdieuian approach which took account of deep levels of context in teachers' and children's lives. In particular it generated examination of the ways in which Polish children conform, in teachers' minds, to the image of a 'model minority' (Li, 2005; Ng et al., 2007) and of how relationships of teachers and Polish children are founded on 'elective affinities' (Grenfell and James, 1998). This revelation of fields operating together supported a richness in the enquiry that fostered outputs beyond my common publication sphere (Flynn, 2013a), and this opportunity as a researcher was both unexpected and profoundly developmental in my thinking.

Dealing with fuzzy logic and responding to determinism

The 'richness' described above was not the product of a straightforward journey using Bourdieu as a framework for interpretive enquiry. The fact that other researchers write of their frustration at misuse of Bourdieu's constructs, habitus in particular, is not without good reason (King, 2000; Nash, 1990). In my early thinking about where Bourdieu's logic of practice might sit in my data analysis the constructs appeared too readily malleable to subjective interpretation by the researcher both in terms of what they represented and in their use in application. The notion of habitus, in particular, appeared contradictory: simultaneously an unconsciously structuring structure (Bourdieu, 1990b) and 'an open system of dispositions that is constantly subjected to experiences' (Bourdieu and Wacquant, 1992, p. 132). This suggests that the habitus is at once the invisible limiter on change and yet subject to change. Finding a path through this anxiety about the value of using the logic of practice was supported largely though the strengths in existing work by Reay (1998) and by Grenfell, whose Bourdieuian take on education resonated with my own understandings of the field. Ultimately, however, the researcher using a Bourdieuian lens will need to grapple with their choice and whether it is one that allows them to simply report subjectively on what they think their data say, or to immerse themselves in first exploring their own habitus as a route to finding objectivity within subjectivity.

Welding the use of constructivist grounded theory to Bourdieu's constructs was the way in which I attempted this open acknowledgement of subjectivity, but this also was not without its problems. In coding the data it was necessary at times to make choices as to where transcript extracts might be housed, and at other times coded extracts obviously belonged to more than one node family. For grounded theory purists this might appear fuzzy and altogether lacking in any methodological rigour. This was definitely a complication in coding but also unavoidable in order to reflect a Bourdieuian view that field, habitus and capital are fundamentally interrelated. Coming to the coding with predetermined overarching nodes could have restricted interpretation, but in fact seeing the data as relational felt liberating and supportive of genuine enquiry.

Nodes relating to habitus and to doxa were particularly difficult to code separately because of the proximity of habitus to doxa conceptually. Indeed at times, it was difficult to house data within any particular node because of the interrelated nature of all aspects of Bourdieu's practical toolkit. The whole thrust of Bourdieuian thinking is that it is not easy to unravel the 'immanent dynamics' between field and habitus (Bourdieu and Wacquant, 1992, p. 140). The extent to which the habitus has internalized the rules of the field means that the two are mutually interdependent and it is recognition of this inseparability that is of itself of interest to research (p. 127). Nevertheless, in interpreting the stories of individuals, it is incumbent on the researcher to represent those individuals as truthfully and honestly as possible (Brinkmann and Kvale, 2005), and the use of Bourdieu as a lens threatened that at times.

The threat came in the form of attempts at generalizations across the group when coding within the nodes related to each of the constructs. While using a Bourdieuian framework layered on to a constructivist grounded theory approach, I was probably unconsciously looking for commonalities and perhaps assuming a group habitus, when much of the time, even in settings where more than one teacher was interviewed, the teachers were very much individuals. Their individuality was rooted in their past histories and their present teaching context, and this was different in every case. There was a movement from the individual to the group and back to the individual throughout the analysis and this is illustrative of the difficulties involved in attempting to deconstruct practice as something logical. However, again, Bourdieu would defend his own theory here and would no doubt criticize the use of grounded theory for being a research tool that attempted to find logic in practice where there is none (Bourdieu, 1990b; Grenfell and James, 1998). Thus, the search for commonality was perhaps more a shortcoming in interpretation and my use of the method, than a failing attributable to the method or the theory in themselves.

The claim that Bourdieuian theory is unacceptably deterministic is supported to some extent by the above commentary. While Bourdieu might describe a theory of practice of seemingly infinite flexibility in its use as an interpretive tool, his view of the world is essentially 'agonistic' (Wacquant, 2008) and this may have led to perceptions of problems for teachers and children where there were none. If, as researcher, I went into this research with a past history of criticism of the curriculum for English, it is possible that I adopted an 'agonized' approach to interpreting the data and unconsciously, or even consciously, sought out tensions and contention. In this way, I may have determined what I was going to see in the data rather than allowing the data to speak for themselves (assuming such a thing were possible).

Resisting any inherent determinism in Bourdieu's way of thinking was particularly important to a researcher with a practitioner background, and this made for findings that at times sat apart from a Bourdieuian interpretation of the classroom. Perhaps most importantly, the teachers saw it as their responsibility to manage the language acquisition needs of their Polish children regardless of whether they felt equipped to do this. They articulated anxieties about their potential to do the best by their pupils, and the revelation of the conflicting fields they were operating in made clear why this was, but it was essential to ensure that their professionalism was reported respectfully. This sense of moral imperative observed in the teachers was at odds with Luke's observation that teachers seek to maintain the dominance of their own language in the classroom, particularly when that language is English (Luke, 2008). Moreover, it did not sit comfortably with a depiction of pedagogic action as symbolic violence when associated with teachers' unconscious attempts to assert the dominance of the language of power (Bourdieu, 1991; Bourdieu and Passeron, 1990). The teachers demonstrated that their craft is about more than a subject and that they seek to put children's needs at the heart of their professional decisions. Holding on to this important positive outcome from data analysis was challenged throughout by the methodological choices I had made.

Moving on with Bourdieu: the theorizing practitioner

Despite some reservations about the use of Bourdieu as a lens for examining the practice of teachers in England, the process of engaging with his logic of practice has revealed several new research possibilities that might otherwise have remained unexplored. The first of these is the use of Bourdieuian ways of thinking to construct analysis of the ways in which the policy for the teaching of English in England is founded on assumptions relating to the value of English as a language. The second is the potential use of Bourdieu to unravel where teachers have been unconsciously subject to decades of centralized curriculum control, arguably a form of symbolic violence, which has reduced if not eliminated their sense of agency to make choices about how and what they teach. Finally, the use of Bourdieu's constructs of capital in particular is valuable for exploring teachers' responses to children from different national and ethnic groups as the minority ethnic population in English schools continues to diversify.

The use of Bourdieu to explore policy, particularly how policy plays out in practice, is potentially acutely powerful in examining education. Something that emerged strongly from my research was the positioning of the teaching of EAL as secondary and subservient to the teaching of English to monolingual learners; the monolingual habitus operated as a structuring structure at both individual and institutional level. This has fostered an interest in exploring how policy positions teachers' thinking about their practice and how that thinking is realized practically. Work by Leung (2001) and Safford and Drury (2013) has usefully identified the problem that the teaching of second language learners is perceived within a monolingual curriculum framework, and also that such teaching is not perceived as important subject knowledge of itself. While recognition of these findings brings much to our practical thinking about multilingual pedagogies, it can be further enriched through a Bourdieuian lens. If we take up Gerrard and Farrell's (2013) exhortation to use Bourdieuian analysis in disambiguating the policy–practice interface, we become better able to explore the complexity in why practice is as it is. To this end, my future research will focus on analysing where the discourse of policy for the teaching of English in England is located in a narrative resting on notions of 'the right kind' of English and a lack of acknowledgement of differences needed in pedagogy for second language learners. In laying bare the fields operating on and shaping the architecture of policy we are better equipped to critique its shortcomings and, more importantly, argue for alternatives in ways that go beyond the understandable lamentations of researchers identifying 'problems' with policy.

As a researcher who identifies with practitioners, while also acknowledging the difference in being a member of the academy and all that brings with it, perhaps the most frustrating and discouraging finding from my study was that of the reduction over decades of teachers' agency as curriculum makers within their own classrooms. In an effort to offload any sense of determinism that might easily overcome the Bourdieuian researcher, my response to this has been to shape research that engages teachers in exploring their pedagogy for EAL at classroom action-research level; this is with a view to publishing guidance for the teaching of EAL learners that marries theory and practice and counteracts the reduction in guidance for non-native speakers in the most recent version of the National Curriculum. It was tempting to continue in breast-beating vein and bemoan the lot of a profession who can only act as blindfolded players in a game where the rules change on the whims of government and the inspector-ate but, perhaps ironically, other policy-related developments have supported a more positive approach to moving on. Publications from the OECD (2011) and the UK government for 'research that provides high-quality evidence to inform policy development and delivery' (DfE, 2013) partner a significant report from BERA/RSA (2014) which indicates a need to engage teachers in researching their own practice. If those of us engaged in research in the classroom want to see teachers take ownership of their professional lives again, we need to work alongside them in order that they become game-makers who create their own rules of the field, and who theorize their practice in ways that enable them to consciously question the institutional habitus of policy where it does not account for the needs of their pupils.

Finally, Bourdieuian analysis led me to fields I didn't expect to occupy in that it forced me to engage with the literature relating to migration studies in an effort to understand the responses of teachers to the migrant families and children in their schools. This was a necessary but not often a comfortable journey. The constructs of field and capital in particular supported revelation of layers of interpretation that went seemingly well beyond the pedagogical and this was challenging for an educational researcher who is not defined as a sociologist. Perhaps, however, this is evidence of just how powerful Bourdieuian analysis is: in openly acknowledging the subjectivity operating at all levels of analysis, the researcher is able to see layers of meaning that may be considerably outside her usual range of sight. The data revealed a need for further exploration of teachers' responses to difference; particularly when those differences are less obvious in children of the 'new migration' (Favell, 2008) who are largely white-skinned. There were assumptions about the nature of Polish children as 'hard-working' that sat at odds with conversations I had around the same time with teachers in Poland, and the complicated construct of the 'elective affinities' between teachers and children has been explored by myself and others (Flynn, 2013a; Kitching, 2011; Sales *et al.*, 2008). But there is more to do here in terms of exploring the stereotypes of nationality that teachers may hold, stereotypes that do not relate to earlier research around pupils from backgrounds associated with England's colonial past, and of how these stereotypes are inextricably linked to fluency in English. Opportunities for interdisciplinary research framed in a Bourdieuian approach appear both obvious and desirable.

Note

1   The term 'node' is used as a noun to describe an emerging theme following the practical process of coding (verb) in the qualitative data analysis programme NVivo.

References

BERA/RSA. (2014) Research and the teaching profession: Building the capacity for a self-improving education system, Final report of the BERA-RSA inquiry into the role of research in teacher education. London: BERA.

Bourdieu, P. (1977) 'The economics of linguistic exchanges' (R. Nice, trans.), *Social Science Information, 16*(6): 645–68.

Bourdieu, P. (1990a) *In other words: Essays towards a reflexive sociology.* Cambridge: Polity Press.

Bourdieu, P. (1990b) *The logic of practice* (R. Nice, trans.). Cambridge: Polity Press.

Bourdieu, P. (1991) *Language and symbolic power.* Cambridge: Polity Press.

Bourdieu, P. (1999) *The weight of the world: Social suffering in contemporary society* (P. Ferguson, trans.). Cambridge: Polity Press.

Bourdieu, P. and Passeron, J.-C. (1990) *Reproduction in education, society and culture* (2nd edn). London: Sage.

Bourdieu, P. and Wacquant, L. (1992) *An invitation to reflexive sociology.* Cambridge: Polity Press.

Brinkmann, S. and Kvale, S. (2005) 'Confronting the ethics of qualitative research', *Journal of Constructive Psychology, 18*(2): 157–81.

Charmaz, K. (2000) 'Grounded theory: Objectivist and constructivist methods', in N. K. Denzin and Y. S. Lincoln (eds), *Handbook of qualitative research* (2nd edn), (pp. 509–35). London: Sage.

Charmaz, K. (2014) *Constructing grounded theory* (2nd edn). London: Sage.

DfE. (2013) *Research priorities and questions: Teachers and teaching*. Nottingham, UK: DfE.

DfES. (1998) *The national literacy strategy framework for teaching*. London: DfES.

DfES. (2006) *Primary framework for literacy and mathematics*. Nottingham: DfES.

Favell, A. (2008) 'The new face of east–west migration in Europe', *Journal of Ethnic and Migration Studies*, 34(5): 701–16.

Flynn, N. (2013a) 'Encountering migration: English primary school teachers' responses to Polish children', *Pedagogies: An International Journal*, 8(4): 336–51.

Flynn, N. (2013b) 'Linguistic capital and the linguistic field for teachers unaccustomed to linguistic difference', *British Journal of Sociology of Education*, 34(2): 225–42.

Gerrard, J. and Farrell, L. (2013) '"Peopling" curriculum policy production: Researching educational governance through institutional ethnography and Bourdieuian field analysis', *Journal of Curriculum Policy*, 28(1): 1–20.

Glaser, B. and Strauss, A. (1967) *The discovery of grounded theory: Strategies for qualitative research*. Chicago: Aldine.

Goldstein, T. (2008) 'The capital of "attentive silence" and its impact', in J. Albright and A. Luke (eds), *Pierre Bourdieu and literacy education* (pp. 209–32). London: Routledge.

Grenfell, M. (1996) 'Bourdieu and initial teacher education: A post-structuralist approach', *British Educational Research Journal*, 22(3): 287–303.

Grenfell, M. (2012a) 'Bourdieu, language and education', in M. Grenfell, D. Bloome, C. Hardy, K. Pahl, J. Rowsell and B. Street (eds), *Language, ethnography and education* (pp. 50–70). London: Routledge.

Grenfell, M. (2012b) 'Bourdieu: A theory of practice', in M. Grenfell (ed.), *Bourdieu, language and linguistics* (pp. 7–34). London: Continuum.

Grenfell, M. (2012c) 'Methodology', in M. Grenfell (ed.), *Pierre Bourdieu: Key concepts* (2nd edn), (pp. 213–28). Durham: Acumen.

Grenfell, M. and James, D. (eds). (1998) *Bourdieu and education: Acts of practical theory*. London: Routledge.

Hardy, C. (2012) 'Language and education', in M. Grenfell (ed.), *Bourdieu, language and linguistics* (pp. 170–93). London: Continuum.

King, A. (2000) 'Thinking with Bourdieu against Bourdieu: A practical critique of the habitus', *Sociological Theory*, 18(3): 417–33.

Kitching, K. (2011) 'Interrogating the changing inequalities constituting "popular", "deviant" and "ordinary" subjects of school/subculture in Ireland: Moments of new migrant student recognition, resistance and recuperation', *Race, Ethnicity and Education*, 14(3): 293–311.

Leung, C. (2001) 'English as an additional language: Distinct language focus or diffused curriculum concerns?', *Language and Education*, 15(1): 33–55.

Li, G. (2005) 'Other people's success: Impact of the "model minority" myth on underachieving Asian students in North America', *KEDI Journal of Educational Policy*, 2(1): 69–86.

Luke, A. (2008) 'Pedagogy as gift', in J. Albright and A. Luke (eds), *Pierre Bourdieu and literacy education* (pp. 68–92). London: Routledge.

May, S. (2012) 'Language policy', in M. Grenfell (ed.), *Bourdieu, language and linguistics* (pp. 147–69). London: Continuum.

Moore, A., Edwards, G., Halpin, D. and George, R. (2002) 'Compliance, resistance and pragmatism: The (re)construction of schoolteacher identities in a period of intensive educational reform', *British Educational Research Journal*, 28(4): 551–65.

Nash, R. (1990) 'Bourdieu on education and social and cultural reproduction', *British Journal of Sociology of Education*, 11(4): 431–47.

Ng, J. C., Lee, S. S. and Pak, Y. K. (2007) 'Contesting the model minority and perpetual foreigner stereotypes: A critical review of literature on Asian Americans in education', *Review of Research in Education*, 31: 95–130.

OECD. (2011) Building a high-quality teaching profession: Lessons from around the world. Paris.

Pahl, K. (2012) 'Seeing with a different eye', in M. Grenfell, D. Bloome, C. Hardy, K. Pahl, J. Rowsell and B. Street (eds), *Language, ethnography and education: Bridging new literacy studies and Bourdieu* (pp. 89–109). London: Routledge.

QCA/DfES. (1999) *The national curriculum for primary schools in England and Wales.* Nottingham: DfES Publications.

Reay, D. (1998) 'Cultural reproduction: Mothers' involvement in their children's primary schooling', in M. Grenfell and D. James (eds), *Bourdieu and education: Acts of practical theory* (pp. 55–71). London: Falmer.

Safford, K. and Drury, R. (2013) 'The "problem"of bilingual children in educational settings: Policy and research in England', *Language and Education*, 27(1): 70–81.

Sales, R., Ryan, L., Rodriguez, M. L. and Alessio, D. A. (2008) *Polish pupils in London schools: Opportunities and challenges.* Middlesex, England: Multiverse and Social Policy Research Centre, University of Middlesex.

Schwandt, T. A. (2000) 'Constructivist, interpretivist approaches to human inquiry', in N. K. Denzin and Y. S. Lincoln (eds), *Handbook of qualitative research* (2nd edn pp. 118–37). London: Sage.

Strauss, A. and Corbin, J. (1998) *Basics of qualitative research: Techniques and procedures for developing grounded theory* (2nd edn). London: Sage.

Wacquant, L. (2008) 'Pierre Bourdieu', in R. Stones (ed.), *Key sociological thinkers* (pp. 262–77) London: Palgrave Macmillan.

Chapter 11

Stimulating conversations between theory and methodology in mathematics teacher education research

Inviting Bourdieu into self-study research

Kathleen Nolan

Over the years, my research in the field of secondary mathematics teacher education over the years has drawn on a number of methodologies and theories and in various combinations with each other. During this time, I have grappled with the relationships and tensions between methodology and theory and myself as researcher. This chapter traces the evolution of that research, ending at a new beginning in the form of a discourse analysis informed by Bourdieu's social field theory and applied, in this case, to my self-study research as a mathematics teacher educator. The conceptualization of this Bourdieu-informed discourse analysis (BIDA) emerges out of my desire to (re)define new relationships and conversations between self-study methodology and Bourdieu's social field theory (BSFT) – ones that resist privileging and separating the threads of methodology and theory in research. BIDA for self-study has several dimensions, each of which will be individually unpacked in this chapter, followed by an application of BIDA in the specific context of my self-study research on my role as a university faculty adviser (supervisor) in prospective mathematics teachers' field experiences.

In the words of Bourdieu (2008, p. v), 'this is not an autobiography' (I hope). Nor is it intended as a genealogy of my research endeavours. It is my intention, however, to draw on my own research story as a means for reflecting on how/why I was drawn to BSFT and how it has shaped theory–methodology conversations in my research.

Research in the field of mathematics teacher education

The field of mathematics teacher education is researched extensively from diverse perspectives, including those interested in theory–practice transitions from university courses to school practicum (Jaworski and Gellert, 2003), those concerned with understanding the skills and content knowledge required by mathematics teachers (Ball *et al.*, 2008; Chapman, 2013), and those focused on identity constructions in becoming a mathematics teacher (Brown and McNamara, 2011; Williams, 2011).

Recently, the field of teacher education research has been paying close attention to the structures and roles of that specific component of teacher education programmes referred to as the school practicum or field experience (Cuenca, 2012; Falkenberg and Smits, 2010). Research indicates that prospective teachers view the practice-based experiences of teacher education as the most important part of their programme and the most significant influence on be(com)ing a teacher and shaping a professional identity (Britzman, 2003; Nolan, 2014a). At the same time, there is research suggesting that the field experience is mostly about compliance and regulation (Brown, 2008) and that school placements are frequently not well aligned with reform-based philosophies and pedagogies being advocated in teacher education programmes (Towers, 2010). Thus, the question of whether prospective teachers have opportunities to try new ideas and approaches in their school-based practicum or merely observe and mimic their cooperating teachers' practice (Britzman, 2009; Clarke *et al.*, 2013) is of great debate.

A sizeable portion of the research on/in field experience calls for a much stronger role to be played by the cooperating (mentor) school teacher, even to the point of calling for a practicum turn in teacher education (Mattsson *et al.*, 2011). It is precisely this practicum turn that is feared by Grenfell (1996) when he critiques governments and policy makers for promoting 'schools as the best place for training' (p. 289), thus reducing theory in courses and proposing practice 'as sufficient for gaining professional competence' (p. 289). Grenfell (1996) further laments that the increased involvement of schools (and corresponding decreased involvement of universities), coupled with the draw to language such as 'training' and 'competence', removes prospective teachers from the space/place where they have opportunities 'to engage with the contradictory elements of teaching and respond in line with their own developing pedagogic habitus' (p. 301), a valuable space/place Grenfell refers to as 'nowhere' (p. 297).

Supervision of prospective mathematics teachers in their field experience is one of the practices characterizing my work as a teacher educator. The research being discussed in this chapter (as an evolving story of my theory–methodology–analysis directions) takes up the issue of mathematics teacher education field experience, beginning with my research into the theory–practice transitions of prospective mathematics teachers as they engage in their field experience, and ending (for the sake of this chapter anyway) with a particular focus on a self-study of my role as faculty supervisor 'in the field'. It is worth noting that the research data itself is not the primary focus of this chapter but instead the story of how my research journey has been shaped and informed by BSFT, critical discourse analysis and self-study methodology.

The draw to Bourdieu's social field theory

Research in mathematics education shows that, in spite of many attempted interventions into the classroom practices of secondary mathematics teachers, traditional textbook and teacher-directed practices dominate (Lerman, 2001; Nolan, 2008). Encouraging prospective teachers to embrace inquiry-based pedagogies in school mathematics classrooms presents many challenges for teacher educators. In my work with prospective mathematics teachers as their supervisor during their field experience, I am perplexed by the complexity of transitions from theory to practice; that is, from university discussions and applications of inquiry-based pedagogies (conducted as part of their curriculum courses) to the actual implementation of the ideas/practices in their field experience classroom. In Nolan (2008), I wondered how it 'might be possible for these becoming teachers to transcend the *habitual* to think the *possible* in mathematics classrooms' (p. 159). Then one day, I stumbled upon a publication by Andrew Noyes (2004) on (re)producing mathematics teachers. From that article, I gained considerable insight into how I was conceptualizing these theory–practice transitions. As Noyes writes,

> Bourdieu's central concept of habitus illuminates the mathematics teacher socialisation context because it explains how embodied life history structures classroom practices. Bourdieu points out here that the agent (in this case the new teacher) can develop practices in the classroom that are transpositions of durable practices that he/she has already developed in other areas (fields) of life.
>
> (pp. 246–7)

An immediate 'aha' moment occurred for me. It wasn't about 'unsuccessful' theory–practice transitions; it was about habitus–field fits (between the fields of their school experiences as students and then as teachers) and misfits (between the fields of university teacher education and school mathematics classrooms). In and through the language of BSFT constructs, including especially an understanding of habitus–field fits, I began to appreciate 'that the habitat in which the student develops their practice has a conforming power, affecting the type of teacher they become' (Noyes, 2004, p. 253).

As a result of this encounter with the work of Noyes (2004), BSFT began to feature prominently as my research theory. Here, I briefly discuss two publications (Nolan and Walshaw, 2012; Nolan, 2012) which feature the use of BSFT to understand and unpack prospective mathematics teachers' experiences of teacher education field experience.

In Nolan and Walshaw's (2012) study of the field of (teacher education) field experience, we make use of BSFT to help 'reveal the ways in which inquiry pedagogy [in mathematics classrooms] is enacted through ambiguous and sometimes contradictory negotiations' (p. 348). Specifically, we draw on Bourdieu's concepts of practice, field, habitus, capital, doxa and misrecognition to understand prospective mathematics teachers' shifts (or lack thereof) towards inquiry teaching. With Bourdieu's theoretical constructs, we studied the social practice journey of one prospective mathematics teacher (Toni) as she negotiated her way in and between two specific fields of practice: the field of secondary schools, particularly mathematics classrooms (F1), and the field of university teacher education, particularly mathematics curriculum courses (F2). In that research, we found that 'in both of these two fields, specific (but quite different) forms of habitus and cultural capital are valued and (re)produced' (p. 349). In F2, promoting and using inquiry-based pedagogical approaches holds considerable cultural capital, while in F1 traditional teacher-directed approaches not only represent valuable cultural capital in that field (because such approaches reflect the cultural arbitrary being reproduced), but also a good habitus–field fit for Toni.

The field of teacher education and the university course, F2, on the one hand, imposed specific categories of being, acting and thinking that promoted inquiry pedagogy. Toni's past experience in school (the field of F1) as a student of mathematics, on the other hand, invested as it was in discursive codes of traditional mathematics pedagogy, established a different set of practices and social relations for the teacher and learner in the classroom. In particular, the image of an organized teacher with a well-structured lesson plan produced a network of structures and relations governing Toni's pedagogic actions in the field of the secondary mathematics classroom (Nolan and Walshaw, 2012, p. 357).

We found that:

> Unsurprisingly, the shift to an inquiry approach is severely bounded by the network of legitimate structures and practices in the field, including those forms of cultural capital that have the most purchase power ... The traditional structures of the field, along with the forms of cultural capital that are currently believed to hold value in the field, persuade teachers away from the dramatic shift in habitus that is demanded of inquiry teaching.
>
> (pp. 357–8)

In other research (Nolan, 2012), I draw on BSFT to present several pervasive discourses, or dispositions, that highlight prospective teachers' negotiations of conflicting habitus–field fits during their teacher education field experience. In that study, I asked the question: 'What are the discourses positioning and regulating prospective teachers in the mathematics field experience practice and how might awareness of these discourses facilitate meaningful discussion and reflection in teacher education programmes?' (p. 202). Using BSFT made me aware that these dispositions are not easily 'shifted', that they denote 'a manner of being, a habitual state (especially of the body)' (Bourdieu and Passeron, 1990, pp. 67–8). In that research text, I note that even though habitus and field are dynamic, a person will feel most comfortable in a field when his/her habitus is a good fit for the logic and operation of the field. The reflections put forth in that paper offer insights into the roles of mathematics teacher educators and teacher education programmes in general. I close Nolan (2012) by reflecting on 'how my practice as a teacher educator and faculty adviser must be (cross)examined as its own site of (re)production' (p. 214), a clear indication of a significant turn inward; that is, a turn towards an interest in self-study approaches to research.

The draw to self-study methodology

Even with the integration of Bourdieu's concepts and habitus–field (mis)fits in my research, I was still not satisfied with my research directions. While I could now understand how the structures and practices in the field limited agency in facilitating change in practice, I realized that I could do very little about it since I was setting out to study how *others* did (or did not) change (from traditional to reform-based teacher). It was a realization that drew me to self-study research methodology; that is, if I could not change others, I *could* focus on changing myself (Nolan, 2010). With a self-study approach, I am presented with opportunities for studying my own learning about what shapes my identity as teacher educator, supervisor and researcher. Thus, instead of focusing pre-dominantly on the habitus–field fit of prospective teachers, I began to explore my own habitus as a teacher educator, supervisor and researcher, focusing on what I could learn in and through my work with prospective teachers, as they construct (and are constructed by) official pedagogical discourses embedded in mathematics classrooms.

Self-study is defined as a methodological approach centred on intentional and systematic inquiry into one's own practice. Self-study has firmly established itself in recent years through its interrogation of pedagogy and practice in teacher education (Samaras, 2002; Sandretto, 2009). Samaras (2002) uses 'the word self-study to mean critical examination of one's actions and the context of those actions in order to achieve a more conscious mode of professional activity, in contrast to action based on habit, tradition, and impulse' (p. xiii). Similarly, Russell (2005) describes self-study methodology as a research design emphasizing 'the importance of attending to the gaps between our professional goals and our professional practices and by suggesting new perspectives for thinking about the processes of professional learning in and from practice' (p. 5).

Bullough and Pinnegar (2001) stress that a key 'aim of self-study research is to provoke, challenge, and illustrate rather than confirm and settle' (p. 20). Sandretto (2009) builds on this aim by proposing that we 'look for useful theoretical tools to do so' (p. 98) because, she states, the self-study of teacher education practices has generally drawn on humanistic discourses. In her study, she seeks to 'highlight the theoretical and methodological tensions . . . in a collaborative self-study using a post-structural theoretical framework' (p. 93). Similarly, other self-study researchers have found their own non-humanistic theoretical lenses, drawing for example on critical race and feminist post-structural theories (McNeil, 2011), theories of identity (Nicol, 2006) and living educational theories (Whitehead, 2009). Framing self-study in a strong theoretical framework like BSFT, however, is still rare in the self-study literature, despite Whitehead's (2009) call for students and teacher educators to engage 'with ideas on the social and cultural influences in learning from the work of Bourdieu . . . [in] repurposing of our professional practices' (p. 107). Though I responded to this call, few others have taken up his suggestion when it comes to engaging with the ideas of Bourdieu (as an exception, see Clift, 2009).

As I drew on both BSFT and self-study methodology, I wrestled with conceptualizing my own positioning and reflexivity as a researcher. Simply put, when I emphasized a strong theory in my research-writing, readers/reviewers did not easily digest a methodological discourse in that same text, and when I placed methodological design front and centre as a frame for my research, it seemed that no one really expected theory (or at least not a 'strong' one). In whatever I wrote, I felt that I was being asked to choose between featuring self-study (as methodology) or Bourdieu (as theory) in my work. I managed to elude this dilemma for a while by dropping all reference to a methodology and highlighting the role of theory (Nolan, 2012). Then, on the side, I pondered methodology–theory connections, referring to 'making sense' of BSFT as methodology (Nolan and Tupper, 2013). I was not content, however, with the separation and isolation of these two key threads of the research process.

I propose that self-study and BSFT are an all too often overlooked pairing of methodology and theoretical lens, a pairing that holds potential for (stimulating) a stimulating conversation together: that is, a conversation where each brings an invaluable and necessary voice to the room, space or text. One conversation starter includes how BSFT can be used to trouble the discursive network of relations in (the field of) university teacher education courses and field experiences, including troubling my own self-constructions of teacher educator/researcher and my inclination to produce orthodoxy in teacher education courses and field experience supervision. I became intrigued by the acts of proposing these theory–methodology conversation starters in the field of my research in secondary mathematics teacher education.

Context for the field of my research: self-study in mathematics teacher education

In the specific context of my university's four-year undergraduate teacher education programme, the culminating field experience is a four-month field (internship) experience in schools. Each prospective teacher (intern) is paired with a cooperating (mentor) teacher in a school and assigned a university supervisor (also called faculty adviser). Each supervisor works with approximately four interns over the internship semester, and is expected to visit, observe and conference with each intern three to five times during this four-month internship. Typically, my supervisory role positions me in the back of a high school classroom, observing an intern's mathematics lesson from start to finish, taking notes on carbon copy 'field experience observation' forms. This note-taking task is preceded and followed by brief pre- and post-conferences with the intern. Research indicates this is a common portrayal of supervision in teacher education programmes (Britzman, 2009; Zeichner, 2009).

I claim that my university's internship supervision model is problematic and 'deficient' for a number of reasons. Primarily, it is challenging to cultivate a mentorship relationship between supervisor and intern (not to mention cooperating teacher) based on only three to five visits over four months. Such limited contact is inadequate to bring about any substantive learning in/from practice, or to disrupt and challenge traditional teaching practices. As a field experience supervisor, my role in this model felt superfluous, even token. To address this feeling of tokenism, I initiated a self-study project to explore how I might expand/enhance my role through a blended real and virtual model for supervision during field experience.

The self-study, initially referred to as the 'e-adviser' project, took on various characteristics as it evolved over the years, and as I adapted my internship supervision approaches in response to research data. During each year of this self-study, a professional learning community was sustained both 'virtually' (through the use of desktop video conferencing as well as online chat and discussion fora) and through 'real' face-to-face professional development sessions with interns and their cooperating teachers. The 'real' professional development aspect of the project uses lesson study approaches that incorporate the recording and analysis of classroom teaching videos. This enhanced model for internship has served to expand my supervisory role, providing me with opportunities to study that role and how I might make it more meaningful to me and, I hope, to the interns and cooperating teachers also. In other words, my expanded and enhanced internship model has an aim of understanding what I can do, as a mathematics teacher educator, to enact my role as a supervisor differently/better/etc.

I would be remiss if I neglected to mention the more critical underpinning for the development of my enhanced internship model. While eliminating my own feeling of being superfluous or token served as the original impetus, the model also provided me with opportunities to challenge and disrupt notions of teacher education programmes as places to 'train' and 'prepare' teachers for the 'real' classroom, with field experience being viewed as the mere 'supervised' enactment of these preparation techniques. I became intrigued by the tensions and disruptions erupting as I endeavoured to move my role as a supervisor beyond tokenism in the field. At the same time, I was drawn to noticing highly complex interactions and relations with/in the field itself.

The draw to networks and graph theory

As I drew extensively on Bourdieu's key thinking tools (for example, habitus, field, cultural capital, doxa, misrecognition and symbolic violence), I became aware of how these thinking tools are much more productive for me in my research when conceptualized within a network of relations in the field (of field experience). With a fresh focus on Bourdieu's networks of social relations in a field, I was drawn to yet another field: the field of mathematics graph theory.

Bourdieu (1990a) claims that a person's habitus, or set of dispositions, in a social practice field are tightly bound up in and by the network of practices and discursive relations within that field. Grenfell (1996) clarifies these relations by offering the following:

> Individuals are embedded, located in time and space, which sets up relations. These relations are not simply self-motivated and arising from individual choices but immanent in the site locations in which they find themselves. Such relations are differential and objectively identifiable. They are structured structures, but, equally, structuring structures in a generative sense.
>
> (p. 290)

My theory–methodology–analysis conceptualization finally started to come together when I focused my attention on *my own positioning* within the network of relations in the field of teacher education field experience. Reflecting on my supervisory role within this network brought Bourdieu's game analogy to mind; that is, that adjustment to the demands of a field requires a certain 'feel for the game' (Bourdieu, 1990a, p. 66). Similar to games, social fields are constructed with specific structures and rules, and the relative smoothness of the game/field often depends upon the players accepting and following these rules without question, regardless of how arbitrary they might seem. At the same time, players/agents in the game/field continually draw on strategies in vying for better positioning within the game/field. This game analogy, along with a parallel flashback to my undergraduate days studying and researching in the field of graph theory, led to my introduction of a graph theory analogy for Bourdieu's network of relations in a social practice (Nolan, 2014b).

In Nolan (2014b; in press), I highlight the metaphorical connections between Bourdieu's conceptualization of social networks in a field and the mathematics field of graph theory. For the purposes of this network analogy, I use the term *nodes* to stand for the sources or agents in the network (including interns, cooperating teachers, and others in addition to myself as supervisor) and *links* (or pathways) to reflect the discursive relations between the various network agents that maintain and reproduce the complex network; all of this is represented by a directed graph with single or double arrowheads (see Clark and Holton, 1991). In Nolan (in press), I present and discuss several data storylines (each one presented as constituting a node and connecting pathway of the network) that convey my efforts to disrupt and reconceptualize the network of relations in teacher education field experience, with the ultimate goal of understanding how (or, if) my own professional practice as supervisor

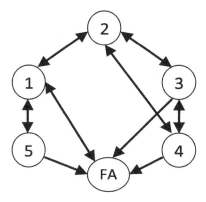

Figure 11.1 Graph theory network diagram
(Nolan, 2014b)

in the field might shape and influence a more dynamic view of these networks. Linking this research analysis to graph theory draws attention to how a mathematical structure such as a graph can be used to model key coupling relations between objects/agents, providing a way to visualize and critique the interactions between the structuring structures in Bourdieu's social networks. A graph theory network diagram, like that in Figure 11.1 (Nolan, 2014b), helps visualize these relations through one possible configuration of a directed graph, or digraph.

Presently, my research focuses on understanding how the network of relations in the field of field experience is shaping me as a supervisor and as a mathematics teacher educator, including how my own identity and learning is being (re)produced. The graph theory analogy is making this an interesting project by creatively drawing on the language of that field (for example, ego network, weighted graph, trivial graph, clique, and quiver) to connect with Bourdieu's field of social practices and networks of relations in my theory–methodology conceptualization.

The draw to more voices in the conversation: critical discourse analysis and Bourdieu's methodological principles

As I contemplated the conversations between theory and methodology (and resisted the pull to tease them further apart), I was also considering the value of critical discourse analysis (CDA) to my work. There is not one specific way to characterize research in CDA. In fact, in addition to drawing from different methodologies, studies in CDA draw from different theories and different forms of data (Wodak and Meyer, 2009, p. 5), not to mention how they define 'discourse' and 'critical' in different ways.

In using the word 'discourse' in my work, I closely associate it with the term 'discursive practice' or even 'discursive relation' since my desire is not to limit the definition of discourse to a strictly language-based, textual description. Instead, the definition of discourse most suited to my Bourdieuian self-study work is presented by Walshaw (2007) when she states that discourse means 'taken-for-granted "rules" that specify what is possible to speak, do, and even think, at a particular time' (p. 19). The primary function of these 'rules' is in 'systematically constituting specific versions of the social and natural worlds for us, all the while obscuring other possibilities from our vision' (Walshaw, 2007, p. 40). What makes my work 'critical' is embracing the tenet that 'social theory should be oriented towards critiquing and changing society, in contrast to traditional theory oriented solely to understanding or explaining it' (Wodak and Meyer, 2009, p. 6). Informed by BSFT, my aim is to critique and propose counter-discourses to dominant traditions in teacher education and in the teaching of school mathematics. Starting with the premise that CDA 'aims to question and critique discourses' (Jäger and Maier, 2009, p. 36), Jäger and Maier outline three areas of focus for CDA (which I adapt here by paraphrasing only slightly): (a) reveal the contradictions within and between discourses, (b) reveal how what can be said and done is heavily regulated, and (c) reveal the means by which discourse makes particular statements, actions and ways of being seem rational and beyond all doubt (despite their contextual nature) (p. 36).

While 'dabbling' in CDA, I was simultaneously engaging Bourdieu's writings at another level. I recognized that I had been drawing on Bourdieu's 'thinking tools' in a rather one dimensional and detached manner; that is, I was endeavouring to understand how his tools were each conceptualized individually as well as how they worked together within a field of relations, but I had much less awareness of Bourdieu's work at the methodological level (Bourdieu and Wacquant, 1992; Grenfell, 2008; Rawolle and Lingard, 2013). Grenfell (2008) synthesizes a number of Bourdieu's methodological writings (including that of Bourdieu and Wacquant (1992)) to arrive at a Bourdieuian methodological approach to research that adopts three guiding principles (p. 220). Rawolle and Lingard (2013), in advising against seeing Grenfell's guiding principles as stages in a research process, state that 'these principles continually interact in the conduct of research working with a Bourdieuian approach to methodology' (p. 131). With a similar focus on highlighting a dialectical relationship between theory and method, Fairclough *et al.* (2010) construct an analytical framework that builds on CDA and Bourdieu's advice for constructing the objects of research. Bourdieu's advice is to name the pre-constructed object of study (in their case, 'citizenship'), followed by 'identifying and characterizing the processes whereby the [pre-constructed object] has been given determinate and/or functional meaning' (p. 414). In other words, Fairclough *et al.* follow Bourdieu's advice to 'shift away from simply using pre-constructed categories or objects, towards exploring the practices involved in their construction and maintenance' (p. 414). These ideas and principles for Bourdieu's approach to socio-analysis can be summarized as:

1   The construction of the research object (Grenfell, p. 220); also described as 'name the pre-constructed object of study' (Fairclough *et al.*, p. 414) and 'the deconstruction of the research object' (Rawolle and Lingard, p. 131).
2   A three-level approach to studying the field of the object of research (the 'three levels represent the various strata of interaction between *habitus* and *field*' (Grenfell, 2008, p. 222)); identify and characterize the process whereby the pre-constructed object has been given determinate and/or functional meaning (Fairclough *et al.*, pp. 414–15); analyse and map the positioning of the field and agents within the field, especially in relation to the field of power (Rawolle and Lingard, p. 131).
3   Participant *objectivation* (Grenfell, p. 220); reflexivity (Rawolle and Lingard, p. 131).

These methodological principles of Bourdieu's approach to socio-analysis confirm that a purposeful weaving of methodology and theory, drawing on several of Bourdieu's key 'thinking tools,' can be used to construct a more formal approach to unpacking self-study research data. In fact, the conceptualization of my BIDA methodological framework represents that more formal approach, one that is heavily based on these descriptions of Bourdieu's approach to the analysis of social phenomena. To construct my BIDA framework, I draw on Jäger and Maier's (2009) areas of focus for CDA, Fairclough *et al.*'s (2010) CDA with Bourdieuian influence, and Bourdieu's own approach to the analysis of social phenomena as portrayed in Bourdieu and Wacquant (1992), Grenfell (2008), and Rawolle and Lingard (2013). Viewing the methodological principles through a critical lens compels me to tweak mildly and 'cherry-pick' the description that I identify with most closely in/for my work, while arriving at a construction that preserves the intent of the Bourdieuian principles and key elements of CDA. Granting significant methodological and theoretical licence to myself, I synthesize and tweak the sources to conceptualize my own BIDA framework for self-study research.

Prior to elaborating on this BIDA framework, I must first note one other significant influence on my work. I construct BIDA for self-study with knowledge of, and insights into, Bourdieu's own self socio-analysis (Bourdieu, 2008), which has been described as 'a very controlled return upon himself' (Bourdieu, 2008, p. x). In acknowledging his positioning as both subject and object of self socio-analysis, Bourdieu declares that a common difficulty of sociological analysis is 'the danger that the "objective intentions", which are brought out by analysis, will appear as express intentions, intentional strategies, explicit projects' (p. 69) of the researcher. While this declaration may have been Bourdieu's way of identifying a weakness in self socio-analysis, I actually interpret Bourdieu's self work as one that helps strengthen and uphold my own project of BIDA for self-study. Simply put, there are not many combinations of methodology and theory where the researcher can be both the research participant (the 'researched') and the one making sense of theory (the 'researcher'). Prior to engaging in self-study I often wondered, along with Britzman (1995), if research theorizing would 'make sense to the people behind my text' (p. 236). In self-study, I am 'the people behind my text,' the one whose conditions are being subjected to critique. Wodak and Meyer (2009) outline a general weakness in CDA critique, noting that the researcher's/analyst's position 'is rarely reflected in [her] understanding of critique' (p. 7). To counter this weakness, these authors proceed to draw on Bourdieu's notion of 'the social embeddedness of research and science', implying 'that critique can by no means draw on an outside position but is itself well integrated within social fields' (p. 7). I contend that these ideas productively position self-study in a strong relationship with CDA and, as noted earlier, also highlight a good fit with a Bourdieuian approach to the analysis of social phenomena. The final outcome: a BIDA for self-study research.

Bourdieu-informed discourse analysis (BIDA) for self-study research

In this closing section, I use the frameworks introduced above, along with my own understanding of BSFT and self-study methodology, to arrive at a conceptualization for BIDA. Following this, I provide a glimpse into how BIDA is presently being applied to self-study research in my role as a supervisor in the field of field experience. Aspects of this analysis have been presented in Nolan (2014b; in press), though those research texts do not explicitly use the BIDA for self-study approach. In fact, this is my first articulation of the three phases (or lenses) for analysis, so I turn to Bourdieu for words of wisdom in conveying how my research work is 'in a state that one may call "becoming", that is, muddled, cloudy, works that you usually see only in their *finished* state' (Bourdieu and Wacquant, 1992, p. 219). The BIDA framework is outlined below:

- Pre-phase: name (which involves both construction and deconstruction of) the pre-constructed object of study.
- Three-phase: study the field of relations, of which the research object is part, through three different lenses:

   a. The lens of the research object habitus and field: identify and characterize the processes by which the research object has been given determinate and/or functional meaning, and how these meanings are heavily regulated and maintained within the networks of social practice; in other words, focus on what the research object *is* and *does* (Bourdieu and Wacquant, 1992, p. 221).

   b. The lens of the role of Others in the network: identify and characterize the contradictions between and within discursive social relations (in field and in cross-field interactions), including a critique of text, actions and ways of being that have been rationalized (doxa and orthodoxies of the field); map the field and positioning (including habitus) of 'Others' in relation to the wider network of power relations.

    c. The lens of reflexivity: identify and characterize possible aspects of bias or distortion in the research process, including researcher positioning and actions that work to (re)produce the research object and discursive relations in the field.

The BIDA framework is presented above in general terms, making it valuable for considering its use in contexts other than self-study. However, since I am presently conceptualizing the BIDA framework in the methodological context of self-study, it is important to note that the outcome of the pre-phase will always be *self*. That said, a further step of qualification is required for an outcome of *self* since all researchers/persons have multiple identities/subjectivities that could become the self-study research (pre-constructed) object. In the research analysis introduced here, the *self* is that of me in the role of field experience supervisor. Hence, the pre-constructed object is that of 'supervisor' of prospective mathematics teachers' field experience.

Having engaged in the pre-phase by naming the research, or pre-constructed object of study (in this case, of self-study) as *self* as faculty 'supervisor', the task ahead is to engage the three-phase approach to studying/interrogating the (*self* as) supervisor within the network of relations. It is valuable to add that the focus of self-study does not assume a coherent, stable self. Hamilton and Pinnegar (1998) note that 'Self-study is the study of one's self, one's actions, one's ideas, as well as the "not self"' (p. 236). It is the 'not self' that encourages me to explore the role of 'others' in identity work. In fact, Walshaw (2012) offers that the identities we construct of ourselves 'are made in and through the pronouncements, interests and investments of others' (p. 107). In addition to reflective researcher journals as data, my self-study research project includes reflective contributions of 'others' involved in the research (primarily prospective and cooperating teachers) in order to describe and critique my own positioning relative to these 'others'.

a.   *The lens of the research object habitus and field*

In this first phase of the analysis, I seek to identify and characterize how supervisor has been given determinate and functional meaning; that is, to identify what a supervisor *is* and *does*. My university's written field experience manual outlines the roles and expectations of interns, cooperating teachers, and faculty advisers (supervisors) during the internship semester. The manual describes the roles and expectations of supervisors using, for example, the language of assist, share, be available, provide, monitor and model. Though it is not possible to cite here the full statements in each case, the meaning underlying the statements points to my role as a kind of 'side service', constructing a habitus as peripheral to the central agents in the field (that is, cooperating teacher and intern).

In addition to official internship manual discourse, interns construct their understanding of the roles and expectations of supervisors and cooperating teachers by listening to stories from interns of past years. These stories constitute a 'pre-constructed script' (Fairclough *et al.*, 2010) for interns. As an illustration, consider the interview I conducted with one intern when I asked her about my role as supervisor and how she perceived it. Her response was:

> Having you there is just kind of extra, I guess. I don't know if it's completely necessary . . . like, if I had had problems with [the cooperating teacher] then I would want you there, I would *need* someone else, but since we got along then the roles kind of seem the same to me.

Other responses over the years have described my role as 'a resource' and 'like a fine-tooth comb'. These metaphors and meanings for supervisor are easily sustained and perpetuated in the network of relations. Garrett (2012) claims that 'the triad is problematic before it even begins its work' (p. 159), stating that the university supervisor 'is "othered" into the third position as the student-teacher and mentor-teacher dismiss "theory for practice"' (p. 159). My involvement as university supervisor is noticeably 'othered', especially when I introduce disruptions in the process of traversing the usual paths in the usual ways in field experience.

A set of discourses, practices, and 'materialities' (Fairclough *et al.*, 2010, p. 415) serve to identify and construct the pre-constructed term of field experience 'supervisor', supplying determinate and functional meanings, often before I have even begun my work. It is evident that the least problematic approach for a supervisor in the field of teacher education field experience is to perform her/his role in agreement with these pre-constructed scripts, as such compliance will provide the most cultural capital among prospective teachers, mathematics teachers, faculty administrators and even faculty colleagues at the university. Fairclough *et al.* (2010) note how the cultural resources associated with the performance of the pre-constructed object 'are the product of a tension and negotiation between the power of the pre-constructed, and the power of situated agency' (p. 415).

b.   *The lens of the role of Others in the network*

BIDA provides an opportunity to draw on BSFT to study the network of 'Others' that carry significant weight in the social practice field of field experience and supervision. The graph theory network diagram presented earlier provides a way to visualize and critique the agents (or nodes) and the possible discursive relations (pathways) sustaining and maintaining that network.

The digraph example was presented in Nolan (2014b), where I name and describe several storylines to convey one possible configuration of agents and discursive relations in the field of field experience. The various agents (and corresponding storyline themes depicting the relations) are: interns (the norm of sitting in the back of the classroom; metaphorically speaking – 'not for the likes of us'), cooperating teachers (avoiding distractions and disruptions to intern's growth), programme structure (intern placement protocols, internship manual roles and expectations), and supervisor, FA (expanding beyond tokenism). Each of these storyline themes (agents and corresponding discursive relations) are further elaborated on in Nolan (in press) and, with limited space, cannot be reiterated here.

The storylines of agents and discursive relations comprise the social practice of teacher education field experience and supervision, drawing attention to the tightly woven network of relations within a field. They reaffirm the core of established and taken-for-granted social practices of field supervision – what could be referred to as teacher education and supervision doxa. Viewing these networked (and doxic) storylines through the lens of BSFT is a reminder of how 'reproduction is achieved because social members internalize the "rules of the game" and so adopt practices that ensure their "unconscious" replication' (Nash, 2002, p. 272). If supervisors exercise agency by introducing 'new rules for the old game', institutional structures and pressures return them to their original form of embodied cultural capital (the dominant discursive dispositions of mind and body). Regrettably, the relations are easily maintained and reproduced as long as agents (particularly those who benefit from them) carry on as if this is 'just the way things are done', thus drawing attention away from the (mostly) arbitrary origins or roots and the promises of constructing alternative pathways in the network of relations.

c. *The lens of reflexivity*

Rawolle and Lingard (2013) describe the third Bourdieuian analysis principle as that of reflexivity, which is meant 'to challenge what Bourdieu saw as three possible aspects of bias or distortion in social science research' (p. 131). These aspects include the positioning of the researcher in the social space, the doxa or orthodoxies of the field and the presence of other actions in the world as more valuable than research (p. 131). As I interrogate the network of field experience relations in my research, I find myself negotiating the well-traversed pathways while also troubling them and exploring new ones. In the language of network theory, the pathways (or discursive relations) of already well-established classroom practices hold valuable cultural capital in the field. I am reminded that cultural capital 'is a credit, it is the power granted to those who have obtained sufficient recognition to be in a position to impose recognition' (Bourdieu, 1990b, p. 138). In my evolving self-study research project (from 'e-adviser' to enhanced internship), I have been cautiously tweaking and extending my role as supervisor in an ongoing manner for more than six years now. Unsurprisingly, my shift to an alternative internship and supervisory approach has been severely bounded by the network of legitimate structures and practices in the field, including those forms of cultural capital associated with current habitus–field matches. As I offer in Nolan (2014b), 'Adopting a reflexive stance in teacher education would aim to expose the socially conditioned and subconscious structures that underlay the reproductive nature of the network of relations (examining the interactions between and among nodes)' (p. 320). However, from a reflexive point of view, even though my articulated research aim is to expose (and reconstruct) that network, in many ways I also comply with its structures and relations. It could be said that I have learned how to be strategic – I am deliberate in my efforts not to disrupt the game of supervision so much so that no one will want to play with me any more. In taking this strategic approach, I admit to my own complicity in (re)producing the network of relations in the field of field experience including, especially, my own positioning as supervisor within.

Closing thoughts

The BIDA framework presented here is conceptualized within the context of research that employs self-study methodology, using aspects of CDA while shaping the research process through key concepts of Bourdieu's social field theory, especially social practice networks and Bourdieu's own methodological principles for socio-analysis. It's quite an amalgamation. In fact, I characterize this blend of methodology, theory, and analysis as 'it ain't heavy, it's just awkward' – the idea of carrying Bourdieu's social field theory into self-study methodology framed by CDA.

The 'awkward' amalgamation, however, is proving valuable as I move forward in my research. The use of BIDA highlights the competing and conflicting demands on me as a teacher educator working to reveal the arbitrary and contingent nature of the discursive relations in the network of field experience supervision. The social practice of teacher education field experience and supervision constitutes a network of relations so inextricably linked to, and implicated in each other that disrupting or dismantling that network is a challenge. This is not a project without hope, however, as 'social agents can experience change in fields when there is a disjunction between their habitus and the current conditions within the field' (Thomson, 2008, p. 79). Perhaps such disjunctions will eventually transpire when teachers, prospective teachers, and teacher educators all recognize that 'the game that is played in fields has no ultimate winner, it is an unending game, and this always implies the potential for change at any time' (Thomson, 2008, p. 79). In my own research and in my development of BIDA for self-study, I hold on to the conviction that 'even when the agents' dispositions are as perfectly harmonized as possible and when the sequence of actions and reactions seems entirely predictable from outside, uncertainty remains as to the outcome of the interaction' (Bourdieu, 1990a, pp. 98–9).

Conceptualizing this BIDA framework as a three-phase (tri-focal) lens guides an interrogation of self-study data, identifying and consolidating the key threads of a dialectical methodology–theory construction. Ultimately, BIDA for self-study opens critical spaces for me to tackle the question of how the field of mathematics teacher education can study itself and unpack learning by inviting Bourdieu into the conversation.

Acknowledgements

This research was supported by a Social Sciences and Humanities Research Council (SSHRC) Insight Grant. Perspectives and conclusions expressed herein are the author's and do not necessarily reflect the views of the granting agency.

References

Ball, D., Thames, M. and Phelps, G. (2008) 'Content knowledge for teaching: What makes it special?', *Journal of Teacher Education*, 59(5): 389–407.

Bourdieu, P. (1990a) *The logic of practice* (R. Nice, trans.). Stanford, CA: Stanford University Press.

Bourdieu, P. (1990b) *In other words: Essays toward a reflexive sociology* (M. Adamson, trans.). Cambridge: Polity Press.

Bourdieu, P. (2008) *Sketch for self-analysis* (R. Nice, trans.). Chicago, IL: University of Chicago Press.

Bourdieu, P. and Passeron, J.-C. (1990) *Reproduction in education, society and culture* (2nd edn) (R. Nice, trans.). London: Sage.

Bourdieu, P. and Wacquant, L. (1992) *An invitation to reflexive sociology*. Chicago, IL: University of Chicago Press.

Britzman, D. (1995). ' "The question of belief": Writing poststructural ethnography', *International Journal of Qualitative Studies in Education*, 8: 229–38.

Britzman, D. (2003) *Practice makes practice: A critical study of learning to teach* (revised edn). New York: State University of New York Press

Britzman, D. (2009) 'The poetics of supervision: A psychoanalytical experiment for teacher education', *Changing English: Studies in Culture and Education*, 16(4): 385–96.

Brown, T. (2008) 'Comforting narratives of compliance: Psychoanalytic perspectives on new teacher responses to mathematics policy reform', in E. de Freitas and K. Nolan (eds), *Opening the research text: Critical insights and in(ter)ventions into mathematics education* (pp. 97–109). New York, NY: Springer.

Brown, T. and McNamara, O. (2011) *Becoming a mathematics teacher: Identity and identifications*. Dordrecht: Springer.

Bullough, R. and Pinnegar, S. (2001) 'Guidelines for quality in autobiographical forms of self study research', *Educational Researcher*, 30(3): 13–21.

Chapman, O. (2013) 'Investigating teachers' knowledge for teaching mathematics', *Journal of Mathematics Teacher Education*, 16(4): 237–43. doi: 10.1007/s10857-013-9247-2.

Clark, J. and Holton, D. (1991) *A first look at graph theory*. Singapore: World Scientific.

Clarke, A., Triggs, V. and Nielsen, W. (2013) 'Cooperating teacher participation in teacher education: A review of the literature', *Review of Educational Research*, 20(10): 1–40.

Clift, R. (2009) 'Repurposing my professional practice: Learning from my students over time and place', *Studying Teacher Education: A Journal of Self-study of Teacher Education Practices*, 5(2): 129–41.

Cuenca, A. (ed.) (2012) *Supervising student teachers: Issues, perspectives and future directions*. Rotterdam: Sense.

Fairclough, N., Pardoe, S. and Szerszynski, B. (2010) 'Critical discourse analysis and citizenship', in N. Fairclough (ed.), *Critical discourse analysis: The critical study of language* (2nd edn), (pp. 412–36). London, UK: Pearson.

Falkenberg, T. and Smits, H. (eds). (2010) *Field experiences in the context of reform of Canadian teacher education programs*. Winnipeg, MB: Faculty of Education, University of Manitoba.

Garrett, J. (2012) 'Rethinking the spaces of supervision: Psychoanalytic considerations', in A. Cuenca (ed.), *Supervising student teachers: Issues, perspectives and future directions* (pp. 157–68) Rotterdam: Sense.

Grenfell, M. (1996) 'Bourdieu and initial teacher education: A post-structuralist approach', *British Educational Research Journal*, 22(3): 287–303.

Grenfell, M. (ed.). (2008) *Pierre Bourdieu: Key concepts*. Stocksfield: Acumen.

Hamilton, M. and Pinnegar, S. (1998) 'Conclusion: The value and promise of self-study', in M. L. Hamilton (ed.), *Reconceptualizing teaching practice: Self-study in teacher education* (pp. 235–46). London: Falmer Press.

Jäger, S. and Maier, F. (2009) 'Theoretical and methodological aspects of Foucauldian critical discourse analysis and dispositive analysis', in R. Wodak and M. Meyer (eds), *Methods of critical discourse analysis* (pp. 34–61). London, UK: Sage.

Jaworski, B. and Gellert, U. (2003) 'Educating new mathematics teachers: Integrating theory and practice, and the roles of practising teachers', in A. Bishop, M.A. Clements, C. Keitel, J. Kilpatrick and F. K. S. Leung (eds), *Second international handbook of mathematics education (part two)* (pp. 829–75). Dordrecht: Kluwer Academic.

Lerman, S. (2001) 'A review of research perspectives on mathematics teacher education', in F.-L. Lin and T. J. Cooney (eds), *Making sense of mathematics teacher education* (pp. 33–52). Dordrecht: Kluwer Academic.

McNeil, B. (2011) 'Charting a way forward: Intersections of race and space in establishing identity as an African-Canadian teacher educator', *Studying Teacher Education: A Journal of Self-study of Teacher Education Practices*, 7(2): 133–43.

Mattsson, M., Eilertsen, T. and Rorrison, R. (eds). (2011) *A practicum turn in teacher education*. Rotterdam: Sense.

Nash, R. (2002) 'A realist framework for the sociology of education: Thinking with Bourdieu', *Educational Philosophy and Theory*, 34(3): 273–88.

Nicol, C. (2006) 'Designing a pedagogy of inquiry in teacher education: Moving from resistance to listening', *Studying Teacher Education: A Journal of Self-study of Teacher Education Practices*, 2(1): 25–41.

Nolan, K. (2008) 'Imagine there's no haven: Exploring the desires and dilemmas of a mathematics education researcher', in T. Brown (ed.), *The psychology of mathematics education: A psychoanalytic displacement* (pp. 159–81). Rotterdam: Sense.

Nolan, K. (2010) 'Playing the field(s) of mathematics education: A teacher educator's journey into pedagogical and paradoxical possibilities', in M. Walshaw (ed.), *Unpacking pedagogy: New perspectives for mathematics classrooms* (pp. 153–73). Charlotte, NC: Information Age.

Nolan, K. (2012) 'Dispositions in the field: Viewing mathematics teacher education field experiences through the lens of Bourdieu's social field theory', *Educational Studies in Mathematics, 80*(1): 201–15. doi: 10.1007/s10649-011-9355-9.

Nolan, K. (2014a) 'Discursive productions of teaching and learning through inquiry: Novice teachers reflect on becoming a teacher and secondary mathematics teacher education', in L. Thomas (ed.), *Becoming teacher: Sites for teacher development in Canadian teacher education* (pp. 258–88). E-book published by the Canadian Association for Teacher Education at www.sites.google.com/site/cssecate/fall-working-conference

Nolan, K. (2014b) 'Survival of the fit: A Bourdieuian and graph theory network analogy for mathematics teacher education', in P. Liljedahl, C. Nicol, S. Oesterle and D. Allan (eds), *Proceedings of the 38th Conference of the International Group for the Psychology of Mathematics Education and the 36th Conference of the North American Chapter of the Psychology of Mathematics Education* (Vol. 4, pp. 313–20). Vancouver, Canada: PME.

Nolan (in press) 'Beyond tokenism in the field: On the learning of a mathematics teacher educator and faculty supervisor', in *Cogent Education*. London: Taylor & Francis.

Nolan, K. and Tupper, J. (2013) '"Field" trips with Bourdieu: Making sense as research methodology in teacher education', *International Journal of Humanities and Social Science, 3*(6): 11–19.

Nolan, K. and Walshaw, M. (2012) 'Playing the game: A Bourdieuian perspective of pre-service inquiry teaching', *Teaching Education, 23*(4): 345–63.

Noyes, A. (2004) '(Re)producing mathematics educators: A sociological perspective', *Teaching Education, 15*(3): 243–56.

Rawolle, S. and Lingard, B. (2013) 'Bourdieu and educational research: Thinking tools, relational thinking, beyond epistemological innocence', in M. Murphy (ed.), *Social theory and education research: Understanding Foucault, Habermas, Bourdieu and Derrida* (pp. 117–37). London: Routledge.

Russell, T. (2005) 'How 20 years of self-study changed my teaching', in C. Kosnik, C. Beck, A. Freese and A. Samaras (eds), *Making a difference in teacher education through self-study* (pp. 3–17). Dordrecht: Springer.

Samaras, A. (2002) *Self-study for teacher educators: Crafting a pedagogy for educational change.* New York: Peter Lang.

Sandretto, S. (2009) 'Theoretical and methodological tensions in a poststructural, collaborative self-study research project', *Studying Teacher Education: A Journal of Self-study of Teacher Education Practices, 5*(1): 89–101.

Thomson, P. (2008) 'Field', in M. Grenfell (ed.), *Pierre Bourdieu: Key concepts* (pp. 67–81). Stocksfield: Acumen.

Towers, J. (2010) 'Learning to teach mathematics through inquiry: A focus on the relationship between describing and enacting inquiry-oriented teaching', *Journal of Mathematics Teacher Education, 13*: 243–63.

Walshaw, M. (2007) *Working with Foucault in education*. Rotterdam: Sense.

Walshaw, M. (2012) 'Reformulations of mathematics teacher identity and voice', *Journal of Mathematics Teacher Education, 15*: 103–8.

Whitehead, J. (2009) 'Self-study, living educational theories, and the generation of educational knowledge', *Studying Teacher Education: A Journal of Self-study of Teacher Education Practices, 5*(2): 107–11.

Williams, J. (2011) 'Teachers telling tales: The narrative mediation of professional identity', *Research in Mathematics Education, 13*(2): 131–42.

Wodak, R. and Meyer, M. (2009) 'Critical discourse analysis: History, agenda, theory and methodology', in R. Wodak and M. Meyer (eds), *Methods of critical discourse analysis* (pp. 1–33). London, UK: Sage.

Zeichner, K. (2009) *Teacher education and the struggle for social justice*. New York: Routledge.

Chapter 12

Conclusion

Method as theory – (re)exploring the intellectual context of education research

Cristina Costa and Mark Murphy

Introduction

Throughout his career Bourdieu tried to reconcile theory and practice as interdependent entities, a key theme of his work overall and also a guiding theme throughout the chapters included in this edited text. This final chapter reflects on the different ways the contributions in this collection have applied Bourdieu's ideas in educational research as both an object and means of investigation. We use this space to respond to some of the critical theory/ method issues raised by the different contributions, in particular exploring the benefits and drawbacks of applying Bourdieu in real-life educational contexts that do not always lend themselves easily to intellectual investigation.

In order to facilitate this exploration, the chapter will outline key benefits and drawbacks of applying Bourdieu in the context of the four areas of education research included in the book:

- Identities
- Equity
- Leadership and management
- Teacher education.

Such an approach, while summarizing and clarifying some of the issues raised in more detail, can also help to identify the ways in which research *context* matters in theory application – for example, are there different kinds of challenges when applying Bourdieu in leadership research as opposed to research in teacher education? The chapter reflects on the significance of context while also illustrating the ways in which such forms of applied research can be taken forward in future research investigations.

Bourdieu and research on educational identities

The section on educational identities presents three very different approaches as to how Bourdieu's conceptual tools can be applied to the understanding of social identities. This not only shows the plasticity of Bourdieu's concepts in exploring different social phenomena, it also provides us with original applications and subsequent interpretations of the contexts studied.

What this edited collection shows in relation to the study of identities in education is that there is not one single way through which such a topic can be researched with Bourdieu in mind. Michael Mu's work on heritage language and ethnicity proposes a break from classical social psychology, with habitus offering both an alternative interpretative lens and a new method of exploring Chineseness. This presents both advantages and challenges when compared with how the ethnic identity of Chinese people has been explored before. If on the one hand, it provides a different approach to the idiosyncratic representations of Chineseness in Australia, on the other hand it raises methodological questions regarding how to depart from psychological approaches to proceed with habitus as a research tool. In the case of Mu, the applicability of habitus to empirical work results in a mixed methods approach to studying individuals' histories within their continuities and variability; at the same time it allows him to excavate deeper into the perceptions and dispositions individuals embody. The design and application of surveys to studying habitus is itself an important contribution to the field given the reluctance of many Bourdieuian scholars to develop social understandings through quantitative methods. Yet, what Mu shows us is that habitus can – at least to a certain extent – be quantified. The result is an understanding of the demographic diversity of the population being studied. This, in turn, provides a sense of the dual habitus that characterizes research participants – the habitus that is inscribed in their DNA and the dispositions participants internalize throughout their life journeys – and to which he returns with follow-up interviews. Mu's work makes a valuable methodological contribution to the application of habitus in that it challenges the perceptions of scholars in 'capturing' habitus through less common approaches. Habitus as a system of dispositions inscribed in the body is more often left to understandings mediated by participants' voices, with narratives and interviews being a commonly used method by the scholarly community. Although Mu too makes use of interviews, he challenges the assumption that the reconstruction of participants' habitus can only be made qualitatively. He encourages us to also think quantitatively. And he shows that quantitative methodologies not only allow us to survey the field, but they also equip us with useful knowledge for the subsequent phases of the research process. This is what he did by conducting regression analysis of the data collected quantitatively. In moving forward with his research he had a more concrete idea of how participants' habitus influenced their identity perceptions and how to explore this aspect of the research.

Jo Warin's research also offers a unique perspective on the study of identities, not only due to the fact that she looks at capitals to arrive at understandings of identity, but also because she conducted a longitudinal study on the subject. This presents challenges to the researcher and the researched, as during the long research period both parties are likely to evolve in their ideas and practices. So, even if indirectly, what Warin is disclosing here is not just the identity trajectories of her research participants but also her journey as a researcher. As she admits, her encounter with Bourdieu's work came after the start of the study, which could in itself explain why instead of using habitus as its main form of inquiry – given that longitudinal studies offer an invaluable opportunity to look at participants' journey during extended periods of time – she opted to study identities through the notion of capital. This, per se, presents an advantage but can also be a disadvantage. The fact that the study was not developed with Bourdieu in mind, created space to look at the phenomenon under study through a much broader lens; yet, the process of inductive recovery of the data with Bourdieu in the background can only stretch so far. Nonetheless, Warin provides a pertinent account of the reproduction of social advantages and disadvantages through the application of capitals to her conceptual framework. In doing so, she shows how young people's articulation of their own identity is related to the opportunities and resources they have at their disposal. Innovative in Warin's methodological approach is also the use of time lines and visuals, such as photos and video, to elicit narratives of the self; these are techniques that can be appropriated to other Bourdieuian tools, such as is the case of habitus. What Warin's methodological and theoretical approach to her research shows is that Bourdieu's theory-method is flexible and useful at different stages of the research process. What this work also evidences is that there is not only one way to apply Bourdieu; his conceptual tools can be applied from the onset of the research, and they can also be introduced at a later stage when the critical approach his work provides is required. Once again Bourdieu shows that there is not only one way to perceive and apprehend the social world, but rather as many ways as there are researchers wanting to challenge the methods through which they access and (de)construct social reality.

The third chapter on identities transports us to a context less popular with Bourdieu's followers – that of digital scholarship practices. This might be so because Bourdieu did not live to see the development of the web as the space of participation and cultural production that it has become. Therefore he never produced any work in this area. However, the contribution of this chapter is beyond the novelty of the topic being explored. By looking at the concepts of doxa and hysteresis in combination with reflexivity Costa and Murphy provide an account of how such constructs can be operationalized to research changes in scholarship practice and the effect such practices have on scholars' perceptions of their profession and professional selves. The authors assert that doxa and hysteresis provide a different perspective on the dialectical relationship between structure and agency by looking at the taken-for-granted approaches agents transport from one field to the other, and which creates the hysteresis effect as the habitus of one field comes in contact with the habitus of another field. This is made apparent through the doxic approaches individuals display through their approaches to practice. Their intention of operationalizing such concepts as theory-method is developed through reflexivity practices and mediated through narrative inquiry techniques. This chapter encourages the development of methodological strategies through which hidden mechanisms of change can be disclosed and understood. In doing so, their purpose is to look at the heterodoxy of practice through less conventional key concepts. Moreover, such an approach encourages researchers to move their understandings beyond the reproduction of practices and analyse the circumstances via which change occurs. The original contribution of this chapter is in employing Bourdieu's concepts to deviate from the conventional debates regarding the reproduction of cultural practices and develop new understandings of how and why the identities of scholars engaged in less conventional practices diverge from the norm.

In summary, the study of identities can take on different forms and perspectives. This is not only related to the contexts in which the research is conducted, but also connected to the methodological decisions researchers make when preparing for fieldwork and/or analysing research data. What the three examples outlined above show us is that Bourdieu offers a flexible research framework that enables a variety of applications. What the Bourdieuian toolkit then prompts is a reflection of how it can be best put to use within our research needs and goals. Bourdieu's methodological legacy is thus not one of reproduction of his theory but rather one of re-discovery of his concepts with every new application.

Bourdieu and research on educational equity

As with the chapters on identities, the three chapters included under the banner of equity illustrate the diverse ways in which researchers have taken to Bourdieu – the underachievement of Afro-Trinidadian boys (Ravi Rampersad), the impact of parental social capital on children's education (Maria Papapolydorou) and an argument for the importance of doing critical ethnography in education research (Katie Fitzpatrick and Stephen May). Of course it should come as no surprise that scholars have adopted Bourdieu in this field, given his own explicit focus on this theme. This would help to explain why Bourdieu is the social theorist of choice for so many education researchers – compare his standing to Habermas for example, who, while exploring issues of relevance to education, did not focus on educational issues explicitly in his career.

The three chapters in this section show why educational equity research has taken to the likes of capital, habitus and field: such concepts allow researchers to explore the ways in which inequalities manifest themselves and are reproduced via the *processes* at work in educational activities. Emphasis here is on processes as education is not a static entity but rather a set of evolving mechanisms via which the broader structures of stratification and culture are played out in the lives of pupils.

This, according to Ravi Rampersad, is one of the reasons why he was attracted to using Bourdieu in the first place. As he puts it in the chapter, 'Crafting an accurate picture of the educational experience of Afro-Trinidadian boys' required grasping both the structures of society and how they are manifested on the individual level, the interplay between the macro and micro.

This is why he combined Bourdieu's conceptual tools with the ideas of critical race theory, a combination that allowed him to operationalize Bourdieu via what he terms 'racialized facilitative capital'. This concept is his own adaptation of Bourdieu, made possible by the interplay of different theoretical approaches. Such an approach illustrates the benefits of adapting social theory to suit the needs of the researcher rather than the other way around. Given the results and analysis of his qualitative research, it pays not to be too concerned with doing Bourdieu 'correctly'.

Having said that, Rampersad acknowledges the challenges faced with such 'cherry-picking' – that it was not always easy to combine different intellectual traditions in the study of one social grouping. But it has allowed him to consider the implications of his current work for other concerns such as the psychic landscape of pigmentocracy and also the ways in which male role models are imagined in society. These kinds of spin-off effects of social theory and its applications should be acknowledged more often, as these kinds of contributions to alternative conceptions of social phenomena are part of the rationale for social theory in the first place.

Part of the rationale for Rampersad's work was to interrogate intersectionality in relation to inequality, which is also a theme developed in Maria Papapolydorou's chapter on parental social capital. She looks specifically at the interplay between parents' differential access to social capital across class and ethnicity lines, and how these factors impact on the educational opportunities of children. Her approach to this issue employed a mixed methods analysis, combining statistical and qualitative forms of inquiry, an approach that proved fruitful in that it helped to further tease out some of the intellectual vagueness around the concept of social capital. Helped in particular by her use of regression analysis, social capital moved from being viewed as a coherent entity to a complex variable with multiple dimensions, many of which are unrelated to one another. As her analysis moved back and forth between the qualitative and quantitative data, it became clearer that there is not merely one type of parental social capital but instead a combination of various types mobilized in more than one context. Such mixed methods approaches to operationalizing Bourdieu illustrate the kinds of benefits of taking a non-partisan approach to the qualitative/quantitative divide, so often a regressive force in educational research.

The final chapter in this part is by Katie Fitzpatrick and Stephen May, who make a strong case for critical ethnography in the style and spirit of Bourdieu. Bourdieu himself employed ethnography as a methodological tool, and was keen to emphasize the critical aspect – in particular the importance of the researcher in taking a reflexive stance and being aware of their own positionality. This is an issue they explore in some detail in their chapter while also detailing their own work and that of others in the area of 'physical' capital – not an area focused on to any great extent by Bourdieu but one that has been taken up by other researchers keen to make associations around embodiment, habitus and equity issues. Their discussion of the topic shows that Bourdieu's idea can be stretched out to explore a broader range of topics, especially when some research objects lend themselves to such investigations. This is the case here – a focus on the body is ready-made for theorizing around habitus and field (as they suggest). Bourdieu doesn't suit all objects, but when it does, it can be highly illuminating and facilitative of more nuanced approaches to the topic at hand.

Researching leadership and management

Bruce Kloot's paper covers both aspects of leadership and management, in his case the position of foundation programmes in South African universities and their influence on the sector. Given their introduction into a racialized environment, the content of this chapter could easily have been framed about issues of equity, but 'leadership and management' as a header works more effectively for a project exploring the mechanisms of reproduction and transformation at work within the university sector. His narrative inquiry approach, using interviews with 21 staff members across two institutions, reveals the influence of the institutional context and also how the struggle over the likes of language, culture and 'race' at national level moulds the field of higher education. Aside from the overview of his own research, Kloot's chapter also contributes a balanced approach to the benefits and drawbacks of using narrative inquiry in educational research. While the benefits include the relatively straightforward nature of documenting personal narratives, the capacity of narrative to characterize habitus and to uncover hidden aspects of the field, the 'dangers' of using narrative accounts, as Kloot puts it, should not be underestimated. This is particularly the case when it is all too easy to take personal narratives at face value and to move too quickly from the personal to universal truths. Without more thorough understandings of the specific contexts under examination and the multiple narratives at work in construction of power relations, narrative inquiry can find itself clutching at methodological straws.

Kloot argues that this is one of the key reasons why a grasp and application of the full range of Bourdieu's conceptual apparatus can help avoid such one-sided approaches to educational research, providing something of a bulwark against biased forms of research methodology. Scott Eacott in his chapter on researching educational leadership agrees with this approach to Bourdieu, while also making the point that Bourdieu allows scholars such as himself to 'think anew' about his own disciplinary field. His chapter provides a thoughtful account of his 'finding' of Bourdieu in a field relatively unpopulated by critical thought, and how his thinking has progressed through the opening of research avenues and ways of thinking made possible by Bourdieu's critical sociology. What is striking when reading this chapter is that Eacott's journey to Bourdieu and beyond finds parallels in the careers of many other scholars, each looking for ways to combine rigorous research methods with sharper intellectual tools.

Researching teacher education

Teacher education as a field of inquiry is unsurprisingly receptive to Bourdieu's legacy given his career-long focus on education. The two chapters on teacher education do, however, present rather unanticipated approaches to how research can be operationalized and conducted in this field, as summarized below.

Naomi Flynn's chapter explores the teaching of the English language with non-native speakers. Flynn reports on the challenges of conducting such research, not only because of her subjective position as researcher, but also because of the methodological decisions she is led to make. Focusing on a grounded theory approach that did not include the Bourdieuian lens from the onset, she faces the challenge of coding without the Bourdieuian theory in the background. Yet, after deciding to introduce the Bourdieuian lens in the coding of the data, she had to fight off the dilemma of confining her sociological gaze to the tensions and conflicts typically portrayed in Bourdieuian studies. In this sense, Flynn elaborates on the problems that derive from coding data that can belong simultaneously to different node families, especially when accepting the interrelation between field, habitus and capitals, or even assuming a group habitus. Nonetheless, she also outlines the advantages and possibilities of using Bourdieu's work. This relates to the Bourdieuian tradition of thinking methodologically which requires a deep understanding of how the mechanism of analysis is devised.

Kathleen Nolan's chapter focuses on secondary mathematics teacher education and her incursions into researching a mentoring programme for teachers on placement within the capacity of researcher–participant. Employing a self-study methodology, Nolan's research sets out to study change, and most importantly, how she could be both the object and facilitator of such change. Such a daring approach implies a study of her own habitus. The challenges of working within the field of the self starts, as she reports, with the concept-ualization of her own positionality and reflexivity as the researcher–participant of the study. Moreover, she also elaborates on the constraints of simultaneously combining the roles of the researcher and the researched and of initially choosing between methodology and theory. An important aspect of this chapter is the realization that the debates around methodology and theory, although often conducted in separate realms, are two aspects of the same research reality and should therefore be considered in connection with each other. This draws the author to consider network and graph theory as she observes her own network of relations and ponders how it affects her own practice. In trying to arrive at an understanding of her own complex reality, Nolan employs critical discourse analysis with Bourdieu's theory in the background (BIDA) in an attempt to critique her own practice rather than merely providing an interpre-tation of the phenomenon being studied and of which she is part. What Nolan does with such an intricate approach is to employ a rather advanced method of eliciting self reflexivity which in the last instance will provide her with knowledge about what needs to be changed. Such an elaborated research framework is a much needed development, one that brings Bourdieu's tool of reflexivity to a much deeper level of application and one that other researchers can work with and build on.

Although these two last chapters focus on the same theme – teacher education – they take very different approaches regarding how to tackle the research contexts they aim to explore. This is not solely due to the genesis of the topics that is different; it is also because the research needs reported in these two chapters are quite peculiar. Both chapters add another layer of complexity to organizing, operationalizing and analysing research as an iterative process that requires deep reflection about the processes deployed and the role the researcher plays in it. In their own way, both chapters present a great level of complexity to the application of the Bourdieuian lens. Whereas Flynn delves into the short-comings of research analysis by weighing the advantages and disadvantages of using Bourdieu's work, Nolan concerns herself with how best to develop a mechanism of self-analysis that may trigger change in the self. Both chapters offer original contributions to the ongoing debate of applying Bourdieu's legacy to the field of educational research.

Conclusion

This book has, we hope, demonstrated that education as a field of inquiry continues to provide a fruitful ground for the application of the Bourdieuian approach. This collection of essays shows that Bourdieu's work has continuously evolved and that his legacy represents the starting and not the end point of more sophisticated and far-reaching approaches as to how research can capture and conceptualize different phenomena in education.

The innovation and usefulness of this book resides precisely in this. With the purpose of moving the discussion of educational research beyond its theorizing objective, the book engages in conversations around application from multiple and varied perspectives. Bourdieu's key concepts are a powerful instrument with which researchers can work both methodologically and theoretically. And it is this interplay between the two – between theory and method – that moves Bourdieu's work forward with each new research application carried out by his followers.

In this sense we did not aim to revive the Bourdieuian tradition in educational research with the book – because it does not lack popularity – but we hope we have provided the reader with stimulating, new ways with which to think and report about research practice alongside the findings that come of it. By making explicit how we think about method(ology), we aim to bring to the forefront the Bourdieuian legacy of theory-method and how one feeds into the other. Moreover, we hope that through this collection we have been able to challenge ingrained perceptions of the incompatibility of certain methods with given Bourdieuian concepts. The authors of the different chapters have put forward exactly the opposite, not only by experimenting with (and sometimes combining) both quantitative and qualitative approaches, but also by devising new mechanisms through which Bourdieu's key concepts can acquire a deeper and more explicit meaning.

Index